Is The Euro Crisis Really Over?

Will doing whatever it takes be enough?

Edward Hugh

Copyright © 2014 Edward Hugh

All rights reserved.

ISBN: 1502343436
ISBN-13: 978-1502343437

DEDICATION

To my brother David, my son Morgan and Vicenta, each of whom, in different ways, bears some of the responsibility for what you will find within.

CONTENTS

	Acknowledgments	i
1	Introduction	1
2	All Quiet on the Western Front	9
3	Deflation, What Deflation?	21
4	The "Good Deflation" Phenomenon	41
5	If Only They Had Their Own Currency!	56
6	Easy To Get Into Trouble, Hard To Get Out Of It	80
7	Labour Mobility at Last!	107
8	Is It All Germany's Fault?	135
9	Zero Bound and Then What?	159
10	Does QE Stop Deflation?	172
11	The Expectations Fairy	199
12	Just Give Me The Facts!	217
13	Towards A Transfer Union Without Transfers?	230
14	Where Do We Go From Here?	243

ACKNOWLEDGMENTS

I would need to thank a lot of people if I were to provide a complete list of those who have helped make this book possible. Nevertheless I would like to make special reference to Claus Vistesen, Uldis Zelmenis, Mikel Abasolo, Jonathan Tepper, Simon White, Bernat Vila, José Contreras, Guiomar Parada and Detlef Güertler. A further name should perhaps be added here, that of Nobel Economist Paul Krugman. As the reader will note, frequent references are made throughout this book to lines of thought he develops. It will also become evident that I have a kind of love hate relationship with many of his arguments, since while I think he is digging in exactly the right place, and his diagnosis is light years ahead of the consensus discourse in terms of its recognition of the depth of the problems we all face, I find his approach unnecessarily polemical, his conclusions often excessively simplistic and the occasional lack of consistency between one argument and the next singularly frustrating. Nonetheless Paul, I am glad you are there, since this way I feel less alone.

1

All Over Bar the Shouting?

The euro zone crisis is not back --, at least not yet it isn't.

The "mini turmoil" in global financial markets that occurred in the summer of 2014 following rising concerns about Portugal's banking system in the wake of the Banco Espirito Santo scandal produced an immediate knee jerk reaction on the part of many hardened economic observers: is **it** back? It in this case was, of course, the Euro Area sovereign debt crisis.

These initial tremors were followed by further stronger ones, both at the start of December as it became obvious Greece was headed for new elections, and at the end of January 2015 following the announcement of the election result. Even though signs of market stress over the Greek situation are not lacking the conclusion that the crisis is really back again would, at this point, still be premature. Just as premature however would be the conclusion that the day won't come when it really is.

Naturally the dramatic shift in market perceptions of Southern Europe which has taken place since the height of the crisis has surprised many. For some the level of investor appetite for shares and bonds in what was previously deemed an economic disaster zone is a sure sign another bubble is on the way, this time in government bonds[1]. For others it is proof that the debt crisis is now well behind us, and indeed that the most seriously affected economies have now "turned the corner"[2].

The question this book will try to address is the extent to which either of these views is valid. There is no doubt that both the countries concerned and the Euro Area itself have made significant institutional advances during the crisis, not least among these the creation of a Banking Union. Running a currency union involving 18 members was never going to be easy, and progress was always going to be slow.

But has enough been done, or has one-can-after-another simply been kicked firmly down the road? Certainly the unresolved issues are not hard to identify: low GDP growth, rising sovereign debt levels, creeping deflation, growing political discontent, how to handle the problem of ageing and declining workforces. So there are plenty of potential sources for more crises; the issue is whether the will to address them before something unfortunate happens exists or whether the driver will, yet one more time, fall quietly asleep at the wheel.[3]

The latest market tensions over Greece illustrate the uncertainty which still hangs over the region, with the perennial doubt about

---

[1] See: Don't Go Potty on the Periphery, The Economist, 19 April, 2014, http://www.economist.com/news/leaders/21600981-southern-europes-economies-are-worse-shape-tumbling-bond-yields-suggest-dont-go-potty#sthash.dZTIXKYK.dpbs

[2] See: IMF praises handling of Spain's economy but warns on joblessness, 10 July 2014, http://www.ft.com/intl/cms/s/0/3cf3da58-0840-11e4-acd8-00144feab7de.html#axzz3Aod2XNR9

[3] Phrase used initially by Herman Van Rompuy, Task Force On European Governance, Press Conference, 8 June 2010, http://vloghvr.consilium.europa.eu/?p=1713

whether a so-called Grexit will finally occur raising its head over and over again. On the other hand the most notable feature of the current Greece crisis is the way in which bond yields in the other periphery countries[4] have continued to head downwards, leading many to conclude that the "contagion" threat is now a thing of the past. In principle the ECB initiating a programme of quantitative easing (QE) involving sovereign bond purchases lies behind the drift in yields. In Japan, where QE has been activated for some years now, yields on 10 year government bonds have already been below 0.5% for some considerable time. But the uncertainty remains: what if the ECB eventually terminates the purchases, or even tries to end them early under a Federal Reserve type "tapering" process, what will happen to bond spreads then? The bund, where ten year yields at the time of writing stand at 0.2 percent (and falling) is perhaps not a problematic case since if the deflation risk increases in Europe interest paid on them will surely fall further while if periphery spreads start to unwind under an inflation scenario then German instruments will continue to attract investment as a "safe haven"[5].

From an investor perspective the easy part is now over. Riding on the back of what is known in the business as a yield compression[6] wave many bondholders enjoyed substantial capital gains as the interest rate on the bonds they were holding fell. But as these yields have hit ever lower levels they have increasingly faced the

---

[4] Most notably Ireland, Spain, Portugal, Italy and Greece, but also Slovenia and potentially other countries in Eastern Europe who now form part of the Euro.
[5] Safe havens are countries whose assets can move in the opposite direction to market sentiment during moments of financial turmoil. Thus demand for bunds would increase if markets were, for example, to put pressure on, say, Italy.
[6] The value of a bond in secondary markets moves inversely with the yield, as yield rises the tradeable value falls and vice versa. When yields fall as they have done recently on Europe's periphery those holding bonds receive capital gains accordingly.

question of whether the return they are receiving justifies the added risk they assume, especially now yields on many bonds have even turned negative. And the decline has often been spectacular. In the case of Portugal 10-year bonds – which currently trade at around 1.7% - fell by 50% - from just over 7 percent to under 3.5 percent - in a matter of months. Given that as interest rates fall the resale value of bonds rises savvy investors were given the opportunity to make windfall profits on what was effectively a one-way-bet-no-brainer once the full impact of Mario Draghi's July 2012 speech had become crystal clear.

But now with each further decline the advantages of holding in anticipation of further declines become less obvious, while the risks being assumed continue to mount as debt levels in some of the key countries go on rising. Portugal, Italy and, of course, Greece[7] are now reaching levels of government debt as a proportion of GDP which are clearly not sustainable in the longer term. Really there are only two alternatives: either the ECB continues to implement a version of full-blown QE indefinitely and effectively swallows a significant part of all the accumulating periphery debt, or there will have to be some sort of private sector bondholder "bail-in" despite declarations that what happened in Greece won't happen again. As time passes and talk of eventual ECB "tapering" grows, those holding the most potentially distressed bonds are likely to get increasingly nervous.

Recent economic data has started to systematically surprise on the upside, and forecasts for Euro Area growth in 2015 and 2016

---

[7] Greece forms something of a special case though, since after the fiasco of the first Troika rescue the country now has a form of "debt guarantee" from its Euro partners. See my The Second Battle Of Thermopylae, 19 June 2013, http://edwardhughtoo.blogspot.com.es/2013/06/the-second-battle-of-thermopylae.html

have been hastily revised upwards. Indeed at the press conference where the initiation of the programme was announced Mario Draghi was so bold as to claim the programme had achieved many of its intended objectives even before it started. [8]

So it is useful at this point to think about the difference between a very short term scenario wherein the Euro Area will undoubtedly outperform expectations, and a longer run one in which many of the old problems – which are deep and structural - will undoubtedly resurface. Given that a significant part of the drop in inflation is the result of the sharp negative price shock from energy costs the headline number is sure to rise in the second half of 2015, especially taking into account the large drop in the value of the Euro. However, even if outright deflation is avoided inflation will be very, very low and will continue to remain so over a considerable period of time. Which means nominal GDP – GDP before inflation adjustment - may barely grow in the years to come, with the nasty consequence that sovereign debt levels (as a percentage of GDP) will continue to move onwards and upwards, especially in the most indebted economies. Previously all official sector projections had periphery debt levels peaking either this year or next, but now these estimates will need to be revisited. Italian gross government debt, for example, hit 131.8 percent of Italian GDP in September 2014, up 5.4 percent on a year earlier, while its Portuguese equivalent hit 131.4%.

Naturally the "Mario Draghi ultimately has my back" feeling continues to prevail, but with markets increasingly financing debt

---

[8] See "Draghi Declares Victory For Bond-Buying Before It Starts, Bloomberg, 5 March 2015 http://www.bloomberg.com/news/articles/2015-03-05/draghi-declares-victory-for-bond-buying-before-it-even-starts

levels that many recognize as ultimately unsustainable nervousness will rise that the size of the pill – and German resistance to the process - may become just too big for the ECB to comfortably swallow, leaving the specter of private sector involvement (PSI) in debt restructuring to once more rear its ugly head.

At the same time, long term issues about the sustainability of Europe's economies are emerging, largely for demographic reasons. Unable to adjust via a classic devaluation, and unwilling to bite the bullet of a sizeable adjustment in relative prices via an internal devaluation, economies in southern Europe are correcting via the long-wished-for route of transnational labour mobility. But as we will see in Chapter 5, the associated migration process is not without problems in an era when working age populations are tilting downwards and elderly population ratios steadily on the rise.

One possible solution to many of these problems would be a complete federation of all Euro Area member states: the long talked about full political union. This wouldn't be an instant cure all for the region's problems but it would make the correction of country level imbalances much more manageable. Unfortunately there seems to be little appetite for such a move on the part of those countries which would be large net contributors to any major move towards fiscal union, and hence this outcome seems unlikely over the relevant time horizon.

More likely in the short term is a battle between periphery and core Europe politicians over getting the ECB to continue with full blown government bond-buying QE. One of the ways this issue could be resolved to the core's satisfaction would be via a substantial PSI type "bail-in" of bondholders prior to any extension of the ECB QE programme. The possibility of this outcome will be explored in the final chapter.

Whom the Gods Would Destroy

The Euro should not exist, but it does. I am certainly not the first, and surely will not be the last observer to notice this otherwise trivial historical detail. According to Lombard Research Chief Economist Charles Dumas, the Euro is a form of "suicide pact"[9], but the Hellerian Catch 22 twist which makes this pact so, so special is that the threat of ending the Euro could easily -via contagion and balance-sheet effects - transform the event from being simply a local European piece of collective insanity into a thoroughly global affair. That is to say, we do have much of a choice, the great beast having been brought into existence we can now either all be hung out to dry separately, or we can be hung out together, and at one and the same time. Unfortunately, at this stage of the game there are no neat and easy solutions left, which is not the same as saying there is nothing to be done. The ECB now seems to have been called to play a decisive, even critical role in holding things together, but what that means is we are all now embarked on a path whose endpoint we cannot even discern.

To anticipate the conclusions reached at the end of this book, no sane person would willingly leave the Euro System as it is currently constituted on an individual, go it alone, basis, whether the agent in question be one of those supposedly problematic pupils, or one of the apparently sound teachers who has simply

---

[9] City Wire, 2012. Why Germans and Dutch will exit 'suicide pact' Eurozone, http://www.citywire.co.uk/money/why-germans-and-dutch-will-exit-suicide-pact-eurozone/a559322?ref=citywire-money-latest-news-list

become tired of the energy drain associated with having to discipline so many irremediably naughty children. For a variety of reasons which will be explained as we advance neither one nor the other will chose to move-on being of sound mind, since an amicable divorce is not imaginable and a conflict ridden one, however contained the event, would have serious negative consequences for all parties. Which leaves us with the other possibility: "whom the gods would destroy they first make mad". The big risk of the current policy mix being applied by Europe's political leaders and the IMF (through the so called Troika, now appropriately renamed "the institutions") is that they may simply end up politically destabilizing a number of EU countries – whether on the periphery or in the core – in a way which leads to a growing adoption of more extreme solutions and the implementation of policy decisions with which rational agents would normally not wish to be associated. In this regard, while Mario Draghi's measures have surely underpinned the stability of the Euro Area financial system the same cannot be said for its political counterpart, as we are currently seeing in Greece.

2

All Quiet on the Western Front

Legendary hedge fund supremo Ray Dalio was in ebullient mood during the summer of 2012. It was a defining moment, and he knew it. So he was relishing every second as he proudly proclaimed to Bloomberg TV[10] that, in his opinion, the euro was now "likely" to stay together. At the time this statement really was news, since up to that point most financial specialists, and in particular those in the hedge fund industry, had been more inclined to believe some sort of (at least partial) break up – in particular a Greek exit, or Grexit – was more or less inevitable. Indeed many in the investment community had been so convinced of such an outcome that they had been visibly backing their intuitions with their money by purchasing Credit Default

---

[10] See: Bridgewater's Dalio: Euro Will Survive Region's Crisis, Bloomberg, 21 September 2012, http://www.bloomberg.com/news/2012-09-21/bridgewater-s-dalio-says-euro-will-survive-region-s-debt-crisis.html

Swaps (a sort of non-payment insurance contract) on the sovereign debt of several of the leading candidates to be right in the firing line.

In hindsight the decision of influential figures like Dalio (who runs the Bridgewater Associates fund) to carry out what was effectively a 180° turn marked a watershed in the Euro debt crisis, a turning point after which some of the things which had been rapidly getting worse started to get steadily better. What lay behind this Saul on the road to Damascus en-masse conversion of the Hedge Fund Industry was the growing perception that Draghi's statement meant the European Central Bank (the ECB) had crossed some sort of Rubicon, and Bridgewater's founder had the prescience to realize this very quickly. The conclusion he and others drew from what they were hearing was that the emphasis on confidence-building but growth-constraining austerity measures of the kind which originally characterized the joint approach of the EU Commission and IMF would gradually be softened as policy moved steadily towards an increasingly accommodative monetary stance and even eventual money printing. With the benefit of hindsight, this judgment seems to have been absolutely spot-on.

The result was that the cutting edge of the investor community started to decide the time had come to sell off all those meticulously acquired CDS positions and start instead to do the exact opposite: buy into Euro periphery assets. Three years later, and with the whole economic universe now debating whether or not it is Europe that is going Japanese or Japan that is about to follow Europe into negative interest rates following the implementation of quantitative easing (QE) at the ECB, we can now begin to see just how visionary this original Dalio judgment really was.

His cue was, of course, ECB President Mario Draghi's "whatever it takes to save the Euro" pledge[11] and the day in July 2012 when Mr. Draghi chose to calmly inform a London investors conference that, "Within our mandate, the ECB is ready to do whatever it takes to preserve the euro. And believe me, it will be enough."

Since that time this game-changing statement has been qualified and clarified, and re-qualified and re-clarified innumerable times, but still the essence remains unchanged. The ECB President wasn't talking about any specific programme of bond purchases or exceptional liquidity measures when he made his promise, he was talking about doing "whatever it takes", and Ray Dalio for one took him at his word.

In fact, what the ECB President could see, again as few others could, was that "enough was enough" and that something had to be done to create the structural underpinnings the common currency so badly needed, and if the bickering politicians couldn't do it in Brussels, then he damn well would do what was needed in Frankfurt instead. In the process Mr Draghi has earned the immense admiration of all those who feel letting the Euro fall apart would mean a collective disaster for all Europeans and the animosity of those, who in one way or another, don't really want the thing to work as a full monetary and fiscal union.

What Bridgewater's founder was getting at when he said what he made his call on Bloomberg TV is that there is now no meaningful

---

[11] See, for example, ECB's Mario Draghi Vows to Save the Euro, France 24, 26 July, 2012
http://www.france24.com/en/20120726-european-central-bank-mario-draghi-pledges-save-euro-spain-italy-borrowing/

limit – beyond what can ultimately be squared with the bank's mandate - being placed on what the ECB might eventually do. Even the mandate could be changed if Europe's political leaders were to see fit, but even if they don't it seems the bank's President will always find a way to work around the one he has. Thus his reply to a December 2014 ECB press conference question about the legality of QE: not to pursue the bank's price mandate (in the face of ultra-low inflation) is what would be illegal. It is just this kind of pragmatism which characterizes the boldness of Mr Draghi, whether you agree with him or not.

In this sense it is easier to envision the ECB's governing council tweaking their interpretation of the bank's mandate than it is to envision an EU Treaty change to establish, for example, a full fiscal union. In particular given the background of growing euroscepticism which makes it hard to believe that any fundamental alteration will be made to the EU institutional structure in the foreseeable future. For now the ECB has become the in-tray into which all the politically tough or unpalatable and thus unresolvable issues ultimately get dumped. This state of affairs – as we will see below – is not without significant risk for the future balance sheet of the bank.

How we got here

Naturally the ECB didn't start out in life with the commitment to do whatever it takes inscribed on its forehead, especially now that the "whatever" includes the massive and unconditional purchase of member state sovereign bonds (QE). The narrative as to what may or may not be permissible for the bank to do under its mandate has evolved in tandem with the crisis. Indeed, anyone who had been familiar with the late 1990s Maastricht-based prohibition of monetary financing and then gone on a voyage to outer space would be little short of astonished to come back to earth in 2015 and discover what was now going on.

Over time there has been a gradual, but subtle shift in how the justification for policy decisions is expressed, and this shift has not a little to do with the change in leadership at the helm. While in 2009 Jean Claude Trichet could still claim "The ECB's actions since the onset of the financial crisis have been bold, and yet firmly anchored within the medium-term framework of our monetary policy strategy,"[12] it is most unlikely that Mario Draghi would continue to express himself in such terms.

At the start of the crisis the ECB's monetary policy was manifestly based on a "two-pillar" strategy whereby decisions are formulated via a systematic examination of both current monetary factors and macroeconomic risks to price stability in the short to medium run. Policy involves a combination of interest rate adjustments based on the economic analysis and geared to keeping inflation expectations within a desired band, and liquidity decisions (related to the prevailing monetary conditions) driven by the need to either increase or decrease liquidity to help the bank maintain the desired market rate.

At the heart of this traditional division of function lay the bank's so-called Separation Principle[13]. In the words of former ECB Governing Council member José Manuel Gonzalez-Paramo this principle "relates to the dichotomy between the ECB's monetary policy and its liquidity policy or, in other words, to the distinction

---

[12] Jean Claude Trichet, The ECB's enhanced credit support. Keynote address at the University of Munich, 13 July 2009. Available http://www.ecb.int/press/key/date/2009/html/sp090713.en.html

[13] Those interested in delving deeper into this topic might find Christian Bordes and Laurent Clerc's "The ECB's separation principle: does it 'rule OK'?" both useful and informative, http://www.sml.hw.ac.uk/documents/newsevents/clercbordes.pdf

between the formulation and the implementation of monetary policy".[14] In effect The ECB made a clear separation between, on the one hand the determination of the monetary policy stance and, on the other hand, its implementation using liquidity operations.

Traditionally liquidity operations were conducted via one or other of the bank's two standing facilities - the marginal lending facility and the deposit facility. Over the years banks have been able to use these facilities if they either need to increase their liquidity or, au contraire, want to park excess liquidity. Both facilities have an overnight maturity and are available to banks on their own initiative. The deposit facility is used for mopping up liquidity from the banks at rates which normally are substantially below market ones, while the marginal lending facility provides liquidity to banks at rates that – under normal conditions – tend to be slightly above market rates.

In the course of their meetings the ECB's Governing Council customarily adopts (or reaffirms) a "monetary policy stance" which is determined on the basis of current data, forecasts etc. so as to serve the bank's primary objective, namely the maintenance of price stability. As Jean Claude Trichet put it, "the implementation of the stance through liquidity operations aims at steering very short-term money market rates close to the ECB's key policy rate (the minimum bid rate in the Eurosystem's main refinancing operations)". But that was back then, and how things were intended to be.

With the arrival of the financial crisis everything changed. ECB

---

[14] J. M. Gonzalez-Paramo, Credit Market Turmoil in 2007-08: Implications for Public Policy, speech at Eleventh Annual International Banking Conference, Federal Reserve Bank of Chicago, 25 September 2008.

liquidity operations were increasingly conducted not with the intention of achieving a given interest rate, but with the objective of ensuring ongoing financial stability. Although the first massive move by the bank – the 335 billion euros injected during the 5 days following 9 August 2007 – could be seen as both guaranteeing liquidity in the wake of the sub-prime crisis and maintaining the targeted interest rate, the distinction between these two objectives grew as the crisis evolved.

In fact at one point the bank raised its main refinancing rate[15] (due to concerns about price stability) even while it retained and even expanded liquidity provision. It was only after the demise of Lehman Brothers in October 2008 that the bank finally began to reduce its key interest rates and this time it did so to historically low, and ever lower, levels. Between October 2008 and May 2009 the main refinancing rate was cut by a total of 325 basis points and reduced to an unprecedented 1 percent. The Governing Council also made a linguistic innovation and started talking about the application of "nonstandard measures".

The first of these - subsequently referred to as Enhanced Credit Support – focused primarily on banks. After the failure of Lehman Brothers in September 2008 the inter-bank money market effectively shut down. Amid significantly impaired markets and elevated counterparty credit concerns, demand for liquidity rose sharply while interbank lending declined rapidly. The objective of Enhanced Credit Support was to provide banks with unlimited liquidity through a procedure known as "fixed rate, full allotment"[16] at longer maturities than had previously been available (up to six months), with an extended participation (the number of eligible

---

[15] In July 2008 by a quarter point to 4.25 percent.
[16] Full allotment means the ECB places no limit on the amount of cash they are willing to lend to counterparties

counterparts was broadened from 140 to around 2200) and an easing of collateral requirements (accepting a broader range of private assets). Since these measures allowed banks to exchange a broader range of (illiquid private) assets on their balance sheet for longer-term (three and six month) central bank liquidity, the ECB viewed the effects of its unconventional measures to be similar to those of the various classes of credit easing adopted elsewhere.

In doing this the ECB was not generating new credit, but rather allowing banks to refinance existing loans. At a time when market-based solutions were not available the central bank stepped in to plug the gap. It would be an error to see this move as an example of "money printing". An existing river of credit transactions was simply re-directed through the halls of the central bank. Having said this the sheer volume and duration of the new measures inevitably meant changes were afoot. The series of small incremental ad hoc measures was surely going to lead eventually to a much more profound policy shift. For example, given that banks could use the increased access to ECB liquidity to buy government bonds some started talking about "QE by stealth": effectively the ECB was staying within the letter of the monetary financing prohibition law while sailing straight over its spirit.

Then in May 2010, following a bout of significant turmoil in the sovereign debt markets, the ECB broke what was clearly new ground by taking the decision to initiate what was called the Securities Market Programme (SMP) "to address the severe tensions which existed in certain market segments." The key difference between SMP and earlier central bank interventions is that the ECB committed itself to outright bond purchases, rather than lending to commercial banks against collateral so that they could buy.

The launching of SMP marked the opening of yet another stage in the consolidation of nonstandard measures as an integral part of monetary policy, a stage which was to take central bank policy ever further away from its earlier liquidity/interest rate separation principle. Under the auspices of SMP the ECB started intervening in the secondary market for some euro area government bonds – Ireland, Greece, and Portugal - in order "to ensure depth and liquidity" and "restore an appropriate monetary policy transmission mechanism".

Following an initial wave of purchases the policy seemed to be working as yields stabilized for a time, leading interest in the programme to lapse. However, a new and more severe outbreak of negative sentiment – this time towards Spain and Italy – lead the programme to be hurriedly re-activated in August 2011. The primary goal of the SMP was to address what was seen as a malfunctioning in certain market segments, those for stressed sovereign bonds, and the objective was to improve functioning by ensuring there was sufficient depth and liquidity. The bank believed that these "severe" market tensions, if left untreated, would create unacceptable downside risks to Euro Area price stability – at least that was the official justification given. The decision to establish the SMP was not accompanied by explicit targets in terms of volumes to be purchased or yield levels to be attained. Indeed ECB policy-makers on numerous occasions emphasized that the purpose of SMP was not to change the monetary policy stance but rather to facilitate the monetary transmission mechanism in the face of turbulent and exceptional market conditions, i.e. to ensure that there was sufficient liquidity in specific markets to hold prevailing market interest rates near to the targeted ones.

At the end of 2012 the amount of government securities at the ECB balance sheet due to the SMP was 208.3 billion euros.

In addition, faced with renewed recession in November 2011 the ECB Governing Council (which had actually raised interest rates twice during the year[17]) initiated a further loosening of monetary policy - in two quarter-percentage-point steps – which took the main refinancing rate back to 1.00 percent (where it had been up to April) by the end of the year. The bank also introduced further liquidity-enhancing measures in the form of two Long Term Refinancing Operations (LTROs), each with a 3 year maturity and the option of early repayment after one year, one in December (€490 billion lent to banks) and the second in February 2012 (a further €530 billion injected).

Finally, and following Mario Draghi's "whatever it takes" statement, on 2 August 2012 the Governing Council of the ECB announced its Outright Monetary Transactions (OMT) programme which included the possibility of purchases in secondary sovereign bond markets in return for strict conditionality for the country concerned, attached to an appropriate European Financial Stability Facility/European Stability Mechanism (EFSF/ESM) programme as agreed with the Euro Partners. Again, the justification for the OMT programme – which was never in fact activated – was the safeguarding of the monetary policy transmission mechanism and the avoidance of fragmentation in the application of monetary policy of the kind which could put the unity of the single currency at risk.

---

[17] The various interest rate rises implemented by the ECB during the crisis must surely count as classic examples of the bank's failure to adequately read the implications of its own macro analysis.

Thus far, and despite the application of a wide variety of non-standard measures, the ECBs beloved "separation principle" had remained more or less intact. And so it seemed it would stay, until in early 2014 a chance combination of three developments lead to a profound change in the policy tack. In February the German constitutional court finally gave its ruling on the legality of OMT under German law. At the same time the ECB Governing Council began to recognize that there was a growing risk of undesirably low inflation (and even deflation) in the Eurozone while the main refinancing rate – which had been cut three times during the recession - was languishing at only 0.25 percent, perilously close to the so called "zero bound".

The German Constitutional Court effectively put a question mark over the legality of OMT, while the fact that price stability was threatened when further monetary easing along classic lines was all but impossible opened the possibility that nonstandard measures could be used not to supplement monetary policy but as the core tool for implementing it. This was a sea change that went right to the heart of the separation principle.

As Wolfgang Munchau pointed out at the time[18], the German court ruling effectively left OMT - which only ever had a virtual existence and was increasingly seen as an empty bluff since it was clear no one was going to accept the conditionality side - deader than that infamous dead duck. Karlsruhe's objection to the existing bond buying programme was that it went beyond the ECBs mandate since directly financing government debt is prohibited under Maastricht, and the objective of OMT was to

---

[18] Wolfgang Munchau, Germany's constitutional court has strengthened the eurosceptics, Financial Times February 9, 2014
http://www.ft.com/intl/cms/s/0/8a64e3ac-8f25-11e3-be85-00144feab7de.html#axzz38PGOk6rj

help governments finance at an affordable price.

Hence the court concluded that OMT violates the German constitution while at the same time accusing the ECB of surreptitiously extending its mandate. In addition it argued that the scheme endangered the underpinnings of the Eurozone rescue programmes and even went so far as to suggest it undermined deep principles of democracy. Were it to be used, the court stated, it would deprive the German parliament of its fiscal sovereignty by forcing it to accept any losses the scheme generated. The ruling explicitly considered OMT to be debt monetization, indeed, as Munchau put it, "it is hard to think of any act short of a military coup that could violate so many important constitutional principles all at once."

With bond-buying in order to correct damage to the monetary transmission mechanism essentially outlawed and break-up risk - which could have offered an alternative justification for OMT - off the table following the effectiveness of Draghi's initial promise, the court decision left OMT without definitive legal justification and in practical terms the emperor visibly had no clothes. Had the markets decided to wake up to that fact things might have turned out differently. But they didn't.

Instead everyone started worrying about deflation.

3

Deflation, What Deflation?

According to the history books the British Admiral Horacio Nelson, on receiving an instruction with which he did not agree, simply placed his telescope over his blind eye and declared, "I see no signal". We do not know whether Mario Draghi used a telescope or a microscope when it came to studying the data which lay behind the bank's economic analysis during the summer months of 2013 but whatever the instrument he used the result was the same. At one post- Governing Council press conference after another[19] he blithely declared that, when it came to deflation, "I see no sign, anywhere".

But in similar fashion to the case of the famous sailor, despite his obstinacy the signal was there. For example, in September of that

---

[19] For example, at the September press conference, in answer to the question "do you see any risk of deflation in Europe or in some European countries like Portugal?" Mario Draghi replied: "if we define deflation as a generalised fall in the price level across broad categories of assets and sectors in a context of self-fulfilling expectations, we do not see deflation in any country in the euro area. We see price falls for selected commodities or sectors which are due to a variety of reasons, whether you have some waning of the one-off effects of the indirect taxation, or you see other local effects of different kinds, or you see genuine price readjustments or relative price adjustments. We do not see deflation basically. We do not see deflation for any country at this point in time."
https://www.ecb.europa.eu/press/pressconf/2013/html/is130905.en.html

year no less than nine EU countries had annual inflation of below 0.5%, and three of those were in negative territory (Bulgaria, Greece, and Latvia). So while deflation had far from arrived, the risk that it might do was clear enough.

So why the prevarication? In part the issue is one of definition.

What exactly is Deflation?

According to Mr. Draghi, answering press questions after the June 2013 ECB meeting, "deflation is a protracted fall in prices across different commodities, sectors and countries. In other words, it is a generalised protracted fall in prices, with self-fulfilling expectations. Therefore, it has explosive downward dynamics".[20] This is more or less the standard ECB definition and the bank's President has stuck by it through thick and thin as the issue as progressed.

Leaving aside the small quibble that for self-fulfilling expectations about an ongoing fall in prices to set-in prices first need to start falling, and before they actually start falling inflation needs to drop to an unacceptably low level, there is nothing especially questionable about this definition as such. For deflation to be a problem it needs to be a protracted and not a short term phenomenon, and it needs to be accompanied by a shift in expectations towards accepting that wages and prices will continue falling almost indefinitely. Under conditions of inflation it makes sense to borrow money to buy something now before

---

[20] Introductory statement to the press conference (with Q&A), Mario Draghi, President of the ECB, Vítor Constâncio, Vice-President of the ECB, Frankfurt am Main, 6 June 2013
https://www.ecb.europa.eu/press/pressconf/2013/html/is130606.en.html

the price goes up. A good example of this process at work was in the Spanish housing market between 2002 and 2007. In the latter years of the boom mortgage credit was growing at over 20% a year, and something like 600,000 new homes were being sold. Then the trend changed. Prices that were formerly going up started to come down. Now fast forward to 2014, house prices have fallen 40%, mortgage credit growth is negative, and new home sales are around 150,000 a year. Those who need somewhere to live are renting from the existing stock of houses, and construction activity remains at a very low level.

This is an example of deflation in one single sector, but the impact is still pretty devastating given that it was formerly the key sector in the country's economy. Regional deflation occurs when this phenomenon spreads across countries. As Draghi also says deflation which spreads across an entire economy, and sets-in to stay, has explosive downward dynamics due – as we will see below – to its impact on debt.

If it were not so, where would be the problem for consumers or savers with having falling prices? Falling prices mean ever cheaper products, as has happened over the last decade or so in some technology sectors - and those who buy these products are hardly complaining. Also generalised deflation means the value of money goes up – money can buy more – so again anyone with savings could – in theory – stand to benefit (depending on what happens to interest rates).

In order to see where the problem is, you need to think about how GDP is calculated. The final GDP reading you see in the press is arrived at by applying an instrument known as the GDP deflator to convert nominal (current prices) GDP into real (comparing apples with apples and not with pears) GDP, since it is an attempt to remove the impact of price movements (inflation or deflation) from the final benchmark reading. Let's take an example. If nominal GDP grows 5% and inflation is 3% then real GDP has grown by 2%. If inflation is subsequently re-estimated to have been 2% then real GDP growth turns out to have been 3%, and so on. Adjusting data for deflation is when things start to get more complicated, and doing so when nominal GDP is either stationary or negative is the moment when the world starts to get really wonky.

Let's take the case where nominal GDP grows by 2%, and deflation is 1% - then real GDP grows by no less than 3% (you have to add the deflation number, not subtract the inflation one: if in difficulty ask the Japanese for help, they have been doing this for years). Now let's imagine a case where quarterly nominal GDP growth is zero, but the GDP deflator is estimated at minus 0.4%. Then in this case real GDP grows on the quarter by 0.4%. Supposing that later you revise the deflator estimate to minus 0.2%, then GDP growth is halved at a stroke, since it also becomes 0.2%.

And when I say that when nominal GDP moves close to zero things get wonky, I mean it. Normally nominal GDP grows by more than real GDP due to the impact of inflation. So regardless of how much actual growth there is people feel they have more money in their pockets. This is called by economists "money illusion". But under conditions of deflation things can reportedly be getting better even while people have less money in their pockets and shopkeepers less takings in their tills. Everyone is that little bit better off simply because the value of money has risen. The same quantity of it buys more. Naturally the person in the street has a great deal of difficulty getting their head around this, and something like "reverse money illusion" operates whereby people feel less well off than they actually are. Effectively in the longer run deflation undermines economic sentiment.

Naturally for the person with debt the problem is much worse, since falling cash wages and incomes mean debts become more onerous and more difficult to service. For individuals and companies this is a major problem, but for heavily indebted governments trying to stimulate a deflation ridden economy it becomes a massive one. Which is why deflation is a place it is better not to go, even for a visit. This has been the lesson almost everyone has drawn from the recent Japanese experience.

The Risks of Getting It Wrong

Observers have often noted how Japan's sustained deflationary slump was very much unanticipated by Japanese policymakers, and many have argued this was a key factor in the authorities' failure to provide sufficient stimulus to maintain growth and sustain positive inflation. It is clear that once inflation turned negative and short-term interest rates approached the zero-lower-bound, it became much more difficult for monetary policy to reactivate the economy. In fact the seminal study[21] on how Japan got into the mess it is in concluded that "the general lesson from Japan's experience is that when inflation and interest rates have fallen close to zero, and the risk of deflation is high, stimulus, both monetary and fiscal, should go beyond the levels conventionally implied by baseline forecasts of future inflation and economic activity."

---

[21] Preventing Deflation: Lessons from Japan's Experience in the 1990s, Alan Ahearne; Joseph Gagnon; Jane Haltmaier; Steve Kamin, Federal Reserve Board International Finance Discussion Papers
2002-729 Washington, June 2002

Mario Draghi has referred several times to the Japan experience over the last year, mainly in an attempt to mark a distinction and try to underline how current concerns about a protracted period of low inflation in the Euro Area are quite very different from the situation which faced the Bank of Japan in the late 1990s. On various occasions Mr Draghi has argued i) that the ECB has acted much earlier than the Bank of Japan; ii) that bank balance sheets are not in such poor state as their Japanese equivalents were; and iii) and most importantly of all that inflation expectations are better anchored than they were in Japan.[22]

The first assertion is debatable, the second quite probably the case, but the third is more than questionable. As Ahearne et al state in their seminal study, "observers were generally slow to adjust downward their forecasts for inflation. Although analysts for the most part foresaw a period of disinflation for the mid-1990s, the descent into deflation in 1995 appears to have caught analysts off guard. In fact, private sector analysts continued to project positive inflation rates until late in the decade."

In fact expectations for inflation in the Euro Area have not better anchored than they were in Japan, and – as the Brussels think tank Bruegel point out during the summer of 2014 in an exhaustive study of the topic[23] – they were continually being

---

[22] In this context Mario Draghi's 2014 Jackson Hole speech marked a departure since for the first time he recognized that medium term inflation expectations were not firmly anchored. The significance of this will be explored in the final chapter.

[23] Addressing weak inflation: The European Central Bank's shopping list, Grégory Claeys, Zsolt Darvas, Silvia Merler and Guntram B. Wolff, Bruegel Brussels, May 2014 http://www.bruegel.org/publications/publication-detail/publication/826-addressing-weak-inflation-the-european-central-banks-shopping-list/

revised down from mid-2012 in the wake of lower than anticipated inflation. Indeed Mario Draghi finally admitted as much after the September 2014 ECB meeting.

It is now clear to everyone that, over the relevant horizon for ECB policymaking, inflation expectations have become seriously de-anchored from the close to 2 percent target. Indeed it was probably the failure to act in a decisive way even when the ECB's own medium-term inflation forecasts fell below the two percent threshold more than likely contributed to the downward revision of longer-term market-based inflation expectations.

As Ahearne et al argue, the cost of deviations from the central bank's current inflation baseline is asymmetric: the downside risk is the one which should be prioritized. The track record of inflationary forecasts and expectations suggests that significant changes in inflation are often unforeseen, and the lesson to be drawn from the Japanese experience is that long-term market expectations can be persistently upward-biased.

The fact that long-term inflation expectations in the euro area had not deviated too far from the desired two percent in the period between the summer of 2013 and the decision to implement QE at the start of 2015 was no guarantee that inflation was going to return to the two percent level without additional monetary policy measures, and it now may not do so even with them. In Japan, long-term inflation expectations remained around the one percent mark between 1996 and 2013, even though actual inflation was slightly below zero. According to the study carried out by Bruegel analysts the average error for the 6-10 year inflation forecasts made in Japan between 1996 and 2003 was 1.1 percentage points.

Another argument that Mario Draghi advanced was that price developments in the euro area have been significantly different from the ones found in Japan during the critical period. At the February 2014 monthly press conference, for example, the ECB's President stated that the bank does not see "much of a similarity with the situation in Japan in the 1990s and early 2000s" as "during the period of deflation in Japan, over 60% of all commodities experienced a decline in prices" while "the percentage for the euro are much lower."[24]

Eurostat data show that the number of items used in the calculation of the EU harmonised index of consumer prices (HICP) that are in deflation has been increasing, and at the time of writing stands at about 40% of the total. This share is still lower than that found in Japan where about 50-60% of items were in deflation between 2000 and 2004[25]. On the other hand headline Euro Area consumer price inflation has now fallen below zero and stayed there for three months, so while we aren't in full-on deflation yet the risk that it could finally arrive has clearly risen, which is why Mario Draghi's decision not to put the telescope over his good eye in the summer of 2013 is, with hindsight, an unfortunate one.

Going back to his aforementioned definition that, "deflation is a protracted fall in prices across different commodities, sectors and countries," the last detail is especially important in the context of a monetary union like the one which lies behind the Euro. Just as in the case of inflation, where the needs of one country may differ

---

[24] See Mario Draghi, Introductory statement to the press conference (with Q&A), ECB, Frankfurt am Main, 6 February 2014
https://www.ecb.europa.eu/press/pressconf/2014/html/is140206.en.html
[25] Is there a risk of deflation in the euro area, Grégory Claeys, Pia Hüttl and Silvia Merler Bruegel Blog, 3 April 2014

considerably from another, "one size fits all" monetary policy has its problems even if the policy concerned is a nonstandard one.

The problem for ECB monetary policy at this point is that some Euro member countries actually need "mild" deflation of the non-noxious kind - if, that is, such a thing exists - since they need a relative price correction to restore competitiveness with their partner countries. Normally this issue is thought of as a "core" versus "periphery" problem, with countries like Ireland, Portugal, Spain, Greece and Italy being seen as needing a substantial period of below average inflation.

The difficulty is that these countries are all heavily indebted, with sovereign debt in each case now over 100% of GDP (and rising) and this is where the dangerous and destructive spiral that Mario Draghi referred to comes in. For this price correction to be achieved without the negative price effects it is important that average inflation in the Euro Area be sustained over 1.5%, or even better at or around 2%. This would enable these countries to have very low inflation levels and regain competitiveness without falling into deflation. But with the inflation average hovering around 0.5% this outcome is not possible.

As Mario Draghi told journalists at the January 2014 press conference: "Even when we look at individual countries we may actually see negative inflation rates in one or two countries, but then we should also ask how much of this is due to the necessary rebalancing of an economy that had lost competitiveness and had gone into a financial and budgetary crisis?" [26]

---

[26] See Mario Draghi, Introductory statement to the press conference (with Q&A), ECB, Frankfurt am Main, 9 January 2014
https://www.ecb.europa.eu/press/pressconf/2014/html/is140109.en.html

So the ECB, even after Mario Draghi's "road to Damascus" moment at the central bankers Jackson Hole 2014 meeting, is not preoccupied by the risk of outright deflation as such, but rather with the prospect of a long period of very low inflation. The drawback of such long-drawn-out low inflation, especially in a common currency region like the euro area, "is that it makes the adjustment of imbalances much more difficult. It is one thing to have to adjust relative prices with an inflation rate which is around 2%, another thing is to adjust relative prices with an inflation rate which is around 0.5%. That means that the change in certain prices, in order to readjust, will have to become negative."[27]

Weaker Than Expected Recovery

But why should such a sustained period of ultra-low inflation be a possibility, the Euro Area is, after all, in the midst of an economic recovery? The simple answer is that the recovery is not as strong as the ECB initially expected and continues to remain fragile. In central bank speak downside risks predominate. Another way of putting this would be that unemployment remains too high, while domestic demand continues to be weak. Given that most countries are making serious efforts to improve productivity there is a constant problem of continual oversupply and an ongoing pressure on margins to ensure that what is produced is sold, which feeds through to the fact that price growth is at best weak and at worst negative.

The fact that the ECB is fully cognizant of this weakness is evidenced not only in their monthly economic analysis, but also by the fact they have cut their main refinancing rate twice in the

---

[27] See Mario Draghi, Introductory statement to the press conference (with Q&A), ECB, Frankfurt am Main, 3 April 2014
https://www.ecb.europa.eu/press/pressconf/2014/html/is140403.en.html

last eighteen months: in November 2013 and June 2014. With the rate now at 0.05% that's about as far as you can go in conventional interest rate policy terms.

But why should the recovery be so weak, and why should many refer to the Euro Area as a potential second Japan? The answer to this question isn't so hard to find, although it may be more difficult to explain and understand. Most Eurozone countries are suffering under the impact of one of two problems (and in several cases they are weighed down by both of them): heavy indebtedness and ageing and declining working age populations.

In the aftermath of the crisis we can all sense that some things have changed, perhaps forever, but we hardly dare to ask ourselves what exactly it is and what the future holds for us. Most hang on to the idea that one day or another things will return to "normal". But while they wait their lives - like that of the soldier Drogo in Dino Buzzati's novel the Tartar Steppe who waited decades in a frontier fortress for an invasion that never came - just go by. And with them our dreams for the future.

Perhaps the time to ask some of the harder questions about the recent crisis has come. Perhaps the answers we find, although disappointing in relation to our most optimistic expectations in the past, will not be as painful as we fear. If the recovery that is taking place across the world's more developed economies - in Europe, in Japan, even in the United States - is not unfolding as classical theory suggests it should, then there must be some reason for this. Such a generalised stagnation cannot simply be the result of a wrong policy here or a lack of global competitiveness there.

If the conceptual framework with which many economists analyze the economic world did not foresee such a development the conclusion that we ought to draw is that there is a problem within the theory and not a problem with reality simply because it does not fit the most widely accepted theory about what should happen. Even less coherent is the idea that we need to sacrifice and introduce risky policies to try to return our economies to a path which may no longer exist.

In many ways this has been the pitfall into which central banks and major multilateral institutions like the IMF, the OECD and the European Commission have fallen. They have tried to turn back the tide of history instead of learning to manage the flow. Much to the surprise of all present this is exactly the conclusion drawn the U.S. economist Larry Summers appeared to draw at last fall's IMF research conference[28].

The Era of Secular Stagnation?

At that event the former US Treasury Secretary said two things worthy of note. In the first place he indicated that had he been a member of the "official sector" he would probably have spoken about topics like "the importance of moving rapidly in the face of financial crises, the importance of providing liquidity decisively, the importance of not allowing financial problems to languish, the importance of erecting sound and comprehensive frameworks to prevent future crises".

But since, he went on to say, he was not a member of the official sector, he did not intend to speak about those sort of things but

---

[28] IMF 14th Annual Research Conference In Honor Of Stanley Fisher, International Monetary Fund, November 8, 2013
http://larrysummers.com/imf-fourteenth-annual-research-conference-in-honor-of-stanley-fischer/

rather – and this is what turned the few short words he had to say into discourse-defining – he would draw attention to the fact that in the four years since the end of the crisis in the US, "the share of adults who are working has not increased at all... [and]... GDP has fallen further behind potential, as we would have defined it in the fall of 2009." And what's more, "Japan's real GDP today is about half of what we believed it would be, what the IMF believed it would be at that time, what the World Bank believed it would be."

All of which lead him to wonder "whether a set of older ideas ...[ones].... that went under the phrase "secular stagnation" -- are not profoundly important in understanding Japan's experience, and may not be without relevance to America's experience".

What Summers was getting at was that while monetary policies implemented to combat the financial crisis were successful in so far as they avoided a widespread panic and a financial sector collapse, when we look at their impact on the level of economic activity there is nothing like so much justification for feeling satisfied.

The reality is that trend growth rates in most developed economies have been falling now for years, but it needed the arrival of the crisis for us to recognize it. Something similar happened with inflation rates, far from skyrocketing they trended downwards in most developed countries during what was surely the biggest speculative boom in recent history. It's only in the post crisis world that we are beginning to recognize that it may be possible to generate bubbles even without provoking inflation.

Before the crisis, for example, trend GDP growth in countries like Portugal and Italy was barely in positive territory. Even theoretically stronger countries like Japan and Germany hardly saw their GDP hardly rise by much over 1% per year. Those countries where growth was of 2% per annum or above on average were countries benefiting from housing and credit booms – and much as some hope against hope for it to happen such growth will not be coming back again. It is for this reason that Larry Summers used the term secular stagnation suggesting a our economies had entered a durable stagnation, one which could easily last for decades.

Whatever explanation we give for this pronounced shift in the trajectory of economic growth, the sooner we accept that the environment in which we live is changing and begin to adapt ourselves to the situation, the sooner we can start to get on with our lives again, initiating and developing projects based on a greater degree of realism. As we must all have learned to our cost, constant perusal of the continuous stream of data seeping almost daily from the Eurozone economies is not a particularly invigorating experience. There is much talk of recovery, but just when we think we are seeing its confirmation we get another piece of data which pours cold water on our expectations. Apparently economic revival is everywhere, but for some strange reason it does not give convincing evidence of its presence in the data we receive or the in feelings we have when we look for work or want to go shopping.

If we look more closely it is not difficult to note the change, it is almost as if the whole economic machinery was moving forward with the handbrake locked firmly on. There are no shortage of indications that something is going on and the change very clearly goes well beyond any straightforward cyclical movement. Perhaps awakening from our slumbers would be easier if we could imagine that in a year, or perhaps two, the situation would improve, but the sad reality is that it won't and that what we are facing is a new idea of what "normal" is. Even the emerging countries of Eastern Europe which before the crisis grew at rates between 4% and 6% annually today grow to 1% or 2%. It isn't simply a problem about the Euro.

In the Eurozone, the Greek economy has now been going backwards for more years than we care to remember, but we are now inured to this, and are not surprised in the least to read yet another series of shocking figures emanating from what was once the country of Homer. More surprising, perhaps, is the performance of European economies usually considered to be "strong" – the so called "core" – countries like Germany, Finland and the Netherlands. While Germany is faring much better than its peers, growth remains far from spectacular and there seems to be an almost permanent recessionary threat lurking in the background. The other two countries I mention have recently suffered quite long recessions and continue to experience slow growth suggesting that their economies have been severely weakened by the crisis. And of course, we are talking here about what are normally considered to be highly competitive economies, where there is no special problem with the flow of credit. Yet if things do not change in these latter two countries perhaps Mr. Schäuble will begin to insist that their finance ministers begin to attend the same kinds of economics classes that have been launched in Brussels for their Greek, Italian, Portuguese and Spanish counterparts.

However, as Larry Summers says, and moving beyond the irony of the situation, perhaps what we are seeing should lead us towards a deep reflection, a reflection that goes far beyond the debate over austerity versus stimulus, or whether the ECB is conducting an appropriate monetary policy. We need to situate ourselves in the era in which we live. It is not simply a question of whether this government or that one has fiscal and structural policies which are more or less adequate. Finland, for example, continues to win awards for being an exceptionally business friendly country making it clear that the recent economic downturn there is not easily understood in traditional terms.

History of an Idea

The background to the secular stagnation argument (as originally, even if prematurely, explored by Alvin Hansen[29], Günar Myrdal[30] and even John Maynard Keynes[31] himself in the 1930s) is that the population dynamics set in motion by the industrial revolution of the late 18th century have reached a historic turning point. In the two centuries or so that have elapsed since what many term the modern growth era got going three related but distinct processes co-existed in time:

1/ positive trend population growth

2/ positive trend economic growth

3/ steadily accelerating technical change

You could call these the three "stylized facts" which characterize and define what we have come to call the modern growth era. Now though, the secular tendency in two of them is about to

---

[29] Alvin Hansen (1939), "Economic progress and declining population growth," American Economic Review.
[30] Gunnar Myrdal: The Effects of Population Decline. Godkin Lectures, Lecture VI, 1938
[31] John Maynard Keynes: Some Economic Consequences of a Declining Population, Galton Lecture, 1937

undergo a seismic shift. At some stage during the 21st century global population will peak, and then gradually start to decline, probably forever more. In fact in some countries (principally in Eastern Europe, but also Japan, Germany, Spain, Portugal, and Greece) population is already falling. All of Europe will likely head in this direction sometime in the 2020s, although there is considerable uncertainty still about the actual path dynamics of this process since in addition to birth rates immigration rates also play a part. At the present time some countries in Europe (the UK, Germany, and Switzerland) are in receipt of large numbers of migrants annually, while others are losing working age population precisely to the aforementioned trio.

We are not talking here about some one-off problem (although often observers have spoken about Japan in just these terms), but a generalized phenomenon, a (demographic) transition, something which eventually will affect all countries on the planet and even our entire species. Previously people have tended to use the expression "demographic transition" to refer to the increase in the proportion of working age population and total population that accompanies the drop in fertility from high levels in less developed economies. The expression "demographic dividend" has often been used to describe the boost to economic activity this shift entails. Normally people assumed that this process would come to a halt around the 2.1 total fertility rate (Tfr) replacement level, but in one developed economy after another this hasn't happened, and those in which it has have been more the exception than the rule. So now reality pushes us towards a broadening of the definition of that transition towards acceptance of a later phase wherein populations age rapidly, and ultimately decline, a process that is greatly accelerated in those countries which have experienced long term very low fertility.

What Alvin Hansen and others started to think about in the 1930s was what the consequence of this development would be for the second of the secular processes which have characterized the modern growth era (positive economic growth). What happens if populations (or better put working age populations) start to shrink? The kernel of their argument is summed up by Paul Krugman[32] as follows:

"To have more or less full employment, we need sufficient spending to make use of the economy's potential. But one important component of spending, investment, is subject to the accelerator effect: the demand for new capital depends on the economy's rate of growth, rather than the current level of output. So if growth slows due to a falloff in population growth, investment demand falls — potentially pushing the economy into a semi-permanent slump."

Pretty simple really, but isn't this just what Keynes says at the start of the General Theory, sometimes the simplest things are the hardest to see. Especially if our natural intellectual disposition leads us towards assuming the opposite. Apart from the theoretical simplicity, the idea is backed by plenty of empirical evidence. It has become clear in one country after another that there is a steady falling off of economic growth after the rate of working age population growth peaks and then starts to decline.

The Japan case is clear enough, but the start of the process is already observable in China, where working age population is currently peaking, and where growth rates have now fallen from the earlier double digit levels to ones which are much nearer to

---

[32] Paul Krugman: Demography and the Bicycle Effect, New York Times, 19 May 2014 http://krugman.blogs.nytimes.com/2014/05/19/demography-and-the-bicycle-effect/

the 6%/7% range. People are even alarming themselves with the "outrageous" idea that we'd better get used to 5% growth in China. In fact this easing in growth rates has little to do with a housing slowdown or other much publicized problems. Rather it is structural and long term, and Chinese growth rates will eventually fall to the level of Japanese ones - does anyone seriously think China can keep going on the basis of attracting immigration?

What we are seeing then is that as working age population growth drops towards zero, so GDP growth weakens. The question is, as it turns negative will GDP growth (as opposed to GDP per capita growth) also turn negative? The answer would seem to be "it depends". A simple approximation to a growth accounting model of the type used by IMF, OECD etc. to calculate trend growth in an economy would be the following:

GDP growth = growth in working age population + TFP (total factor productivity) growth

Now, if working age population growth turns negative, then GDP growth can only be positive if productivity grows faster. One conclusion is very obvious: handling the later stages of the demographic transition is going to be all about managing the rate of working age population decline. This can be achieved to some extent via lengthening the working life, raising the participation rate, or having immigration. Even so, we may arrive at a point were GDP trend growth rates drop below zero. This situation is very near to being the case in Japan, Italy and Portugal, among others.

In addition, and this is where we get back to where we started, the structural deficiency in demand which this decline in working age population produces is what increases the likelihood of encountering structural deflation. It is this structural deflation which seems to be arriving in the Euro Area right now, and this impression is confirmed by the fact that many East European countries – where levels of indebtedness are not so high as in the south – are also finding themselves entering deflation territory. Even countries like the Czech Republic and Hungary which have their own currencies are facing similar problems as their Euro Area counterparts. The problem of deflation is not simply a southern periphery problem, or even a Euro Area one: it is a problem which will eventually face each and every country as their working age populations start to decline.

4

The "Good Deflation" Phenomenon

Spain's domestic economy is booming, or so the story goes, and in no small part this boom comes thanks to the arrival of what is being termed the "good kind of deflation", the sort everyone would like to have, a world where prices fall, real incomes rise, jobs are created, and everyone gets to live happily ever after. Let's not worry ourselves too much that in the process the recovery is steadily being transformed from an export lead one into a domestic consumption - or import driven - one.

"Deflation is like cholesterol", the country's Economy Minister Luis De Guindos told CNBC at the World Economic Forum in Davos[33], "There are two kinds.....The bad one and the good one. In Spain, you know, we have the good kind." So appealing was the story he told I'm surprised many of those in his audience didn't immediately get on a plane for a visit to try to discover what the secret was. After all, sounds like the next best thing to a free lunch. Wouldn't anyone want some of that?

---

[33] Deflation is like cholesterol, we have the good kind, interview with CNBC, 23 January 2015. http://www.cnbc.com/id/102363479#

Or again, we have Bloomberg's Maria Tadeo, who temptingly told her readers that "Madrid is ready to party again."[34] A strengthening economy and a pickup in consumer spending, she said, "are energizing nightlife in the Spanish capital after a perfect storm of record unemployment, tax increases and a smoking ban put more than 400 venues out of business since 2008."

"Madrid is a great place to be," Javier Bordas, owner of popular disco Opium told the news site. He now plans to open his night club seven days a week. "You've got the football players, celebrities, and people love to party. We're optimistic."

It makes you wonder why on earth support for the radical Podemos party is surging at the polls. Surely there must be a catch here somewhere?

Of course, Maria is only doing her job and covering a story, an upside-bullish Spain-recovery one, and she does point out that Spain's 23.7% unemployment rate is the second highest in Europe after Greece, but still, it couldn't be that all the intense talking-up of Spain's recovery in domestic demand is also helping to sell some of the 3.34 billion Euros worth of retail commercial property that went under the hammer in 2014, now could it?

Certainly the story must be a lot more palatable to the clique of property consultants who are currently doing the selling than it is to one of the 4 million Spaniards currently on the credit blacklist run by credit consulting firm ASNEF, who normally can't get hold of credit under any circumstances and will have a hard time joining in the current consumer "boom" even if they do find a job.

---

[34] Maria Tadeo, Madrid Ready to Party as Spain's Recovery Lifts Mood, Bloomberg News, 11 February 2015. http://www.bloomberg.com/news/articles/2015-02-11/madrid-ready-to-party-as-spain-s-recovery-bolsters-spending-mood

Spain's Economy minister Luis De Guindos put it even more graphically.[35] "It's hard not to defer purchases when you've got no money for them in the first place," he told reporters at Davos, "in the case of Spanish unemployed I think they've got more worries than waiting for a new sofa suite to drop by €50."

Nor is the "good deflation" argument especially convincing to anyone with sufficient economic common sense to understand that deflation in a heavily indebted economy can **never** be unequivocally "good". I doubt there are too many mortgage holders out there busily applauding the ongoing fall in house prices.

If there is such a thing as "good deflation" it surely comes from falling prices in the wake of productivity gains rather than from "downward stickiness" in wages and pensions. But this is not the Spanish case since employment is growing faster than output. Spain's economy grew by 1.4% during 2014, yet employment was up 2.5%, suggesting that labour productivity actually fell during the year. So Spain's drift downward in prices is being fueled more by a demand shortfall than by supply side improvement: it's hard to see what is so "good" about that.

My intention here, however, is not to argue that Spain's economic recovery has been hopelessly one sided, which it has, but rather to try and pick my way through the ideologically-loaded minefield of arguments which are currently being advanced about the significance and meaning of the deflation phenomenon in Spain.

---

[35] Spain's de Guindos says there is no deflation in Spain, Forex Live, 26 November 2014. http://www.forexlive.com/blog/2014/11/26/spains-guindos-says-there-is-no-deflation-in-spain-26-november-2014

So, Is Deflation A Problem?

"Deflation is a protracted fall in prices across different commodities, sectors and countries. In other words, it is a generalised protracted fall in prices, with self-fulfilling expectations. Therefore, it has explosive downward dynamics."
Mario Draghi

One of the reasons the arrival of deflation in Spain has generated so much controversy is that many doubt the country is actually suffering the phenomenon at all. Bank of Spain Governor Mario Linde stated, for example, in November 2014 that "deflation risk in Spain continues to be low."[36] Economy Minister Luis De Guindos was no less explicit a few days later, "Spain is not at risk of sliding into deflation."[37] But even beyond policy makers and those who have economic interests in "talking up" the Spanish recovery there is also little perception that it is a real issue, possibly because many have come to doubt so many of the things the administration says that they aren't even sure yet prices are actually falling. Leaving aside petrol and house prices the fall is so comparatively small it's not that easy to perceive, especially when reductions are not shown in the form of like-for-like changes, but in the form of more complex "offers" and "discounts" or "two-for the price of one" promotions.

In fact statistics show that consumer prices were down in January by 1.5% over January 2014, while the GDP deflator for the whole of 2014 (the figure that is used to estimate the impact of inflation on overall output) was estimated at minus 0.7%, meaning that the

---

[36] El Banco De España Descarta Deflación y Recessión en España , Te Interessa, 25 November 2014http://www.teinteresa.es/dinero/BANCO-ESPANA-DESCARTA-DEFLACION-RECESION_0_1255075857.html
[37] http://www.channelnewsasia.com/news/business/spain-not-sliding-into/1528816.html

inflation corrected rise in GDP of 1.4% was only half that number in non price-adjusted (nominal) terms. So, statistically speaking at least, deflation is important.

But beyond those who simply - perhaps for definitional reasons - doubt that Spain is experiencing deflation rather than simple disinflation there is another group: those who doubt falling prices really constitute a problem. This is the so-called "good deflation" argument. The FT's Tobias Buck sums up many of the arguments in his article "Spanish Consumers Defy Deflationary Gloom"[38] article.

The gist of the "good deflation" case is pretty simple: on the one hand countries like Spain need falling prices and some kind of "internal devaluation" in their ongoing attempt to restore international competitiveness with other members of the Euro Area. On the other consumers aren't "so" rational as to engage in long and complex calculations across generations and infinite time just to work out whether it is better to purchase now-or-later products whose price is falling by only 1% a year.

At this point it is perhaps worth reminding ourselves of just what Mario Draghi actually says deflation is. "Deflation", he tells us, "is a generalised **protracted** fall in prices, accompanied by **self-fulfilling expectations** which has explosive downward dynamics."

In this sense little in the way of conclusions can be drawn from Spain's initial contact with falling prices, since it hasn't been that protracted (yet) and certainly has not developed self-fulfilling expectations: most people in Spain regard the situation as

---

[38] Tobias Buck, Spanish Consumers Defy Deflationary Gloom, Financial Times 21 January 2015 http://www.ft.com/intl/cms/s/0/aa1c7bbe-a159-11e4-bd03-00144feab7de.html#axzz3QgTQz9Hp

transitory. The self-fulfilling part of the definition relates to the possibility of a downward wage-price spiral which mirrors the kind of self-reinforcement we see under inflationary dynamics but in the opposite direction. As prices fall, then wage reductions can be offered - as has been evident in Japan - to maintain real wages constant and these wage cuts then fuel further drops in prices. None of this is to be seen in Spain so far, even if wages have fallen at some points in the crisis, and this being election year, the process is unlikely to take hold in 2015.

As for those "explosive dynamics" Mr Draghi mentions, the explosive part refers to the impact of a wage-price downward spiral on debt affordability, since debt to income ratios are constantly pushed up as incomes go down.

The idea that economies move into an outright contractionary spiral simply because a small fall in prices is repeated over a number of years is a curious one, whose origin isn't clear, and whose reality is to some extent denied. As FT Alphaville's Matthew Klein points out[39] in a post entitled "Did Japan Actually Lose Any Decades", Japan's economy is widely believed to have performed "tolerably well" all through the deflation years, with weaker consumption growth being more due to declining population (a problem which may also affect Spain in the future) than it is to a supposed phenomenon of "purchase postponement". It's only when you start to look at Japan's 245% government debt to GDP level that you get to see where there might be a problem.

Even in the case of technological products, where price falls are

---

[39] Mathew Klein, Did Japan Actually Lose Any Decades, FT Alphaville, 4 December 2014. http://ftalphaville.ft.com/2014/12/04/2059371/did-japan-actually-lose-any-decades

constant and significant, people seem more likely to look for a combination of price and performance, since improvements are ongoing and unending, yet even so people do buy.

So if there is general agreement that small but constant price falls don't, in and of themselves, produce widespread purchase postponement, and in addition that Spain needs weaker inflation than Germany, then, you might ask yourself, why on earth are policymakers worried by the phenomenon? Yet worried about it they are, since if they weren't why would the German government be acquiescing in sovereign bond purchases by the ECB (which in principle it is opposed to), purchases whose aim is to try to stop the phenomenon digging in for the long haul?

Assuming you don't write this institutional concern off as yet another example of things only economists worry about, and go on to ask the question seriously then you are likely to encounter three basic explanations: i) not all price falls are small, ii) there is an interest rate impact and iii) those who are burdened by debts become even more burdened as time passes.

Spanish housing offers us a clear example of something whose price has fallen considerably, around 40% since the 2007 peak, and whose price continues to fall (currently in the 3% to 5% per annum range).

Far from this fall in prices having stimulated demand - the deflation "consumption boom" argument - we are witnessing exactly the opposite effect: demand has collapsed, and is not recovering significantly. This is not surprising, since housing is a special sort of good (combining both use and investment) and the market is one where price movements tend to be self-reinforcing.

The Spanish housing market is still far from functioning normally -

the number of new houses purchased in December 2014 was just over 7,000 - the lowest monthly level in more than a decade. True, the number of second hand houses being purchased is rising, but even the combined total is far from showing a sharp rebound.

The problem with the arrival of deflation in Spain is this is going to create an environment where it becomes even more difficult for the housing market to really recover. In the meantime, constantly falling prices have had one consequence: Spaniards now prefer renting to buying, they have become more aware of the risk involved in owning a property. So perhaps rather than thinking about the impact of deflation as being the initiation of a simple purchase postponement process what we should be trying to identify is the way it might induce a broader set of behavioral changes over the longer term.

In any event, given the importance of the Spanish housing market to the economy in general - 75% of the country's household wealth is tied up in property - the situation cannot be ignored: ending deflation in Spain would help push house price movements back into positive territory, and in so doing would give a significant boost to the Spanish economy.

Then There Are Borrowing Costs

Moving beyond the issue of the supposed "purchase displacement effect", Mario Draghi has a rather more powerful argument: the interest rate impact. Consumption growth in modern economies is as much about credit as it is about spending from current income. Too many people are still stuck in the bad habit of thinking about economic dynamics in terms of confidence and money stored under the mattress. Credit plays a major, possibly a decisive role in modern economies, as was evident during the recent "credit crunch". As consumer credit accelerates, economies grow, and normally when this happens central bankers start raising interest rates to slow credit growth. In general I think it is fair to say that those who think there is "good deflation" in Spain and those who think Spanish deflation is "not so good" agree about this.

Yet, curiously, the credit phenomenon is all about the temporal displacement of purchases. When credit is cheap, and inflation is expected to be present, a majority of consumers tend to advance purchases by borrowing. I don't know whether anyone wants to challenge this, but it is the cornerstone of any kind of interest rate policy. It is what gives the central bank, under normal conditions, the ability to apply counter cyclical policies in the face of recession. If this mechanism doesn't work, then there is a problem in the whole way we have been thinking about things.[40]

Once interest rates reach the zero bound (I think it is impossible to separate discussion of deflation from the issues which arise in the context of a zero bound) then this mechanism hits a limiting factor, since while price movements are in negative territory conventional central banking theory makes bankers reluctant to follow by taking interest rates into negative territory (although, it should be said, we are now increasingly seeing the negative nominal interest rate phenomenon in countries like Sweden, Denmark and Switzerland).

As Mario Draghi put it answering questions[41] at the ECBs

---

[40] Some would argue that savers suffer during periods of low interest rates, as their income falls, which is why I say on aggregate, a majority, since normally the increase in borrowing far outweighs the drop in consumption from savers.
[41] Mario Draghi, Introductory statement to the press conference (with Q&A),

December 2014 press conference:

"Now, let me make absolutely clear that we won't tolerate prolonged deviations from price stability, and the main reason is that if these deviations feed into inflation expectations, they'll cause a drop on medium to long-term inflation expectations, which by the way still are within a range consistent with medium-term price stability. But if these were to feed into inflation expectations, these lower outcomes of inflation, were to feed into lower inflation expectations, we would have a zero lower-bound nominal interest rate. This would be tantamount to an increase in the real interest rate."

Here we find some keyword type expressions: **prolonged deviations from price stability, lower long-term inflation expectations, increase in real interest rate.** This situation is rather different from the one described by the Spanish economist Javier Andrés in the Tobias Buck article I mentioned earlier: "The fall in prices", Andrés argued, " is not strong enough, nor is it perceived to last that long, as to make it worthwhile for consumers to postpone the purchase of goods."[42] In Spain at the moment the deviations from price stability have not been strong enough or perceived to have lasted long enough to have an impact on consumer expectations. Indeed Spain's citizens seem to have a kind of "inflation bias" after many years of elevated inflation, and simply refuse to believe that prices really have started falling.

ECB, 4 December 2014
http://www.ecb.europa.eu/press/pressconf/2014/html/is141204.en.html

[42] Tobias Buck, Spanish Consumers Defy Deflationary Gloom, Financial Times 21 January 2015 http://www.ft.com/intl/cms/s/0/aa1c7bbe-a159-11e4-bd03-00144feab7de.html#axzz3QgTQz9Hp

Mr Draghi, however, is worried (although not it seems Mr Linde, or Mr De Guindos, as we have seen) that if the current trend is not corrected Spain's citizens might eventually begin to believe in the presence of price declines and indeed come to expect them, forcing special offers and price reductions on retailers in order to attract customers. This is why the ECB President gives more importance to the issue than his critics do and is taking measures accordingly.

In addition he argues that falling inflation expectations raise real interest rates by influencing the perceived cost of credit into the future. If consumers anticipate inflation, then that makes borrowing cheaper and people tend to advance purchases.

Conversely expected price falls make the cost of borrowing greater, and make the desirability of advancing purchases via credit less. In this sense falling future inflation expectations constitute a form of monetary tightening in the here and now. I am aware of an ongoing debate about whether interest rates really are a key factor influencing investment decisions, but I have never seen an argument suggesting that the cost of credit does not influence consumption.[43] And so it is in Spain, since the demand for household borrowing is not surging, even though the country's banks keep telling us they are now ready to lend.

Deflation Favors Savers Not Debtors

Deflation obviously favors those with money in the bank (unless that is the banks start charging negative rates on time deposits)[44]

---

[43] Well, I have seen one, from Michael Pettis in the Chinese context, due to the very high household saving rate. But in this case, as in so many others, China is a special case.

[44] As is happening now in some European countries, see Chapter 5.

since the value of money – in terms of what it will purchase - steadily goes up. It is not so kind on those with debts, since as prices and incomes go down, debts remain unchanged and the burden of paying them increases.

Spain is an indebted country - the net international investment position (NIIP) is negative to the tune of around 100% of GDP - so it isn't the first place that comes to mind when you think of some kind of "good deflation" process. Japan, in comparison, has a positive NIIP of around 50% of GDP, making it a very different case.

The various sectors in Spain's domestic economy are also very highly indebted, and the combined debt of government, households and the business sector comes to about 275% of GDP, not that much less than it was at the start of the crisis. This is because while household and corporate debt has reduced, government debt has increased considerably. All of this means that if deflation sets in it will be a serious problem for Spain.

Spain's external correction still has some way to go in terms of price competitiveness, but having so called "good" competitiveness recovering deflation is not the way to do it at this point, due to the debt impact. This is why ECB policy is directed towards trying to stimulate Euro Area inflation, since obviously if countries like Germany had 2% annual inflation and Spain and others had 0.5% the correction would be a lot less fraught with problems.

So What Is It - Good or Bad Deflation?

At the moment Spain's citizens have mainly seen only the good side of deflation: wages and pensions went up during 2014 while prices fell. Spanish hourly wages rose an annual 0.2% according to the national statistics office, while pensions were up 0.25% (despite the pension system running a loss of 1.3% of GDP). Consumer prices on the other hand fell 1.1% during the year. In addition 400,000 new jobs were created. It is little surprise then to discover that the statistics office reported that price corrected household consumption was up 3.9% on the year at the end of 2014.

The question is, what happens next? Do workers and pensioners continue to receive above cost-of-living wage and pension increases? This being election year the chances are they do, which means more pressure on profit margins and more withdrawals from the pension reserve fund. But in the longer run, is this sustainable, or will wages and pensions start to fall in line with prices, producing the so called "spiral"?

To get answers to these questions we will need to wait to see what happens in the years to come, but in the meantime important changes may be occurring in consumer behaviour, not only in attitudes towards house purchase, or in terms of any supposed "postponement" activity, but simply in the way people are becoming more sensitive to price movements and bargains. In this context, an article by Justin McCurry in the Guardian[45] recounting the Japanese experience - Spectre of deflation horrifies bankers, but Japan now has a taste for it - makes interesting reading. McCurry concludes that:

---

[45] Justin McCurry, Spectre of deflation horrifies bankers, but Japan now has a taste for it Guardian, 11 January 2015.
http://www.theguardian.com/world/2015/jan/11/japan-deflation-consumers-falling-prices-gyudon

"*Spending habits honed over 20 years die hard. And if Japan's experience can teach Europe anything, it is that government attempts to haul consumers out of the deflationary abyss are fraught with difficulty. An entire generation has come to embrace the deflationary devil they know. For the population at large, what started life as a reluctant thrift habit borne of necessity has quietly become the economic version of the Stockholm syndrome.*"

An article in the online magazine Money Morning - The Real Housewives of Japan: Shopping for Bargains ... Driving Deflation? - highlights how years of deflation have lead customers to expect price discounts, and have come to leverage online and social media in the search for ever better bargains[46].

"*Could,*" they ask, "*70,000 Japanese housewives tip this Asian giant into a deflationary spiral? ... As farfetched as that sounds, it's become a major cause for concern in this nation of 128 million, which has been in an economic funk for two decades. These "real housewives" are part of a user-driven, social-networking site called Mainichi Tokubai, which delivers the best prices on specific grocery-store items to the fingertips of Tokyo-region consumers.*"

And they go on to say, "*To hear frustrated Japanese policymakers and retail executives tell it, these bargain-minded consumers and their equally frugal social-networking site are almost-single-handedly undercutting the Japanese economy.*"

The above articles caught my attention precisely because this online bargain hunting is a phenomenon which is increasingly to be seen at work in Spain: people are starting to shop around a lot

---

[46]Keith Fitzgerald, The Real Housewives of Japan: Shopping for Bargains ... Driving Deflation? Money Morning, 8 July 2010
http://moneymorning.com/2010/07/08/real-housewives/

more and are coming to expect bargains, using online media to help them in their search.[47] In deflationary times a mounting body of evidence suggests there is a rise of a kind of "consumer power" where people come to expect permanent sales and discounts and virtually force these on retailers, to the great disadvantage of the small, local shop. This kind of behaviour obviously fuels deflation and when entrenched it is hard to change. As New York Times correspondent, Stanley White, noted:

"A bargain-hunting psychology is so entrenched in Japan — after two decades of stop-start economic growth, 15 years of falling wages and nearly 15 years of deflation — that the government will struggle to convince people that their incomes will improve enough for them to buy more expensive goods."[48]

Spanish policymakers take note, and think twice in future before you say Spain is simply suffering from a bout of "good deflation".

---

[47] Rebajas y compras online: ¿cómo es la situación en 2015?, Zenith Blog, 7 January 2015. http://blogginzenith.zenithmedia.es/rebajas-y-compras-online/
[48] Stanley White, Deflation a Determined Foe in Japan, New York Times, 17 December 2012 http://www.nytimes.com/2012/12/18/business/global/deflation-a-determined-foe-in-japan.html?_r=1&

5

If only they had their own currency?

It is now reasonably obvious to everyone that having a single size monetary policy that did not make allowance for the specific needs of individual countries played a significant part in blowing credit bubbles and facilitating competitiveness-loss on Europe's periphery. So far so good. But having noted this, it's worth considering the possibility that simply letting countries return to the status quo ante may well not have the strong beneficial effect which many observers all too readily assume. The world we live in today is not identical to the world of the early 1990s when the essentials of the Euro architecture were first thrashed out.

As we shall see, financial globalisation and mass migration flows have significantly changed the environment in which monetary policy operates. One of the first to draw attention to the way things were changing was the Danish economist Carsten Valgreen who coined the expression Global Financial Accelerator to describe one of the most important of the new phenomena.[49]

---

[49] Valgreen, Carsten. 2007. The Global Financial Accelerator and the role of International Credit Agencies, Paper presented to the International Conference of Commercial Bank Economists, Madrid, July 2007

The thought involved is really quite straight forward: real economic decision makers are increasingly isolated from local monetary conditions and more sensitive to global ones like the transnational willingness for credit extension (or, if you prefer, global risk sentiment). Valgreen gives the following arbitrary example:

"A Polish household wants to buy a second home in France. To do this they contact their local bank (which happens to be the subsidiary of a Swedish based banking corporation) in order to obtain mortgage finance. They then chose to borrow the money in Swiss Francs and Yen. This action is likely to have a large impact on the future income streams and net asset value of this Polish household, and – hence – its future behaviour in the real economy. However, as long as free capital flows are maintained the Polish central bank has limited influence on the transaction. None of it is in Polish Zloty. And the credit decision of the private banking corporation extending the credit is taken based on a credit model maintained in Stockholm in Sweden. What will matter for the family is the future currency and rate moves in Swiss Francs and Yen. And the price developments for second homes in France. And perhaps also the future credit attitude of a Swedish based credit institution."

The point of Valgreen's example is to show just how powerless national monetary policy can actually become, especially in small open economies, in a world of fluid cross-border financial flows. In order to illustrate his point further he selected two countries – Iceland and Latvia - both of which were later to gain a certain degree of notoriety. As it turned out neither the Icelandic nor the Latvian central bank were able, via recourse to conventional monetary policy tools, to control the rate of credit expansion in their countries. The end result in each case was surprisingly

http://books.google.es/books/about/The_Global_Financial_Accelerator_and_the.html?hl=es&id=O-guMQAACAAJ

similar despite the fact that one country had a floating exchange rate while the other was operating a currency peg with the Euro.

The Icelandic central bank could control the prevailing interest rate on loans in Icelandic Krona. But that did not matter much for households, non-financial companies or banks who were all busily borrowing in foreign currency. Neither does it seem to matter too much today that the official currency of Croatia is the Kuna - the country has one of the most Euroised economies outside the actual Euro Area.

As Valgreen argues in the Icelandic case, as long as the local banks maintain a high credit rating and are perceived as sound by the international markets, credit flows easily to them in a liquid global environment. "Perversely", he noted, "it even seems as if a stronger currency stimulated the Icelandic economy in the short run, as consumer spending reacts to increasing external buying power and as exports are concentrated in price insensitive commodity sectors."

What seems to matter more than ever before is global liquidity, and global risk sentiment, as can be readily seen at the present time in the growing market for Italian and Portuguese government bonds even though the debt burdens facing the respective governments hardly seem sustainable.

While Valgreen was probably the first to identify this "perverse" rising-currency stimulating credit-growth (financial accelerator) phenomenon, it was later to gain much more attention following Ben Bernanke's various attempts to put the pedal-to-the-metal on US credit demand via systematic quantitative easing. His policy was most successful in generating credit expansion, not as he had intended in the United States, but in countries as far apart as Thailand, India and Brazil. Reserve Bank of India governor Raghuram Rajan's revealed his frustration when he went to Frankfurt last year and complained to his audience: "We seem to be in a situation where we are doomed to inflate bubbles elsewhere."[50]

Policy reactions in the worst affected countries were swift and to the point. Indeed they provoked nothing less than a revolution in economic thinking, as Dani Rodrik proudly heralded at the time:

"In the world of economics and finance, revolutions occur rarely and are often detected only in hindsight. But what happened on February 19 [2010] can safely be called the end of an era in global finance. On that day, the International Monetary Fund published a policy note that reversed its long-held position on capital controls. Taxes and other restrictions on capital inflows, the IMF's economists wrote, can be helpful, and they constitute a 'legitimate part' of policymakers' toolkit."[51]

Naturally, in this case the IMF were prepared to contemplate the use of capital controls to make it more difficult for money to enter (not leave) a country, for the simple reason that raising interest rates to slow an overheating economy was having the perverse consequence of attracting even more money, pushing up the currency in the process, and giving nascent manufacturing industries a hefty dose of the Dutch disease[52]. Unfortunately, most of the "unorthodox measures" deployed had little effect (so powerful are these flows), and after the rise came the – more or less – inevitable fall. While from 2010 to 2013 Emerging Market

---

[50] See Raghuram Rajan's tough battle against bubbles, MoneyLife 21 October 2013 http://www.moneylife.in/article/raghuram-rajans-tough-battle-against-bubbles/34956.html

[51] Rodrick, Dani. 2010. The End of an Era in Finance, Project Syndicate, 11 March 2010 http://www.project-syndicate.org/commentary/rodrik41/English

[52] Dutch disease is a way of describing the apparent relationship between the increase in the share and value of natural resources in an economy and a decline in manufacturing sector competitiveness.

economies from Indonesia to Brazil and from India to Turkey steadily inflated, following the announcement of Federal Reserve tapering intentions in May 2013 the perfectly foreseeable crisis occurred as investors started withdrawing their money and economic activity slumped. Apparently no one had noticed the large current account deficits which were being built up while risk sentiment was so clearly "on". Not a case then of "once bitten twice shy", since this was simply a repeat performance of what had earlier happened on the European periphery.

And it isn't only in Emerging Markets that the Global Financial Accelerator is causing problems. Mark Carney at the Bank of England has recently talked of the need for macro prudential measures in the UK due to the large quantity of money entering the country and seriously distorting the London housing market. Indeed, forward guidance suggesting a growing possibility of interest rate hikes only further pushes up the currency and attracts more inflows in a pattern reminiscent of what happened in Iceland.

The Arrival of Negative Interest Rates

One of the principal driver of these phenomena is the abundance of global liquidity. The latest central bank to plan for a large increase in its balance sheet is the ECB, and the arrival of QE in Frankfurt is now having substantial consequences all along the frontier of the monetary union. There are identifiable currency impacts in countries as diverse as the UK (GBP hit a 7 year high against Euro in March 2015), Switzerland, Denmark, Sweden, the Czech Republic and Poland.

While Switzerland and the UK saw their currencies appreciate during the existential Euro crisis due to their "safe haven" status, what is happening now is a quite different phenomenon. During the earlier crisis money was fleeing the currency union fearing conversion risk, now it is being driven out by as part of an explicit policy from the central bank. At the very same moment Greece was being pushed near to the point of introducing capital controls to stop capital flight, Denmark was rumored to be near to introducing them to stop similar inflows.[53]

The build-up towards ECB QE has been the essential backdrop to such phenomenon. The ECB is implementing a policy which is intended - however much the bank denies they target any given currency level - to make the Euro weaker, based on the idea that this should stimulate growth by encouraging exports, and raise inflation by making imports more expensive. This is the process we have seen at work in Japan. One of the main channels through which QE achieves this effect is via the so called portfolio effect. The central bank action (or even the promise of it) lowers yields on bonds since they become virtually risk free given the presence of the central bank as purchaser of the last resort, making them ultimately less attractive for investors. Faced with this, and with the fact that as the Euro weakens the USD value of such investments falls, the hope is investors offload the bonds they have in their portfolio to the ECB and put the money thus freed-up to use elsewhere. In fact the bank even introduced a negative deposit rate for those commercial banks storing money in its vaults to try to induce this effect.

In principle it is hoped that the additional liquidity generated ends up financing lending in the struggling economies on the Euro Area periphery, but in practice it is more likely the funds move offshore (at least while the Euro is trending down), in the process

---

[53] Denmark Dismisses Report It Could Consider Capital Controls , Bloomberg News, 23 February 2015 http://www.bloomberg.com/news/articles/2015-02-23/banks-do-reality-check-on-report-of-capital-controls-in-denmark

weakening the currency. The challenge for investors under these circumstances is to find currencies whose value is likely to rise as the Euro falls: enter the Swiss Franc and the Swedish and Danish Crowns.

The Swiss National Bank hit the headlines in January when it unexpectedly removed the 120 cap on the Swiss Franc exchange rate with the Euro, a policy measure which had been in place for more than three and a half years. Within minutes of the announcement the CHF surged, and was up by 30% at one point during the day, although it did eventually settle down at a level of 0.98 to the Euro, a rise of nearly 20%.

At the same time the SNB lowered the deposit rate on money paid to central banks from -0.25% to -0.75% taking it deeper into negative territory. The decision caused havoc in financial markets and was widely criticized for its abruptness, although it is hard to see how, once you have such a measure in place, you can remove it other than abruptly. The move hit those who had been foolhardy enough to borrow in Swiss Francs hard, and will probably hit Swiss exporters even harder over time, but given the relative sizes of the two central banks the country had little alternative. Now Switzerland will import some of the deflation the Euro Area wants to export.

Swiss government bond yields soon followed the deposit rates into negative territory. And it wasn't only the 10 year bond, those of shorter duration went to ever lower levels. On the 22 January the 1 year bond yield hit -1.38%.

Negative rates have even started to reach corporate bonds, raising the possibility that companies could eventually be paid to borrow money and then proceed to use it to carry out share buybacks. On 3 February, in a first move of its kind a 20 month Nestle bond started trading below 0%.

Seeing the havoc - and trading opportunities - that were created in markets by the Swiss Cap removal investors did not need much convincing to put themselves to work looking for other possible "volatility" candidates, and it didn't take them too long to stumble upon the Danish Krone's peg with the Euro.

Voters in Denmark rejected Euro membership in a referendum at the start of the century. As a consequence the Danish krone now forms part of the ERM-II mechanism, with an exchange rate which is tied to a band of plus or minus 2.25% around a rate of 7.46038 to the Euro. The question is, are the Danes enjoying this situation? Would they like, as many in London assume, to move to a free floating currency? Looking at the determination of the Danish central bank to resist the pressure of those who would break the peg, the answer seems to be no. The Danes, and especially their important export industries are anxious not to follow along the Swiss path. Yet the cost of trying not to do this is not negligible.

In the first place, and despite having an already over-leveraged household sector, you can get paid in Denmark to take out a mortgage. Danish households owe their creditors 321% of disposable incomes, according to the Organization for Economic Cooperation and Development. "That's the highest ratio in the world and a level that's prompted warnings from both the OECD and the International Monetary Fund to rein in borrowing. Danish authorities argue that households aren't at risk thanks to high pension and household equity levels. Meanwhile, even years after Denmark's property bubble burst, house prices in the country's biggest cities are already higher than at any point in recorded history.

The backdrop to the situation has been the Danmarks Nationalbank's constant lowering of the deposit rate (it did so 3 times in the same number of weeks in February) to a current global record low of minus 0.75%. "The main message is that we are ready to do whatever it takes to defend the peg," central bank governor Lars Rohde told the Financial Times, "We have unlimited access to Danish krone and we have no restrictions on our balance sheet."[54]

Asked how low rates could go, Mr Rohde replied: "We have to admit that we are in unmapped, uncharted territory. Of course, we are well aware there are negative impacts on the financial industry of negative interest rates. But our priority is simply to defend the peg and we will do what it takes."

Another unusual result of the policy is that commercial banks are now starting to charge retail customers negative interest on their deposits. In times of negative lending rates "paying our customers zero or positive interest is very bad for profitability," Palle Nordahl, FIH Erhvervsbanks chief financial officer, told the Wall Street Journal.[55] Denmark is itself experiencing very strong disinflation and the central bank is clearly concerned lest this becomes outright deflation, yet breaking the peg and floating would see the currency pushed up, not down as the country needs. The other alternative of joining the Euro – which would be virtually painless at this point – is ruled out by opposition from Danish voters.

---

[54] Danish central bank fiercely defends currency peg, Financial Times, 6 February 2015 http://www.ft.com/intl/cms/s/0/d3c385f6-adc6-11e4-919e-00144feab7de.html#axzz3UqEit0O3

[55] In Denmark Depositors to Pay Interest to Bank, Wall Street Journal 10 February 2015 http://www.wsj.com/articles/danish-lenders-take-unprecedented-steps-to-combat-negative-interest-rates-1423576590

Meanwhile on 11 February the Swedish Riksbank, the very selfsame one that Paul Krugman had referred to as "sado-monetarist"[56] for its 2010/11 rate hikes, surprised everyone by announcing it was cutting its benchmark borrowing rate to minus 0.1%. At the same time the bank announced a QE style programme of bond purchases. In fact, those looking at what had been happening in Switzerland and Denmark should not have been so surprised: bets the country's currency would rise had been increasing at the same time as the country was sinking steadily into deflation. No other central bank has maintained a negative deposit rate as low as the Riksbank has. The bank reduced the rate for commercial banks to -0.85% in Feb after having maintained it at -0.75% since October 2014, just to keep one step ahead of the Danes.

In fact the central bank's monetary policy had been geared towards steadily weakening the currency over the last two years, and in February Bloomberg had the Swedish Crown down as the worst performer (that is the one that has weakened most) among nine major currencies, with a drop of some 12% over the prior 12 months. Naturally all this hard work was being put in jeopardy by the arrival of the big ECB neighbour onto the quantitative easing terrain. As central bank governor Stefan Ingves put it: " It's like sailing in a small boat on a big ocean. That's reality when you come from a midsize fairly open economy."

What makes the Swedish case such a striking one is that the economy is growing quite rapidly - it was up a quarterly 1.1% in the last three months of 2014, and by an annual 2.7%. In addition

---

[56] Swedish Sadomonetarist Setback, New York Times, 5 July 2014
http://krugman.blogs.nytimes.com/2014/07/05/swedish-sadomonetarist-setback/

the housing market is booming making such an expansionary monetary policy deeply problematic. Credit growth was an annual 6.1% in December 2014, while house prices in January were up 9% over a year earlier. And Sweden comes second only to Denmark in the international housing debt league table, with mortgage debt running at around 80% of GDP. Yet such is the fear of negative impacts from the backwash of ECB policy that policymakers felt they had little choice but to go for what they clearly see as the "lesser evil".

Thus the world of international macroeconomics has changed mightily over the last decade, and things are far from being the way they used to be. Which should give us all some serious food for thought when it comes to arguing in favour of a simple return to the status quo ante in the case of the Euro Area countries. The benefits of belonging to a currency union with a more powerful central bank have become greater than before in an era when monetary policy is all about the application of non-standard measures when interest rates are generally round the zero mark.

Economic Capacity Limits Aren't What they Were

Another pioneer in questioning the potency of national monetary policy in a globalised world has been Richard Fisher President of the Federal Reserve Bank of Dallas. As far back as 2005 Fisher was already arguing that:

"Globalization is an ecosystem in which economic potential is no longer defined or contained by political and geographic boundaries. Economic activity knows no bounds in a globalized economy. A globalized world is one where goods, services, financial capital, machinery, money, workers and ideas migrate to wherever they are most valued and can work together most efficiently, flexibly and securely".

So, Fisher asked, "Where exactly does monetary policy come into play in this world?" Well let's see:

"The language of Fedspeak is full of sacrosanct terms such as 'output gap' and 'capacity constraints' and 'the natural rate of unemployment', known by its successor acronym, 'NAIRU', the non-accelerating inflation rate of unemployment. Central bankers want GDP to run at no more than its theoretical limit, for exceeding that limit for long might stoke the fires of inflation. They do not wish to strain the economy's capacity to produce. One key capacity factor is the labour pool. There is a shibboleth known as the Phillips curve, which posits that beyond a certain point too much employment ignites demand for greater pay, with eventual inflationary consequences for the entire economy".

And, as he says, "Until only recently, the econometric calculations of the various capacity constraints and gaps of the U.S. economy were based on assumptions of a world that exists no more".

A world that exists no more. And one that individual countries cannot go back to. The issue being presented is not that individual domestic economies are not subject to price and wage increases following surges in domestic demand, but that they are not subject to these to anything like the degree they used to be. Beyond the domestic supply of raw materials, labour and capital, there now lies a much broader and much deeper factor supply market and unless allowance is made in traditional econometric models for the degree of flexibility in these markets, then prior notions of "capacity" are likely to lead policymakers seriously astray when it comes to estimating the impact of monetary policy changes.

The very idea of capacity itself has become much more elusive and elastic. Indeed it is this very elasticity - i.e. the capacity for local economies to draw on large pools of underutilized labour, and even over long distances (the Global Labour accelerator), and to avail themselves of the increased (and normally cheaper) supplies of capital which are available through global financial markets (and of course in the Eurozone context the European capital markets themselves) - which means they are able to respond to rapid increases in demand without the normal wage and prices pressures coming immediately and visibly into play to anything like the extent that they once did.

To take but one simple example, between 2000 and 2008 the Spanish population increased by six million (from 40 to 46 million). Almost none of this increase was the product of natural birth-death-dynamic factors. Six million people went to live in Spain, some to enjoy the sun and the benefits of a new home, but the vast majority as economic migrants, nearly 5 million of them, looking for work, work which was available due to the workforce needs of Spain's unsustainable property boom, a boom which was made possible by an excessively lax evaluation of the situation by the various credit rating agencies (and the official sector in general), and the availability of ultra-cheap funding in the new European capital markets.

The lesson here is that we live in a non-linear world, where capital flows, warped exchange rates or rapid movements of labour can create dynamics which look very attractive in the short term, but prove to be totally unsustainable over a rather longer one. And when they unwind – as we have seen in Spain – everything goes into reverse gear. That is why Valgreen spoke of a Financial Accelerator and why I am extending this expression to cover that of a Labour one, because the changes are not proportional, they are self-reinforcing: they accelerate till they hit a tipping point. Conventional policy has great difficulty handling the kind of processes involved.

Another recent example might make this situation even clearer. Great Britain has at the present time the fastest growing economy among all industrialized countries. But why should Britain suddenly have become a stellar economy, an exceptional out-performer? All this euphoria in the UK really reminds me of Spain, since Spain in its day was also considered to be an "out-performer", experiencing a major economic miracle.

London house prices are rising at the present time at a rate of about 18% a year, and at the same time the current account balance is negative and worsening. At the moment national insurance data indicate that roughly 600,000 economic migrants are arriving in the UK annually. Not as many as in Spain during the boom times - either in absolute terms or proportionally - but still a significant number. Because the immigration is mainly focused on London, it is leading to large local distortions which then affect the whole economy. The new arrivals need homes, but naturally their starting point is that they are without work and so normally they are not looking to buy. They end up renting - maybe in groups of 3 or 4 - and are thus able to collectively pay rental prices which a normal family cannot afford. As a result the buy-to-rent business suddenly becomes much more interesting.

The big novelty with recent immigration into the UK is that it is largely made up of people coming from other countries in the European Union, among these many from the EU periphery including a significant number of Spaniards. Sadly many of those young Spaniards currently arriving in London (maybe around 60,000 a year) are fleeing the consequences of one bubble only to inadvertently fuel another. Thus, labour mobility has a procyclical effect. When the economy is on the upswing, the economic cycle is lengthened with the aid of migrant labour, wage increases are muted enabling the economy to grow more quickly without the need for interest rate rises. If this upswing is driven by a sustainable activity then the situation is win-win. But in cases where the migration serves to sustain a basically unsustainable activity everything seems to be getting better and better and better, until the day it doesn't, and that day is when the bubble bursts.

Traditionally immigrants went to a country looking for a new home, a new life, and a new society to integrate in. But today the pattern is changing. We are seeing – alongside those with all the classic ambitions - migrants who are looking for work or adventure without any clear plan: locate work quickly, and if a crisis hits then change country would seem to be the driving principle. Possibly this is not a conscious initial decision, but it is how things work out in practice. I have used the expression "Hot Labour" to describe this latter phenomenon.[57]

Many young Spaniards working now in London or Berlin seem to fit this category. They don't really plan to emigrate, they just want to survive what they perceive as a "difficult period" in their home country. Asked in surveys about how they see their future they normally reply that they are working abroad "temporarily" and will eventually return home. In fact they may never return home: emigration is a process which is often not the product of a firm initial decision, but equally these unwitting emigrants may also be forced to move on quickly if the economic recovery in the country where they have found work suddenly becomes volatile.

So the distinction between immigrants and Hot Labour could be thought of as following the same pattern as the one found in analysing capital flows, where people have long distinguished between foreign direct investment and speculative investments, of the kind usually covered by the expression "Hot Money ".

In fact, Spain itself is a good example of what can happen, since the earlier migrant flows have now completely inverted: in 2013 alone approximately half a million people left, most of them former immigrants. The National Statistics Office estimates that the country's population could fall by 2.5 million between now

---

[57] See my blog, The "Hot Labour" Phenomenon, Edward Hugh Blog, 11 June 2014 http://edwardhughtoo.blogspot.com.es/2014/06/the-hot-labour-phenomenon.html

and 2023. The long term consequences for Spain, and the Spanish economy are hard to foresee at this point, but they are hardly going to be positive.

Leaving The Euro – Last Exit To Somewhere?

"Think of it this way: the Greek government cannot announce a policy of leaving the euro and I'm sure it has no intention of doing that. But at this point it's all too easy to imagine a default on debt, triggering a crisis of confidence, which forces the government to impose a banking holiday and at that point the logic of hanging on to the common currency come hell or high water becomes a lot less compelling."
Paul Krugman – How Reversible Is The Euro?[58]

"Some economists, myself included, look at Europe's woes and have the feeling that we've seen this movie before, a decade ago on another continent: specifically, in Argentina" – Paul Krugman: Can Europe Be Saved[59]

On 30 July 2014 Argentina once more hit the global financial headlines since it entered into technical default when it failed to make a $539 million interest payment to bondholders following the failure of 2 days of negotiations with a group of so called "holdout"[60] investors. The payment wasn't made, not because the country was once again insolvent, but because a U.S. judge ruled that it couldn't be made unless the holdouts - a group of hedge funds led by Elliott Management Corp. – first got the $1.5 billion repayment they were claiming.

---

[58] Paul Krugman, How Reversible is the Euro?, New York Times, 28 April 2010
http://krugman.blogs.nytimes.com/2010/04/28/how-reversible-is-the-euro/
[59] Paul Krugman, Can Europe Be Saved?, New York Times, 16 January 2011
http://www.nytimes.com/2011/01/16/magazine/16Europe-t.html?pagewanted=1
[60] See: Argentina v holdouts: plus ça change, Financial Times, 4 August 2014
http://www.ft.com/intl/cms/s/0/2e479696-1bde-11e4-9db1-00144feabdc0.html#axzz3BONHX7Wz

Nonetheless, whatever the ins and outs of the situation, this event still constituted the second default by the country in a little over 10 years, a fact which helps put in perspective some of the statements made about the country like "investors have short memories", or "once you get default over with it is only a matter of time before you are back in the markets".

The details of the current dispute are complex, and involve owners of bonds who refused to accept the Argentinian offers accepted by other bondholders in 2005 and 2010. But the big point is, 13 years after the 2001 default, Argentina is still not back in the international capital markets and is still wrangling over debt obligations which existed at that time. In the meantime the country has been through numerous squabbles with multilateral economic and financial institutions – including a bout of accusations from the IMF and inflation-linked bondholders that the statistics office was falsifying the country's inflation data, and tensions surrounding attempts to expropriate the assets of the Spanish energy company Repsol without paying compensation. Over and above everything such controversies only serve to highlight the continuing poor quality of the country's institutions of governance, an issue which also frequently arises on Europe's southern periphery.

As the above quotes from Paul Krugman suggest, Argentina has often been cited as a reference case for how to resolve Greece's problems. Indeed in a noteworthy blog post[61] in the New York Times the Nobel Prize winner even went so far as to say that country's "recovery following its exit from the one-peso-one-dollar 'convertibility law'" was "a remarkable success story, one that arguably holds lessons for the euro zone".

---

[61] Paul Krugman, Down Argentina Way, New York Times, May 3, 2012
http://krugman.blogs.nytimes.com/2012/05/03/down-argentina-way/?_php=true&_type=blogs&_r=0

And Krugman was far from alone in the romanticisation of Argentina. In May 2011 Mark Weisbrot, co-director of the Washington Based Center for Economic and Policy Research, in an article[62] entitled Why Greece Should Reject the Euro, said the following:

"For more than three and a half years Argentina had suffered through one of the deepest recessions of the 20th century......Then Argentina defaulted on its foreign debt and cut loose from the dollar. Most economists and the business press predicted that years of disaster would ensue. But the economy shrank for just one more quarter after the devaluation and default; it then grew 63 percent over the next six years. More than 11 million people, in a nation of 39 million, were pulled out of poverty"

Now these are strong claims. But let's leave aside the issue of whether or 11 million people were pulled out of poverty or not, and dig a bit deeper into what actually happened in Argentina, and let's do this by comparing it with another country, one which arguably has similar social and economic development characteristics, Chile . At the turn of the century Chile had a population of more or less 15 million, as compared with the 39 million Argentinians mentioned by Weisbrot. In 1998, just before Argentina entered its depression, Chilean GDP was some 79 billion US dollars, while Argentina's was 299 billion US dollars.

Now let's fast forward to 2010, Argentina's GDP at the end of that year was 370 billion USD, and Chile's 203 billion. That is to say, between 1998 and 2010 Argentina's GDP (as measured in US dollars) increased by 24 percent, while Chile's increased by percent %. As they say in Spanish "no hay color" (there is simply no comparison). Especially when you take into account that Chile has only 38 percent of Argentina's population, while it has 55

---

[62] Mark Weisbrot, Why Greece Should Reject The Euro, New york Times Op-ed, May 9, 2011
http://www.nytimes.com/2011/05/10/opinion/10weisbrot.html?_r=1&hp

percent of Argentina's GDP. So over the 12 years between 1998 and 2010 Chile (which maintained a floating currency throughout) evidently did a lot better than Argentina (despite Argentina's abandonment of the peg). And here's another relevant piece of information: between 1998 and 2010 the Argentinian price level rose by 143 percent, while in Chile it only rose by 48 percent.

Now why use USD GDP as the measure of comparison? I do this since it offers us a simple and convenient yardstick (euros would do equally well) of the relative external values of the two economies. This is important, since Argentina's apparently high growth levels have been also associated with high inflation levels, which have been constantly compensated for by devaluing the peso. This is not a specifically Argentinian problem; it happens frequently in countries where there is poor institutional quality such as, for example, Russia. This year the IMF predict 3.5 percent inflation for Chile and 3.6 percent GDP growth, in Argentina the economy may well contract, and inflation is expected to be somewhere over 40 percent. So something more than the mere ability to devalue is needed for countries to move themselves onto a healthy growth path and raise the population's living standards.

This something is really better institutional quality, although these days more often than not the expression "structural reform" is used. Bank of America Merrill Lynch currency strategist – and former IMF economist – Thanos Vamvakidis makes essentially this point in a research note[63] published at the time of the Greece debate:

"In our view, …(the results of our study)…. point to the conclusion that exchange rate devaluations do not lead to permanent

---

[63] Covered by FT Alphaville blogger Tracey Alloway, Devaluation, the Great Greek Damp Squid? FT Aphaville, May 12, 2011
http://ftalphaville.ft.com/2011/05/12/567256/devaluation-the-great-greek-damp-squib/

competitiveness improvements in rigid economies, such as in the Eurozone periphery. In this context, tail risk scenarios about EUR exit are misplaced. Structural reforms are the best bet to improve the periphery's growth prospects, within or outside monetary union".

Does this whole debate sound familiar to anyone? Anyone remember when Italians were paying themselves in million lira notes? In fact, it was precisely to break the Southern European countries from the high-inflation, high-interest-rates, periodic-devaluation dynamic that the Euro was thought to be such a good idea in the first place. It hasn't worked as planned, but that doesn't mean that the most traditional and the most simplistic solutions are necessarily going to be the best ones at this point.

Due to the current ideological debate between proponents of stimulus and those of austerity a separation between on the one hand "macro" monetary, fiscal and currency policies and on the other more "micro" structural reform approaches has become some sort of "new normal" but it needn't be like this. The two policy levels are completely compatible, and indeed arguably they need to be jointly deployed to achieve some sort of progress towards overcoming the economic depression into which much of Southern Europe has been plunged.

The countries concerned need to restore competitiveness, and some sort of devaluation – whether conventional or "internal"- is still going to be needed, but they also need some kind of institutional and political revolution, and to achieve this they need stability and a long term anchor, otherwise we will see more and more new versions of Argentina developing within (or just outside) the frontiers of the EU.

Put another way: if the most valid argument against going back to the Drachma always was that this would imply default, given that Greece eventually defaulted, why was it not allowed to devalue at the same time? There were proposals being advanced to let the country do just that. As former IMF Chief Economist Ken Rogoff put it[64], "I would recommend that Greece take a sabbatical from the euro zone, do massive currency devaluation and then re-enter at a later date, although I realize there is a very strong political commitment not to let that happen."

The reason for this political commitment is, I think, obvious. If Greece were allowed to default, exit the Euro for a time and then re-enter others would surely seek to do likewise, and that would be a very, very costly affair.

But looked at more pragmatically, what matters is not whether Greece defaulted or not (it did, and others will have to do likewise), or whether Greece left and then re-entered the Euro with a new exchange rate – what really matters is whether Greece becomes Chile or Argentina, and you can't see that issue if you insist on blinding yourself by romanticising Argentina.

Why Countries Like Greece Should Not Leave

Belonging to the Euro has obviously negatively impacted the economic progress of several periphery countries, although those who note this often only look at one side of the argument – the economic imbalances one. More often than not they fail to carry out a "contrary to the fact" analysis of what the political and economic profile of the respective country's institutions would look like if it had not been for the EU policy anchor. Naturally they could have remained in the EU without joining the Euro, but they didn't and that fact now forms part of their shared history. Breaking with the Euro in a disorderly fashion – whether the country remained inside or outside the Union – would risk

---

[64] See Kenneth Rogoff, Germany Has Been the Winner of the Globalization Process, Spiegel Online, 20 February 2012
http://www.spiegel.de/international/business/us-economist-kenneth-rogoff-germany-has-been-the-winner-in-the-globalization-process-a-816071.html

undoing all the democratic and institutional gains that these countries have made over the last 20 years.

In fact arguments to the effect that a US type single size monetary policy would never work for these countries – even in the context of a federal Euro Area with a common treasury – are in reality deeply pessimistic ones when it comes to the future of countries on the southern periphery. They seem to imply that the needed institutional changes are impossible to achieve (possibly for cultural reasons), but if this is the case, it is hard to understand why devaluation is advocated as a simple "cure all". Set adrift and left to their own devices they would only go from bad to worse, especially in the context of the demographic challenges they now all face.

In their book Why Nations Fail: The Origins of Power, Prosperity, and Poverty[65], Darren Acemoglu and James Robinson argue that it is not the vagaries of geography, climate, or culture that determine the prosperity or poverty of a nation. It is the quality of that nation's institutions, both political and economic. What they call "extractive states" are locked into a vicious circle of kleptocracy, suppression of technological innovation and economic and personal freedom. In particular they stress how politically powerful rich elites – that some call extractive classes – constitute the biggest barrier to long-run economic growth in countries where they exercise an inordinate level of influence over the central political authority. Southern Europe offers a good example of just how the presence of such extractive networks helps maintain the respective countries in relative poverty. Any

---

[65] Darren Acemoglu and James Robinson, Why Nations Fail: The Origins of Power, Prosperity, and Poverty, Crown Business, New York, 2012

theory which purports to offer a solution to the Euro crisis without addressing the issue of how what it proposes impacts this issue simply isn't doing its job.

As we have seen in this chapter the world of international macroeconomics has changed mightily over the last decade, and things are far from being what they used to be. In addition the arrival of secular stagnation and sovereign bond purchasing QE has – as we will see in a subsequent chapter – also altered the debt balance, meaning other possible solutions to the debt burden problem beyond traditional default are presenting themselves.

Which should give us all some serious food for thought when it comes to arguing in favour of a simple return to the status quo ante in the case of the Euro Area countries. It should also help those living outside the Euro Area who to understand the strong desire shown by voters in Greece and elsewhere to stay in EMU despite all the evident disadvantages. On a worst case scenario Greece could become another Serbia, an outcome few either in Greece or outside would wish on the country, but on the best case one it would become a Denmark or a Sweden, with its monetary policy and its currency value essentially determined elsewhere. They would most definitely not be getting the ability to determine their own future since the days when international capital movements were characterized by simple models like Krugman's eternal triangle are now long gone.[66]

---

[66] Conventionally economists have assumed that small open economies could choose any two out of three possible policy objectives at the expense of the third. Recent experience, however, suggests that in the choice between a stable exchange rate, stabilization policy and adequate liquidity, the urgent need to stabilize the exchange rate may mean the need to forego both of the other two. http://web.mit.edu/krugman/www/triangle.html

6

Easy To Get Into Trouble, Hard To Get Out Of It

One of the greatest difficulties confronting those debating the desirability and efficacy of European Monetary Union has been the fact that the two sides of the argument have often been talking about entirely different things. Perhaps the clearest example of this has been the insistence over the years on the part of both EU Commission and the ECB on using Euro Area rather than individual-country-level data. While many of the common currency's critics were willing to grant that the numbers looked fine on aggregate, it was what was happening at the national level that worried them. It seems the kind of research that came naturally to researchers trained in the US tradition like Fernanda Nechio[67] either did not occur to or was considered taboo by economists employed at the heart of common currency policy making. As former IMF Chief Economist Simon Johnson put it:

"I vividly recall discussions with euro-zone authorities in 2007 — when I was chief economist at the I.M.F. — in which they argued

---

[67] See: Nechio, Fernanda. 2011. "Monetary Policy When One Size Does Not Fit All" FRBSF Economic Letter 2011-18 (June 13)

that current-account imbalances within the euro zone had no meaning and were not the business of the I.M.F. Their argument was that the I.M.F. was not concerned with payment imbalances between the various American states (all, of course, using the dollar), and it should likewise back away from discussing the fact that some euro-zone countries, like Germany and the Netherlands, had large surpluses in their current accounts while Greece, Spain and others had big deficits"[68].

This focus by those who had reservations about the "great experiment"[69] on disaggregating Euro Area data only served to enrage central bank representatives in Frankfurt even further. Time and time again they highlighted how state level differences in the US are if anything greater than those between individual nations in the Euro Area, a point which the critics freely granted. The latter were not impressed since, they argued, this was completely beside the point given the United States was a single nation, "with a universally shared cultural identity, a single language and a central treasury able to redistribute resources between richer and poorer States."[70] Defenders of the single currency promptly pointed to the European Structural Funds, to which the critics in turn responded by comparing the levels of GDP committed to such transfers (under 2% of GDP in the EU

---

[68] Simon Johnson, The French Determination to Run the IMF, Economix Blog, New York Times, 2 June 2011.
http://economix.blogs.nytimes.com/2011/06/02/the-french-determination-to-run-the-i-m-f/?_php=true&_type=blogs&hp&_r=0

[69] The term used by Ben Bernanke in his essay The Euro at Five: An Assessment, in Posen, A. (Ed), The Euro at Five: Ready for a Global Role? Peterson Institute for International Economics, Washington, DC, 2005

[70] Paul Krugman, Can Europe Be Saved?, New York Times, 16 January 2011
http://www.nytimes.com/2011/01/16/magazine/16Europe-t.html?pagewanted=all

case). And so the debate went - (and continues to go) - on and on, and on and on. It seems the two parties are condemned to misunderstand each other until the day when what can only go on for as long as it can, simply can go on no longer.

One of the problems analysts encountered in attempting to interpret aggregate Euro Area data in the pre-crisis world was that some of the traditional "flashing red light" warning indicators (like for example a country's net international investment position or levels of household credit and indebtedness, or current account balances) were no longer up on the table for policy deliberation. With the benefit of hindsight it is apparent that there was something deeply preoccupying about the sizable current account deficits being accumulated in Southern Europe, but at the time when they were being run up the consensus was that since the Euro Area as a whole was more or less in balance, the situation was not especially preoccupying.[71] Far more importance was then attributed to the dangers inherent in the ongoing US current account deficit[72] yet ironically it was to be the (virtually un-noticed) Euro Area ones which brought the global economy near the point of breakdown.

Since the crisis, the EU Commission has tried to remedy this earlier omission by creating a series of economic indicators which

---

[71] Philip Lane & Gian Maria Milesi-Ferretti, 2007. "A Global Perspective on External Positions," NBER Chapters, in: G7 Current Account Imbalances: Sustainability and Adjustment, pages 67-102 National Bureau of Economic Research, Inc.; and Milesi-Ferretti, Gian Maria & Philip R. Lane, 2007. "Europe and Global Imbalances," IMF Working Papers 07/144, International Monetary Fund.

[72] Nouriel Roubini and Brad Setser, Will the Bretton Woods 2 regime unravel soon? the risk of a hard landing in 2005-2006,Proceedings of the Federal Reserve Bank of San Francisco, February 2005
http://ideas.repec.org/a/fip/fedfpr/y2005ifebx13.html

are to be systematically followed and have been included in what is termed the Macroeconomic Imbalance Procedure (MIP).[73] An online Scoreboard has been created[74] which, according to the accompanying documentation, contains data which can be used to identify emerging or persistent macroeconomic imbalances in a given country. Among the indicators which are followed are sovereign debt levels, current account balances, external indebtedness, unit labour costs and private indebtedness. The initiative is a positive move, but has an air of "closing the barn door after the horse has bolted" about it.

The ideal policy would have been to follow these indicators from the moment the Eurozone was created, and to have stopped the imbalance development dead in its tracks. But since those responsible for developing policy didn't see the imbalances as a major issue or risk this was not done. So a number of member countries were able to systematically generate sizeable current account deficits, run up unsustainable levels of sovereign debt, lose competitiveness to a non-trivial extent, and get their banking systems firmly on the hook with unrealistic levels of private sector debt, all without anyone really noticing.

Given low interest rates, high credit ratings (based on the perception that the Euro Area was effectively a single entity, as policymakers were arguing) and the development of highly integrated European capital markets, getting yourself into trouble was hardly difficult. Greece, for example, developed a 15%

---

[73] See EU Commission, Economic and Financial Affairs, Macro Imbalance Procedure
http://ec.europa.eu/economy_finance/economic_governance/macroeconomic_imbalance_procedure/index_en.htm
[74] See Macro Imbalance Procedure Indicators, Eurostat
http://epp.eurostat.ec.europa.eu/portal/page/portal/macroeconomic_imbalance_procedure/indicators

current account deficit, and a negative net international investment position (NIIP) of close to 100% of GDP. The IMF estimate that competitiveness, as measured by the unit labour cost (ULC) -based real effective exchange rate (REER), declined by 20-30 percent in the decade following euro adoption.[75] And despite the fact that the government was later discovered to have been systematically cooking the books to understate the real level of the fiscal deficit, the country managed to accumulate a sovereign debt to the tune of over 100% of GDP even before the crisis broke.

Well, following Tolstoy's dictum that "every unhappy family is unhappy in its own particular way," there were a multitude of ways in which a country could get into trouble during the good times. In Greece the main issue was the lack of international competitiveness and the high level of government debt, but in Ireland and Spain it was private debt which had been fuelled by low interest rates and easy financing for property construction. In fact government debt wasn't an issue in these countries before the crisis, since in both cases it was under 40% of GDP.

On the other hand bank lending was hugely overextended (loan to deposit ratios reached about 180%) with nearly half of outstanding borrowing being financed in the wholesale money markets across Europe. While government debt wasn't high, construction activity generated large (but not sustainable) revenues encouraging excessive and often frivolous spending. Once VAT income from new home sales disappeared (leaving a large hole in government finance) and the banks had to write-off

---

[75] See Greece: Ex Post Evaluation of Exceptional Access Under the 2010 Stand-By Arrangement, IMF, Washington, June 5, 2013
http://www.imf.org/external/pubs/cat/longres.aspx?sk=40639.0

loans to failed developers the level of government debt surged and is now over 100% of GDP and rising in both cases.

Italy and Portugal on the other hand had no boom. They got virtually no growth out of the first 8 years of monetary union, and in fact their ten year average annual growth rate is currently negative.

Despite the lack of growth both countries managed to ramp up debt, in the Italian case sovereign debt and the Portuguese one massive private debt. Now, however, these two countries come second and third in the Euro Area sovereign debt league, just behind the Greek frontrunner.

Spain, Greece and Portugal also ran very high current account deficits – reaching over 10% of GDP before the crisis broke out. Unit labour costs got out of line in all the periphery countries, rising by something like 15% – 20% more than the Euro Area average between 2000 and 2008. In the case of Portugal, the IMF described the situation as follows: the country's "economic imbalances have increased considerably since its entry into the Euro area. The significant fall in interest rates associated with euro adoption boosted non-tradable sectors and caused a significant real appreciation, created large fiscal and external imbalances, and lowered savings."[76]

And they went on to add, "Portugal's ULC-based REER has appreciated by close to 20 percent since 1995, reflecting nominal wage growth in excess of the euro area average (by about 19 percent), and increasingly also a substantial slowdown in labour

---

[76] Portugal: Request for a Three-Year Arrangement Under the Extended Fund Facility, IMF Washington, 7 June 2011
https://www.imf.org/external/pubs/cat/longres.aspx?sk=24908.0

productivity. Profitability in the non-tradable sector has risen, diverting resources from the tradable sector and resulting in large and sustained current account deficits."

In the Irish case the loss of competitiveness was not seen as such a problem, the issue was much more one of exposure of the banking system (and the sovereign) to non-performing private debt.

"The economic and financial pressures facing Ireland are intense", the Fund said at the time of the country's bailout[77]. "At the heart of the problem is Ireland's banking sector, which is over-sized relative to the economy and holds sizeable vulnerable assets". Such deep-rooted structural problems, the IMF argued, "have resulted in a marked erosion of confidence, leading to a loss of deposits and market funding, almost all of which in recent months has been replaced by ECB funding."

Of course, to back up the new Macroeconomic Imbalance Procedure (which has yet to see its real first test case[78]) there have been other major institutional changes and the newly created banking union would surely avoid a repetition of crises such as the Irish one, but it isn't clear that even while old loopholes are being closed, new ones aren't being created[79]. Really full fiscal union and a federal state structure is needed, but both of these are most unlikely developments given the prevailing Eurosceptic mood in the member countries, both core and periphery.

---

[77] Ireland: Request for an Extended Arrangement, IMF, Washington, 16 December 2010 http://www.imf.org/external/pubs/ft/scr/2010/cr10366.pdf
[78] See EU Commission demands German action to balance foreign trade, Deutsche Welle, 5 March 2014 http://www.dw.de/eu-commission-demands-german-action-to-balance-foreign-trade/a-17477201
[79] See discussion in chapter 5 on population drift and the new labour mobility.

What About Mechanisms for Correcting a Crisis?

So getting into trouble was relatively easy, any fool could have done it, but what about getting out of it? It is here that the real difficulty lies, and this is why, despite all the talk of "nascent recoveries" and "improving fundamentals" much of the periphery is still stuck in some form of long term economic depression.

Greece is obviously the worst case example. The economy shrank for six consecutive years (2008-13) – with output falling by around 25%. At the time of writing it is touch-and-go whether or not the run will extend to seven. Despite all the hard sacrifices made by the Greek people exports were down 7.8 percent over a year earlier in the first five months of 2014, retail sales continue to fall and unemployment remains over 26 percent of the economically active population. Even after having gone through a major restructuring gross government debt was still at 175% of GDP at the end of 2013.

Italy and Portugal are not much better. In Portugal the economy contracted in five of the six years between 2008 and 2013 and now stands at around the same level it first attained in 2000. Growth did seem to be recovering steadily in 2014 until the Banco Espirito Santo Crisis hit. Unemployment has improved and stands at around 14%.

Italy is Portugal without the private debt. Italy's main problem is low (almost negative) growth and high (and rising) government debt. Like Portugal, GDP is back around where it was at the start of the century. Now that the large contractions are over, average growth seems likely to hover between 0% and 0.5% annually over the next few years if there are no more external shocks, but with inflation in the plus or minus 0.5% range, nominal GDP growth is unlikely to exceed 1% per annum and could even remain close to zero. Which means debt levels will continue to grow, and if the ECB doesn't intervene and accept responsibility for part of the debt some sort of debt restructuring will become inevitable.

The big problem for these countries now is how do they get back to where they were before they got into this mess while staying inside the currency union? Some would say quite simply they can't and the conclusion to be drawn is that they should leave the Euro. For reasons explored in the last chapter this isn't as easy or as obvious solution as it seems, and in addition many of the other member countries are effectively counterparties on much of the large external debt that has been accumulated, so in the event of non-payment part of the problem would simply change hands.

Any decision by a member country to cut loose from the Euro is unlikely to be welcomed by the creditor nations, making the idea of a voluntary, negotiated departure pretty unlikely, particularly after Mr. Draghi made his promise. The exiting country would have to do so unilaterally, and face the consequences on debt default and sustained lack of access to international capital markets.

It would be a very messy affair. Under these circumstances the only conceivable way a deliberate decision to leave could credibly be envisioned would be as a result of one or more of the respective agents being actually effectively driven "insane" by the constant painful efforts involved in trying to carry out the very large competitiveness correction required while remaining within the currency union.[80]

---

[80] The situation in Catalonia is in fact the reverse of this, since a relatively well-balanced part of a society which is steadily being driven off the rails simply wants out, a development, ironically, which may lead the region to be expelled

By "insane" I mean prepared to vote for a mixture of policies which go well beyond the boundaries of normal EU consensus politics. Could, for example, Hungary's leader Viktor Orban[81] be offering us an early prototype for the kind of road map which some of the participants might need to follow in order to reach the point whereby they actively decide to leave? In Hungary's case, of course, the departure would be from the EU, not the Euro, but the point is effectively the same, since the farewell party for any Euro exiting country would most certainly acrimonious, and the possibility of regulating and managing the exit would be limited. The end product would almost certainly not be a new version of Norway or Switzerland but the initial steps towards the creation of an unstable populist state.

For the inevitably defaulting participants, given the total determination not to have official sector restructuring, leaving the Euro would more or less automatically mean a sharp break with both the EU and the IMF and in all probability with the United States as well. If we take Greece as an example, the only meaningful possibilities for default would be against the official sector – the ECB, the IMF and the EU member states – and clearly such a development would not be well received, among other reasons due to the precedents which could be created for other struggling countries who might wish to follow the same path.

So the list of probable allies for an exiting country – Venezuela, Bolivia, and North Korea come to mind, or nearer home Serbia, Belarus and even Russia itself – would not be entirely alluring. Despite the recent forceful efforts by Vladimir Putin for Russia to

---

from the Euro with very unpredictable consequences.
[81] See: Orban Says He Seeks to End Liberal Democracy in Hungary, Bloomberg News, 28 July 2014 http://www.bloomberg.com/news/2014-07-28/orban-says-he-seeks-to-end-liberal-democracy-in-hungary.html

become a pole of attraction for Western discontents[82] the difficulty is that after the ending of the cold war, the world is rather short of attractive role models for developed economies who want to pursue unorthodox policies, especially if they are engaged in a disorderly default which is causing considerable discomfort for most of their "first world" peers[83].

Long Term Depression

Meanwhile the situation on the struggling periphery is hardly an enviable one. Economies there are condemned to either frequent recessions or one very long depression, depending on how you classify things[84]. The degree of lost competitiveness that was

---

[82] See: Tsipras blasts EU's Ukraine policy in Moscow, Enet English 13 May 2014, "Syriza leader Alexis Tsipras lambasted western policy on Ukraine and expressed support for separatist referendums in the Ukraine during an official visit to Moscow, upon the invitation of the Russian government."

"We believe the Ukrainian people should be sovereign and should decide with a democratic manner and with referendums on its future," Tsipras said, as quoted by the state-run Athens News Agency, of the breakaway referendums that are leading to the country's partition.
http://www.enetenglish.gr/?i=news.en.article&id=1920
[83] See also: Worsening EU-Russia ties leave Greek coalition in precarious position, Macro Polis, 21 August 2014.

Russia's recent decision to place a ban on food imports from the EU left Greek fruit producers facing significant losses....This opened a window of opportunity for SYRIZA, which has sought closer ties with Russia in recent months (leftist leader Alexis Tsipras visited Moscow in May). The opposition party has been highly critical of the government's decision to back sanctions against Russia, which triggered the ban on EU imports."
http://www.macropolis.gr/?i=portal.en.politics.1448
[84] The UK based Centre for Economic Policy Research has a Euro Area recession dating committee which produced a report on 11 June 2014 entitled Euro Area Mired In Recession Pause which concluded that: The lack of evidence of sustained improvement of economic activity in the euro area does, however, preclude calling an end to the recession that started after 2011Q3. Rather, consistent with the concerns expressed by the Committee at its October 2013

inflicted during the early years of the century means that a decade or more may pass before daylight is seen. If it ever is.

This outcome will prove very painful for the respective populations, but to date it should be noted that there is no real sign of any kind of substantial popular revolt. Given Europe's evolving demographics the political process now manifestly favours the over 50s – who effectively have a de facto majority in the electoral system, given the apathy of the young (who find identification with the current generation of politicians difficult) and their relatively smaller cohort size. Thus, condemned to substantial periods of unemployment (or underemployment in relation to their skill level), many vote with their feet by emigrating, thus reinforcing the domination of the "old age" vote, and making it even more difficult for their respective economies to recover sustainable growth paths. Pensioners, it will be noted, are rarely to be found burning down the centres of cities.

The result: an adjustment process which will be long, slow and demoralising. What these countries 15 years ago could have achieved overnight with a short sharp conventional devaluation will now take years. Take Spain: the country has in fact managed to obtain a remarkable improvement in its current account. Over a 5 year period the country has made a transition equivalent to 11 percent of GDP, moving from a deficit of 10 percent in 2007 to a 1 percent surplus in 2013.

Only one other advanced large non-commodity exporting country has ever been through a current account improvement of comparative magnitude: South Korea in the years 1997–98.

---

meeting, the euro area may be experiencing since early 2013 a prolonged pause in the recession that started after 2011Q3.

Naturally Spain's current account improvement is doubly notable given that it was achieved without currency depreciation. South Korea's adjustment was facilitated by a large exchange rate devaluation, an option that is simply not available to Spain. While Spain's real effective exchange rate (REER) did depreciate significantly over the adjustment period when measured in terms of unit labour costs (ULCs), this improvement largely reflected a process of labour shedding. GDP fell by only 7% while employment dropped 20%, meaning that output per head among those who remained was substantially higher. Effectively nearly 20% of the working age population were expelled from the economy, and given that much of the current demand for products can be satisfied by those who still work it is hard to see how many of the displaced employees are going to get back in again. This is why there is so much talk about "high structural unemployment".

The current account adjustment was also partly achieved by massive "import compression" – essentially the country started consuming a lot less which is not surprising with so many "displaced persons" wandering around with little income or consumption capacity. Growing exports and reduced imports naturally lead to an improved current account. What is striking is the way - as soon as employment started to rise again - productivity slowed and the current account worsened[85].

On the other hand, while Unit Labour Costs have fallen, consumer prices have not – so far – adjusted to anything like the same extent in relation to the Euro Area average.

---

[85] See my: Spain and the IMF: Round the Bend or Out of the Woods?, Spain Economy Watch, 15 July 2014
http://spaineconomy.blogspot.com.es/2014/07/spain-and-imf-round-bend-or-out-of-woods.html

In addition important external vulnerabilities still remain, in particular when it comes to the net international investment position (NIIP) which, as we have seen, remains strongly negative. As the IMF noted in their latest country report on Spain[86] achieving both a major improvement in net NIIP and much lower level of unemployment will surely require a substantially lower consumer price level and years of significantly larger current account surpluses. The IMF conclude that despite everything "the real effective exchange rate is some 5–15 percent above the level consistent with medium-term fundamentals and desirable policies." And as they add, "achieving significantly lower unemployment rates closer to international peers in the medium term may require an even larger adjustment in the exchange rate."

What Does Unacceptably High Mean?

In the midst of all the debates about the current "recovery" everyone is at least in agreement on one thing: unemployment in Spain and Greece remains unacceptably high. But what does "unacceptable" mean? Well according to widely accepted definitions normally it means you don't continue to accept the phenomenon so described and do something about it. But while most of the reports published by organisations in the "Official Sector" (IMF, EU Commission, ECB, OECD etc) are reasonably long on praise for the achievements made to date by the periphery countries, they remain pretty short on practical proposals for dealing with what they consider to be "unacceptable". Wouldn't

---

[86] Spain: 2014 Article IV Consultation-Staff Report, IMF, Washington, July 10, 2014 https://www.imf.org/external/pubs/cat/longres.aspx?sk=41733.0

"undesirable" but "unavoidable" be more honest for the people concerned.

Actually things haven't always been like this. Back in the summer of 2013 the IMF Spain Article IV country report[87] advanced a proposal for a form of work sharing which was widely commented on internationally but received short shrift from economic agents inside the country. In a blog post[88] which sought to defend the proposal for a social compact which would effectively have involved a 10% reduction in Spanish wages and salaries, the EU Economy and Finance Commissioner Olli Rehn cited a line from Bob Dylan - "Something is happening here, but you don't know what it is".

He was talking about the evident uncertainty surrounding the kind of economic recovery Spain might be having. But the line could equally be applied to the across-the-board response of Spanish society to those very Fund proposals he was defending. From employers to unions to government and opposition the country has spoken with one voice, "something is going on here and we don't want to know what it is".

Arguments to explain why the proposal was out of place, and even ridiculous, were multiple, but they all forgot one thing: they failed to take notice of the fact that it is Spain, not the IMF or the EU Commission, that is in deep crisis. They ignored the fact that unemployment, and especially youth unemployment, remained unacceptably high, that the country's future is leaving by the day

---

[87] Spain: 2013 Article IV Consultation, IMF, Washington, 2 August 2013, http://www.imf.org/external/pubs/cat/longres.aspx?sk=40842.0

[88] Olli Rehn, Spanish Sketches A.D. 2013: Can Spain achieve what Ireland and Latvia did?, 6 August 2013. http://blogs.ec.europa.eu/rehn/spanish-sketches-a-d-2013-can-spain-achieve-what-ireland-and-latvia-did/

on planes, boats and trains, that the economic growth outlook is pathetically weak, and that, at the end of the day, if worse damage isn't to be inflicted over the longer term then something most definitely needs to be done.

As Spain IMF Mission Head James Daniel put it at that time, "we see a recovery, but only a weak one".[89] Naturally, by 2014 the language on the recovery had changed slightly, but despite all the fuss and euphoria that has been in evidence at times the recovery remains exactly that: weak. What else could you call a situation where industrial output and retail sales are down around 30% from the pre-crisis peak, and won't have regained their earlier level a decade from now?

What the IMF have been saying is that if you leave the situation as it is then growth will not be sufficient to make a significant change in the unemployment rate. Thus they estimate that on the basis of present policies the rate will still be around 20% come 2020.

In addition the Fund drew attention to the way the impact of the crisis has been so unfairly distributed, with those aged under 30, who surely have little responsibility for what actually happened, being asked to carry the biggest part of the burden. Given this, is it really so surprising that many of them are now leaving to seek a brighter future elsewhere? Still being unemployed at the end of this decade is hardly an enticing prospect!

To avoid such a catastrophe, as James Daniel says, "Growth needs to be stronger and needs to become more job rich". This, he argued, is something that requires action in many areas, among

---

[89] Spain: Continue Reforms to Strengthen Recovery, Create Jobs, IMF Survey Magazine, 2 August, 2013
http://www.imf.org/external/pubs/ft/survey/so/2013/car080213a.htm

which he included "increasing wage flexibility so that growth produces more jobs" and creates "a more even playing field between those with permanent jobs and those with temporary jobs".

The IMF proposal for a 10% salary reduction in return for a 7% increase in employment is effectively a work sharing variant of the so called "internal devaluation" that macroeconomists like Paul Krugman, Dani Rodrik and myself have been advocating for some 6 years now. It isn't a perfect plan, having the Euro doesn't make things easy, but it is a damn sight better than doing nothing and watching and waiting while things get worse. Certainly it is a proposal worth studying and discussing and not simply dismissing out of hand, although this is exactly what has happened.

Another possibility, which I have personally advanced inside Spain, would be to temporarily change the retirement regulations to allow people to retire from 60 onwards on the condition that their employer replaces them with someone previously unemployed and under-30 (not obviously job for job) on a long term contract.

Now, you will say, doesn't this roll back the 2010 pension reform which tied retirement ages to life expectancy and saw a progressive increase in retirement age from 65 to 67? This reform was much applauded at the time, and was indeed a core part of the Zapatero government's attempt to regain market credibility. My response to this objection is, indeed it would, but let's think about the situation for a moment, and in particular about the meaning of Keynes's oft cited – but little understood - phrase, "in the long run we are all dead".

What Keynes was getting at with this expression is that we need to be "nimble of thought" enough to be able to distinguish between the different time horizons involved in economic policy. (And not simply shrug our shoulders because "in the long run it will all sort itself out, Adam Smith style[90]). Simply because something is advantageous in the long run, doesn't mean that a policy to promote it is what is needed in the shorter term. There can be a trade-off between interests, and doing something which might be harmful in the longer run (running up government debt), could be not only a palliative in the short run but could lead to a superior long run outcome if it is done wisely. The dilemma we face in Spain was summed up in more theoretical terms by the founder of modern growth theory - Robert Solow - when he admitted in his Nobel acceptance speech, that "the problem of combining long-run and short-run macroeconomics has still not been solved"[91].

In the long run, despite the fact that we will all die, we are all living longer, and having longer working lives makes sense. But in the short run, in a country with 5.9 million people unemployed (half of them for over a year) and over 50% of those between 16 and 24 who are looking for work unable to find it, asking people to work longer doesn't seem to make that much sense.

Letting people retire to be replaced by people with a younger mind-set makes obvious economic and productivity sense, but what about the implications of such a decision for the pensions system? Wouldn't this be moving backwards? Well this is where the second (2013) pension reform comes in. That reform introduced the principle of "sustainability" into the Spanish

---

[90] In fact, due to declining birth rates this time is different: it won't.
[91] Robert Solow, Growth Theory and After, Stockholm, 8 December 1987 http://www.nobelprize.org/nobel_prizes/economic-sciences/laureates/1987/solow-lecture.html

pension system.

Sustainability means - across the economic cycle – that only as much money goes out as comes in. I think this is a good reform, indeed a vital one, since it transforms the Spanish pensions from a defined benefits one (which would be unable to live up to its promise) into an easy to understand defined contributions one. The pension system becomes an implicit contract between those working and those receiving benefits and takes the government (and most importantly its finances) out of the middle. Indeed there is a formula in place to decide how much can be paid in any given time period, so if more people suddenly start claiming pensions naturally pensions will go down proportionately, but there is no systemic collapse, and there will be no knock on effect on government finances.

What both the above proposals have in common is that they involve solidarity and they involve sacrifice, and neither of these seem to be very much in fashion at the moment. But people need to be aware of the longer run consequences of doing nothing. And this is just where expressions like "Spain has turned the corner" don't really help, since they don't put people in the right frame of mind.

If unemployment is unacceptably high then it is an urgent matter to do something more about it. It does not mean just sitting there with our arms folded to see if the IMF forecast of unemployment moving under 20% in 2020 is fulfilled or whether it happens in 2019, or 2021. These kind of outcomes simply won't do, and as we will see below if they do happen they will have very negative long run consequences for Spain.

Long Run Growth Potential

Virtually everybody agrees that the Spanish economy will grow in 2014 at a rate which lies somewhere between 1% and 2%. Naturally a lot of debate and energy has been invested in arguing about just which end of the range will be nearer the final mark, but the focus misses the point. The end result, whatever it is, may well be better than what was expected in 2013 but at the same time it will hardly constitute an economic revolution. No game changer to see here, please move along.

The issue people should be thinking about is what we can expect from Spain in the years ahead, well beyond 2014 and 2015, and in approaching that tricky question there is no piece of current economic data that can help us decide. We need a different approach: growth analysis.

To put things into some sort of perspective on this account it is worth perhaps noting Spanish retail sales were up a mere 0.3% in the three months through May 2014 over the same period a year earlier, while industrial output was up around 2.5% over the same time horizon. The notable difference between these two numbers reflects the fact that at the end of the day the future of Spain's economy is now more linked to the sale of industrial products abroad than it is to the level of shop sales at home. But the second thought to take away is the sobering one that both of these indicators are still down around 30% since 2007, and that at current rates the economy will need over a decade to get them back to earlier levels, if it ever does.

I say **if** it ever does, since the possibility exists we may not **ever** see Spanish retail sales activity in getting back to their earlier pre-crisis highs. The reasoning behind this idea is simple: after rising rapidly in the first decade of the century Spain's population is now falling and aging at quite a rapid rate, and if that rate isn't at least slowed then a decade from now (whatever the reform progress the country makes) it is hard to see the Spanish economy eking out a hell of a lot in the way of growth. Which means if the country doesn't hit those pre-crisis levels soon, which it surely won't, it may never do so.

To see why this could be the case what we need to think about are not the country's short-term economic dynamics, but its growth potential in the longer term. On this issue the authors of the 2014 IMF Article IV Spain report tell us the following:

"Longer-term potential growth prospects also appear weaker than in the boom years. Growth during 1995–2007 was sustained by large accumulation of capital (the credit-fuelled housing boom) and labour (immigration and rising participation rates) hiding a substantial decline in productivity growth. Demographic trends have now turned negative (emigration and the ageing population) and capital accumulation will likely be lower (given the large rise during the boom and falling population). Spain will also need to tackle the negative effects of very high structural unemployment. In this context, potential growth may only be around 1 percent over the medium term."[92]

Over time Spain's growth trend growth rate has been falling, as it has in most developed economies. In the Spanish case while the economy grew by an average of 3.5% a year over the period between 1995 and 2007 there was an important structural shift in the composition of growth taking place. The rate of per capita

---

[92] Spain: 2014 Article IV Consultation-Staff Report; Staff Supplement; Press Release; and Statement by the Executive Director for Spain, IMF, Washington, 10 July 2014 https://www.imf.org/external/pubs/cat/longres.aspx?sk=41733.0

GDP growth started to slump dramatically after 2000 as both population and the employed population surged upwards. In particular growth during Spain's housing boom became increasingly labour intensive.

Before the mid-1990s a significant part of Spain's growth had come from productivity improvements. Even in the second half of the nineties this remained to some extent the case. But between 2000 and 2007 growth was almost entirely explained by increases in the capital stock (the result of construction activity) and higher labour force growth. This is not the direction a country which wishes to raise its living standards by engaging in higher value added work really wants to go.

Now, in the wake of the crisis, the country faces an enormous challenge since it has to start raising average productivity at the same time as it tries to put 3 million low skilled workers back to work. Spain's leaders are proud of the fact that the country has been creating employment on much lower than expected GDP growth, but this is only partly good news since the other side of the coin is that productivity improvements are now slowing. This is what many feared might happen (current account again turns negative, productivity gains weaken) and is a warning signal that the current recovery may not be on such solid ground as some imagine.

But moving beyond the present, the reason we can expect this ongoing fall in trend growth rate to continue in Spain has to do with the composition of growth and how trend growth is estimated. Basically long term growth potential is a function of working age population dynamics and total factor productivity (TFP) growth.

Leaving immigration and emigration aside for a moment, Spain's population is now virtually stagnant, fertility is around 1.3 TFR[93] - meaning each generation has only about two thirds of the children of the preceding one - and the annual balance will soon turn negative. In fact the annual number of births had been rising before the crisis, but has now started falling again. The annual balance between births and deaths also rose to a peak in the boom years only to subsequently fall back. The difference between births and deaths was a record low of 36,181 in 2013, and within a few years the balance will surely be negative.

But we need to remember: in economic growth terms it isn't the size of the population that matters, it is the age structure, and especially the proportion of working age. Spain's working age population will certainly shrink faster than the overall population will, so even on the best of scenarios Spain's workforce is now facing slow and steady decline and this will undoubtedly bring down the trend growth performance.

But Spain isn't facing the best of scenarios. Where once people were arriving, the dire state of the country's labour market means they are now leaving. And once we factor in immigration, things start to get far more dramatic than the natural evolution numbers suggest. According to IMF economists[94]:

"Demographics have turned negative. After expanding at a fast pace until 2007, population growth slowed significantly and turned negative in 2012. This is likely to be a new trend, as INE projects working-age population to continue to decline over the

---

[93] Total Fertility Rate: estimated average number of children that would be born to a woman over her lifetime at current birth rates.
[94] Spain Selected Issues 2014, IMF, Washington
https://www.imf.org/external/pubs/cat/longres.aspx?sk=41734.0

next years........Labour dynamics will make a much weaker contribution to potential output. Demographics will be a drag on growth due to declining working-age population (emigration and ageing). The Spanish statistical agency (INE) expects working-age population to fall by 1 percent a year over the medium term."

During the boom years over nearly 6 million immigrants came to live or work in Spain. The population - which as we have seen is nearly stationary in terms of births minus deaths - shot up from 40 to 46 million. But now, as the IMF say, this dynamic has turned negative. Quite how many people of working age are leaving Spain every year is hard to say. This, in part, is because while the number of former immigrants leaving is known with a reasonable degree of accuracy, the number of young Spanish nationals who do so is much harder to pin down, mainly because you need to go to receiving countries like the UK and Germany to obtain the data since most Spaniards who are working abroad have not registered with the Spanish national authorities.

According to the latest estimates (30 June 2014) the net number of emigrants leaving Spain in 2013 was 256,849. Of these the net number of Spanish nationals leaving was 45,913. But this latter number is confusing since during 2013 some 190,000 former immigrants obtained Spanish nationality and some of these subsequently left for other EU countries. More to the point perhaps, is that these are net numbers. The gross numbers are even more shocking: over half a million people left Spain in 2013 (547,890 to be exact), while some 291,041 new immigrants arrived.

Now I don't want to get into the issue of the enormous tragedy that is taking place daily on Europe's southern borders (and in any event many of the newcomers currently arriving in Spain are doing so as part of family regroupment processes) but the absolute number of people leaving is very large, and those leaving possess a skill set which is vastly superior to that of those arriving, so in the longer run the human capital drain on Spain is massive, again reducing the potential longer term growth rate.

As the IMF point out, projections here are pretty risky, but still the Spanish statistics office (INE) have made an attempt: basically Spain's population will suddenly have become much smaller and much older. Between 2013 and 2023 the population is projected to fall by 2.6 million, and the number of people in the 20 to 49 age group to fall by 4.7 million (or 22.7%). These numbers are large by any historical standard, which is why it is so important to try to do something more and boost employment rapidly.

If nothing is done the impact on long term growth will be sizable, and the pressure to reduce pensions constant. This INE population and emigration forecast is, you could say, based on a no policy change assumption: it tells us what will most likely happen if substantially more is not done. It is the sense of urgency about this "need to do something more" that I - and many others - do not find encapsulated in the phrase "Spain has turned the corner". If these population projections are realized then quite simply it won't have done so.

Pensions, for one thing, will be set on a continuously downward path, which is why I think pensioners could be convinced of the need for them to make sacrifices now, if the situation were better explained to them. For another the debt which is currently accumulating will have fewer and fewer people left to pay it. And let's not even start talking about the impact of this sharp reduction on the value of Spanish property.

The real problem in Spain – and this is the country's true tragedy - is the complete collapse of civic confidence in many of the country's institutions, a lack of confidence which stretches from the Bank of Spain, to market regulator CNMV (remember the Bankia IPO, the Preference Shares scandal), to politicians and political parties (the Barcenas and Pujol affairs, among many others), to the monarchy. It is this crisis of confidence which makes it so difficult to get the consensus to make more sacrifices.

Many say that there can't possibly be 25% unemployment in Spain since if there were there would be a revolution (referring to the existence of the underground economy but conveniently forgetting that the worst years of the 1930s depression were not years of revolution, those came later).

What many people are missing about Spain is the way the credibility of the institutional structure is weakening. Voices talking about a constitutional crisis are growing. The economic crisis basically coincided with the moment when the set-up established - including the return of the monarchy - during the transition from Franco's dictatorship to democracy was increasingly seen as having "run its course". Many observers recognise that major constitutional reform is needed together with some kind of "rebirth" and renovation in the political system. Last month's EU elections were the latest warning signal. The two main political parties (the so called institutional parties) for the first time since the transition failed to get over 50% of the popular vote between them, while the Syriza-like Podemos - who hadn't even been listed in the opinion surveys - surged from nowhere to take 5 seats and 9% of the vote. And in Catalonia a large majority of voters voted for parties who are actively campaigning for independence from Spain. A general election is coming next year, but it is hard to see either of the "old" parties getting a majority without a complex set of coalition partners.

And whither Spain goes, so go the other depression-struck countries on the EU's southern periphery. If I have dwelt long on Spain here this is only because it is the country I know best, and gives some clear examples of what it means to say the Euro makes it "easier to get into trouble than to get out". Similar points could be made about Greece, Italy, Spain or Portugal, and indeed they will be, from time to time in other chapters across this book.

7

Labour Mobility at Last!

"After all that has been said of the levity and inconstancy of human nature, it appears evidently from experience that a man is of all sorts of luggage the most difficult to be transported." Adam Smith, Wealth of Nations[95]

European countries wanting to move towards economic recovery following the Euro Area debt crisis have much to learn from how East Germany responded following the fall of the Berlin Wall. Such was the message Angel Merkel gave to a meeting of party faithful in Mainz in 2013.[96] Of course, she was speaking about the need for reform, something on which all parties – whatever their ideological stance - agree. "At the beginning of the 21st century", she told her audience, "Germany was the sick man of Europe and that we are where we are today also has to do with reforms we carried out in the past…..When we became part of the Federal

---

[95] Wealth of Nations I.viii.31
[96] Merkel Cites East German Lessons for EU's Problem States, Bloomberg News, 19 February, 2013 http://www.bloomberg.com/news/2013-02-18/merkel-cites-east-german-lessons-for-crisis-wracked-euro-states.html

Republic of Germany we had to carry out massive reforms to restructure our economy, also with great upheaval."

But there was one tiny little detail she forgot to mention. During the post-unification reform period East Germany's population went into what was literally melt-down mode. Writing in 2009 the New York Times Columnist Nicholas Kulish[97] put it like this:

"Unemployment in the former East Germany remains double what it is in the west, and in some regions the number of women between the ages of 20 and 30 has dropped by more than 30 percent. In all, roughly 1.7 million people have left the former East Germany since the fall of the Berlin Wall, around 12 percent of the population, a continuing process even in the few years before the economic crisis began to bite."

And the population decline is becoming self-reinforcing, as fewer and fewer children are born in each succeeding generation. The East German birth rate, which was already low (around 1.3 Tfr), all but collapsed in the early post-communist years. Indeed, according to Reiner Klingholz, director of the Berlin Institute for Population and Development the drop is only comparable to those seen in times of war - "For a number of years East Germans just stopped having children."

Kulish also cites the newspaper Frankfurter Allgemeine Zeitung to the effect that that although 14,000 young people earned their high school diplomas in Saxony in 2009, only 7,500 were expected to do so in 2010, and so on. Since 1989, about 2,000 schools have closed across the former East Germany because of a scarcity of

---

[97] Nicholas Kulish, In East Germany, a Decline as Stark as a Wall, New York Times, 18 June 2009
http://www.nytimes.com/2009/06/19/world/europe/19germany.html?_r=0

children.

Now this situation is quite serious, and needs a long term solution, but it is not as serious as the drama that is currently unfolding in countries like Latvia, or Bulgaria, or a number of the other former communist states in Eastern and Central Europe. These countries are also engaged in an ongoing reform process, and obviously the comparisons with the old DDR come readily to hand. But the lesson we should draw from the comparison is far from evident, unless, that is, what Angela Merkel is trying to highlight is the way East Germany managed to salvage something from what would otherwise have been total population wreckage by sneaking in under the shelter of another state, one with a centralized system of support for pensions and health care. Somehow I doubt it, but it could be this is something we need to think more about.

Optimum Labour Mobility Union?

One of the habitual criticisms outside observers have liked to make about the way in which the Euro currency union operated during its first decade of existence had to do with the comparative absence of labour mobility within the region. Indeed labour mobility as an adjustment mechanism in the face of economic shocks has long been a leading – even a "hot" - topic in the economic literature on currency unions. More than 50 years ago, in his seminal paper on optimum currency areas, Robert Mundell[98] stressed the need for high labour and capital mobility as a shock absorber within a currency union: he even went so far as to argue that a high degree of factor mobility, especially labour mobility, is the defining characteristic of an optimum currency area – i.e. one

---

[98] Robert A Mundell, A Theory of Optimum Currency Areas, American Economic Review, 51, 657-665, 1961

that works well. Thus, a key question when evaluating whether the Eurozone is an optimal currency area has always been: how significant is labour mobility as an economic imbalance adjustment mechanism in Europe compared with, say, the United States?

The answer given has normally been that the Euro Area doesn't work well as a currency union in this particular sense: "Europe is still a stay-at-home place compared with America"[99] would be the consensus view. And the facts would seem to back the folklore up. In 2011, 2.7% of North Americans had lived a year earlier in another US state, while only 0.2% of Europeans had migrated within the currency union over the previous 12 months. As the Economist points out people move around (or stay put) for lots of reasons, but "the economic question that matters is how willing workers are to get on their bikes (these days planes) to look for work when times get hard where they live." The basic idea behind the "ease of adjustment" theory is that the more people are prepared to move the more the respective economies will be able to cope with structural changes in economies and the employment imbalances they produce.

A recent study from the OECD[100], however, suggests that "the times" in this regard "may be a changing". If anything, the migration reaction to the post crisis unemployment shock has been stronger in Europe than it was in America. This greater responsiveness appears to have started in eastern and central

---

[99] On the Move, Economist Free Exchange Blog, 13 January 2014, http://www.economist.com/blogs/freeexchange/2014/01/european-labour-mobility

[100] Julia Jauer, Thomas Liebig, John P. Martin and Patrick Puhani, Migration as an adjustment mechanism in the crisis? A comparison of Europe and the United States, OECD WP 155, Paris January 2014

Europe after countries there joined the EU, which expanded its membership from 15 to 25 in May 2004, then to 27 in January 2007 and to 28 last July. What makes this latest study different is that it goes beyond highlighting the impact of wage differences, which have long been a seen as a big factor in longer-term migration. Rather the study focuses on the kind of labour mobility seen in the Baltic states after the global financial crisis hit. When unemployment shot up following the credit bust Latvian workers started looking in increasing numbers for jobs outside their homeland leading to net emigration of about 6% of the population in the years between 2008 and 2012.

Now, in principle, the fact that people are moving around looking farther afield for work is a good thing, isn't it? Simple economic theory suggests it should be. If only life were so simple. Two issues arise in the case of labour migration within the EU that make the situation different to that of movement from one US state to another. In the first place US states are inside one and the same country. This is important when we come to think about things like unemployment benefits, health systems and pension rights. In the second place US fertility still hovers round about population replacement level (2.1 total fertility rate). In most of the countries on the EU periphery fertility levels are significantly below 1.5 children per woman of childbearing age (Tfr), and have been for decades.

What this means is that sustaining health and pension systems in the face of growing elderly populations is the greatest social and political challenge facing these countries. Children are in short supply, and as such a valuable resource. Fully formed and well educated ones even more so. They simply can't afford to lose their young and educated on any ongoing basis. Otherwise long term sustainability – even of the country itself - comes into question.

After many years of complete neglect the IMF has finally started thinking about the demographic side of the European periphery problem. Well, at least in the Latvian context it has. For whatever reason there seems to have been some sort of resistance among economists – at the Fund and elsewhere - to thinking about demographic issues (including migration flows) as part of the core macro picture, yet as can easily be seen above they obviously do, and growth theorists like economics Nobel Robert Solow wouldn't doubt it for a moment.

As the IMF inform us in their appendix to their 2012 Latvia Article IV consultation report[101], the fact the country's population is shrinking rapidly should start to set some sort of warning signal flashing. During 2000–11 it declined by about 14 percent (340 thousand people). Emigration was responsible for about two thirds of this decline while natural change due to low fertility accounted for the remainder.

Emigration: an estimated 200–215 thousand people, mainly young people—roughly 9 percent of the population— left Latvia between 2000 and 2011.

Low fertility: during the same period the population decline for natural reasons was about 125–140 thousand people (5 percent of the population). The number of births has halved since the early 1990s — from around 40,000 annual births to around 20,000 — the birthrate is well below replacement levels (Tfr 1.3) and

---

[101] Republic of Latvia: 2012 Article IV Consultation and Second Post-Program Monitoring Discussions, IMF, Washington, 28 January 2013
https://www.imf.org/external/pubs/cat/longres.aspx?sk=40274.0

since in each generation there are less children who then don't replace themselves population momentum is highly negative.

The number of births has been falling more rapidly since the onset of the crisis due in part to the harsh economic conditions but also aided and abetted by the fact that the majority of the women emigrating are of childbearing age.

So Latvia is facing a massive challenge. A combination of low fertility and emigration mean that the population is shrinking rapidly and at the same time ageing. The proportion of over 65s is set to surge between now and 2030 as it is all over Europe. Naturally with the hole in the pyramid left by the "missing births" and the working-age-population migration-loss the country is bound to become one of the worst case scenarios, far worse than, for example, Japan since Japan has only been resisting immigration, it has not lost population through emigration. Fortunately, the country has a potential solution - it belongs to the EU, has just joined the Euro, and the possibility exists that the Euro Area will become a transfer union over the next decade.

At least that's the theory but, as I keep stressing in this book, I don't doubt the reality could well be different. Really the creation of this transfer union is Latvia's only hope now, and obviously it would be a substantial net beneficiary, since otherwise it is hard to see how the country will be able to offer its elderly population modern minimum-standard welfare services like health and non-poverty-inducing pensions.

The three IMF economists who produced the most thorough post-mortem on the Latvian crisis - Olivier Blanchard, Mark Griffiths and Bertrand Gruss - do try and address some of these issues[102].

---

[102] Olivier Blanchard, Mark Griffiths and Bertrand Gruss, Boom, Bust, Recovery

As they acknowledge, "an important part of the [Latvian] adjustment has taken the form of emigration". As they also point out Latvian emigration long predates the crisis so it isn't simply a product of the crisis. But the problem was made worse by it, so it is reasonable to ask just how far Latvia's longer term future is being put at risk by the form in which the adjustment occurred.

Again the IMF economists do touch on this issue:

> "*The question however is whether this emigration is, in some sense, a failure of the adjustment program. In the United States, migration rather than unemployment is the major margin of adjustment to state specific shocks..... These adjustments are typically seen as good, indeed as the main reason why the United States functions well as a common currency area: If there are jobs in other states, and if moving costs are low, it is better for workers to move to those jobs than to remain unemployed.*"

This is an argument that is commonly advanced in the context of Euro Area issues (let's leave aside for the moment the fact that Latvia wasn't in the Euro during the crisis, since in fact it was pegged to it). As noted above, in an optimal common currency area the sort of labour mobility we are seeing away from Latvia is a good thing – the population move to other areas where the value of their economic activity is higher. In addition let's leave aside the fact that Europe isn't the United States in another sense, that it is a continent made up of nations, and that these nations form part of our identity as Europeans in a way which is hard to quantify economically but which can't simply be wished away by waving a magic wand. The fact of the matter is that the Euro Area quite obviously isn't an optimal common currency one, at least

---

Forensics of the Latvia Crisis, Brookings Papers On Economic Activity, Autumn 2013

institutionally it isn't. To become one of those it would need to have a common treasury and a common unemployment benefit and pension system, etc.

Unfortunately, this is an issue which the IMF authors, like so many before them, simply slide silently past - "the largely permanent departure of the younger and more educated workers may indeed be costly for those who stay" - like a ship in the night looking for open water while at the same time carefully evading the enemy minefield.

"Is the answer [to the above question: EH] different for a small country than for a US state? Some economic aspects are different: Some of the costs of running a country are fixed costs, and thus may not be easy to support with a smaller population. In the United States, many of those costs are picked up by the Federal government (although, as we have seen for Detroit, the remaining fixed costs per capita may become too large for a state or a city to function). This is not the case for a country, which must for example finance its defense budget alone."

The reference to Detroit is of course salutary (this is exactly the problem), although it is curious that the example they take for the fixed costs of having a separate state is defence, an area where Latvia obviously benefits from the existence of external institutions like NATO and the EU. Again, the extent would be hard to calculate, but one of the factors which must have influenced Latvian's in their decision not to offend their EU partners by devaluing the Lat must have been a consideration of just this issue.

It is also striking that they choose the issue of defence, which as I say could be considered to be a double edged sword in this context, and not the glaring and evident examples of health, care of the elderly and pensions.

At the end of the day, more than just ending the emigration what Latvia really needs (like Japan, like South Korea) is immigration to shore up the population pyramid and to make the welfare system sustainable in the longer run, especially since although the country's future currently depends on the creation of an EU transfer union there is no guarantee there is actually going to be one.

Is Labour Mobility the Most Desirable Adjustment Mechanism in the South?

When it comes to southern Europe, the OECD research didn't notice any significant change in pattern between 2006 and 2011 (the year their study ended). More recent evidence, however, suggests that things have been changing in the south, with 2011/2012 marking a turning point in migration patterns and population momentum all across the southern rim. The number of newly registered migrants into Germany from Italy and Spain, for example, rose by about 40% between the first half of 2012 and the first half of 2013. The number from Portugal rose by more than 25% over the same period, and since that time the process has simply accelerated. Numbers for London and Paris reveal a similar pattern.

Unemployment in the Euro Area currently ranges from about 5% in Austria and Germany to over 25% in Greece and Spain, so there is plenty of potential for imbalance adjustment. The consequence is that half-a-century after Mundell's original article was published, the most ambitious attempt yet to create a single currency spanning a wide variety of national boundaries is about to see "optimal" labour mobility. Or is it really so optimal? Is it as desirable as many assume to correct imbalances between countries through working age population flows rather than through devaluation? Is there any way to evaluate outcomes? Are there hidden costs in doing it in the former rather than the latter way?

Well, in theory this is just the kind of problem that macroeconomists should be attempting to explore. As the master of neo-classical growth theory Robert Solow put it in his Nobel acceptance speech[103]: "Growth theory was invented to provide a systematic way to talk about and to compare equilibrium paths for the economy." However, as he pointed out, in attempting to carry out this task the standard theory "failed to come to grips adequately with an equally important and interesting problem: the right way to deal with deviations from equilibrium growth." Thus, "if one looks at substantial more-than-quarterly departures from equilibrium growth........... It is impossible to believe that the equilibrium growth path itself is unaffected by the short- to medium-run experience."

As he says, it is impossible to believe that the longer term path of an economy is unaffected by the trajectory taken during the deviations from trend - whether upwards or downwards. There is no doubt that emigration, and with it negative working age population dynamics, are being promoted by the ongoing labour market crisis in the worst affected countries. Those where unemployment continues to remain at "unacceptably" high levels.

---

[103] Robert Solow, Growth Theory and After, Nobel acceptance speech, Stockholm 1987, http://www.nobelprize.org/nobel_prizes/economic-sciences/laureates/1987/solow-lecture.html

The question is just how far the longer term future of these countries is being put at risk by the form in which the adjustment is taking place. Are we simply substituting short term debt defaults for longer term pension and health system ones?

Young people are moving from the weak economies on the periphery to the comparatively stronger ones in the core, or even out of an ever-older EU altogether. This has the simple consequence that the fiscal deficit issues in the core are reduced, while those on the periphery are only liable to get worse as welfare systems become ever less affordable. Meanwhile, more and more young people follow the lead of Gerard Depardieu and look for somewhere where there isn't such a high fiscal burden, preferably a place where the elderly dependency ratio isn't set to shoot up so fast.

What impact are the migration trends within the Euro Area going to have on trend GDP growth and structural budget deficits in the respective member countries in the longer term? This is an important issue, since such movements seem to be an unforeseen and largely unmeasured by-product of the kind of adjustment currently being favoured by the EU and the ECB, yet the consequences they have shape the long term future of the whole Eurozone, and with it the sustainability or otherwise of the component states.

One of the cornerstones of the boom Spain enjoyed during the early years of this century was the arrival of economic migrants to fuel the growth process. The country's population, as we saw in the last chapter, grew by more than six million (from 40 to 46 million) in the first eight years of the century, raising employment levels in both the formal and the informal economies. Migrants are still arriving, but the flow balance has now turned negative:

according to data from the Spanish National Statistics Office, as of June 2013 the net outflow was 20,000 a month and accelerating. That is to say a quarter of a million people were leaving a year, or a million every four years. And the rate of departure is still accelerating suggesting the outflow in the future could be even larger. Meanwhile the Spanish pension system continues to run deficits.

So a country which already doesn't have enough people working to pay for its pension system now faces having less and less as time goes by, while the number of pensioners looking to claim benefits will only grow and grow. In part this is the end result of sitting back and watching a 1.3-child-per-woman fertility rate running steadily along for over 30 years. But to this grave underlying problem is now being added a new and potentially more deadly one. Those leaving are not only migrants who came earlier. Increasingly, the young, educated Spanish, Greek, Italian and Portuguese are upping and leaving, and unlike in earlier periods many who go now will never return. Not only is there a massive human capital loss involved, trend GDP growth is evidently being reduced as the size of the potential workforce steadily shrinks, while all those unsellable surplus-to-requirement houses become even less sellable.

Which raises the question: are Mario Draghi and his governing council at the ECB really living up to their promise? Are they really doing what it takes to hold the Euro together? The Outright Market Transactions (OMT) policy was intended to try to remove break-up risk in the capital markets. Despite the fact that the programme has not been made operational, it has worked reasonably well in that capital flight has been brought to a halt and even reversed. The bank deposit base in most countries on the periphery is now rising, and the break-up risk component in national bond spreads has been virtually removed.

But as often happens in economic matters, solutions to one problem may inadvertently promote the creation of another. Avoiding radical debt restructuring on the periphery, and going for a "slowly, slowly" correction doesn't necessarily mean that all other things remain equal. The Euro is being held together by allowing unemployment rates to adjust towards a narrower range via population flows. So capital flight is being arrested by turning a blind eye to "population flight".

The question is, is this good news? Obviously in one sense it is, if this is what is needed to make the Euro work it has to happen. But there is a downside: changes in the political process are lagging well behind developments in other areas, and especially in the migration one. It has been clear since the Euro debt crisis that a common treasury was a necessity for the good functioning of the currency union, that all participants would need to make sacrifices in this regard, yet progress towards this objective has been painfully slow, and full of bitter recrimination. The migration problem might just be the issue that brings this simmering conflict right to a head.

If nothing is done to alter the current dynamic Spaniards will wake up one day to discover the country's population has become much smaller and much older. According to national statistics office projections the population will fall by 2.6 million between now and 2023, and the number of people in the 20 to 49 age group will fall by 4.7 million (or 22.7%). This is why it is so important to try to do something more now and boost employment much more rapidly than we be the case under a "no policy change" assumption. Otherwise the impact on long term growth will be sizable, and the pressure to reduce pensions constant.

Typically the native Spanish emigrants are young educated people who can't find work. There is nothing especially surprising in this, since the tendency has long existed for people to move from more depressed areas to economically more dynamic ones. The exodus from Detroit in the United States immediately comes to mind. Or Scottish people getting on the bus to make the fateful journey from Edinburgh or Glasgow to London. The Schengen accord simply extends this process which used to take place within nation states to entire single-market zones, or currency unions. But does this extension have consequences for the participating states which were not anticipated at the outset, and are these consequences all benign?

In addition, this time round something important is different since these movements are occurring in the context of a long and difficult economic adjustment, indeed the people leaving form an integral part of that adjustment. What's more it is hard to accept that this is the kind of adjustment that countries like Spain and Portugal really need. Renovation in these countries implies these young people with all their energy and talent are injected into the local economy to dynamise it, and not shot out of it like water from a high pressure hose with numerous holes. So the big question I am asking here is whether the economic programs which are being implemented in these countries take sufficient account of the demographic impacts they are inducing, and of the fact that the population loss involved - which most likely will become permanent - is going to cast a long shadow over the history of the countries concerned.

In earlier generations, migrants used to leave behind them what were comparatively high fertility societies. There were more children being born than the local economy could absorb. We can still see this phenomenon in the world around us, as highlighted by the constant tragedies off the coast of Lampedusa, Italy. But the EU periphery case is different because the countries people are leaving are going to be short of working age population in a not too distant future.

True, all these countries are suffering excessive levels of unemployment. But unlike the case of, say, Nigeria or Ecuador, this is not because there are too many young people for the economy to absorb, it is because the economy is stuck in a bad place and can't grow sufficiently to generate the needed employment. Structural reforms are needed, but some of the reforms simply don't make sense. What is the point, for example, in lengthening the working life of older, less productive, workers when these very same people are going in increasing numbers to the airport to wave goodbye to their innovative and educated grandchildren who are forced to leave as a result. Surely a better solution would be sustainability in the pensions system - what goes out in total can be no greater than what comes in - and no increase (and maybe even a reduction) in the retirement age in the short term. Yes, this will mean lower pensions in the short term, but if the young leave those pensions will be **even** lower in the long run. There's a problem of priorities somewhere, and an issue about generational imbalance in how the adjustment is being implemented. The current trajectory is not only unfair, it will lead to far from optimal outcomes in the longer run.

The question we should be asking ourselves is whether there isn't a better way of doing things? In order to ask that question we need to overcome some inbuilt prejudices that economists have accumulated over the years. Labour mobility isn't always and everywhere the optimum solution to regional imbalances. Most economists – like the IMF ones I am about to cite[104] - assume that from an economic point of view emigration raises overall welfare:

"In the United States, migration rather than unemployment is the major margin of adjustment to state specific shocks ….. These adjustments are typically seen as good, indeed as the main reason why the United States functions well as a common currency area: If there are jobs in other states, and if moving costs are low, it is better for workers to move to those jobs than to remain unemployed."

Unfortunately, this is the typical "non-answer" we keep getting about this problem in the EU context. Obviously, from the point of view of optimal output, and the maximizing resources across a continent, most probably such movements are beneficial. But even the United States is sensitive about cross border movements of migrants into the country, even if, perhaps, such movements are beneficial to global economic output. People are moving from countries with high levels of unemployment, to ones where there is a much lower one. But when it comes to such analyses economists rapidly switch from being global to being national ones.

The question we should ask ourselves in the EU context is to whom are the current migrant flows beneficial? Which "collective" community is it whose overall welfare is being raised here? Arguably it is not the ones to be found in Spain, Latvia and

---

[104] Olivier Blanchard, Mark Griffiths and Bertrand Gruss, Boom, Bust, Recovery Forensics of the Latvia Crisis, Brookings Papers On Economic Activity, Autumn 2013 http://www.brookings.edu/about/projects/bpea/latest-conference/2013-fall-blanchard-latvia-crisis

Portugal. EU countries are not US states, and a United States of Europe does not exist. It is a theoretical, and even remote, possibility which may come into existence one day. But if the rich countries have too much to lose and the poor ones too much to gain it never will. Only if there is convergence between countries will it become politically possible, one day, to create a union of states like the USA one among the various members on the Euro Area. Yet the current adjustment is moving countries ever further away from convergence towards a common mean.

This point is obvious, and more-or-less agreed on by all, but when the problem this raises in terms of emigration from countries who have been running birthrates well below the replacement level is put on the table all we get is silence.

Now assuming policymakers are not simply stupid[105] this silence suggests that the whole issue touches on some very fundamental raw nerve. There is no answer in terms of sustainability for those countries who are net losers unless there are reverse direction transfers, as under the US Federal system, and that is something no one wants to talk about, at least in public. As the IMF

---

[105] Stupid they undoubtedly are not, but ignorant about the processes taking place under their noses they most certainly are. A good recent example of this "ignorance" was to be found in Mario Draghi's 2014 Jackson Hole speech. Comparing the differing rates of adjustment in the Spanish and Irish labour markets he said: "This diverging performance can in part be accounted for by emigration, especially of foreign-born labour which was much higher in Ireland." This simply is not true. The emigration of foreign born labour (as a proportion) has been much higher in Spain. Irish emigration has largely been of Irish nationals. He also asserted that migrants in Spain naturalized in large numbers.

"While both Ireland and Spain experienced a strong influx of foreign-born labour in advance of the crisis, an important difference between the two counties is that in Spain a large proportion of these workers were naturalized. This in part accounts for the different emigration dynamics since the crisis."

This simply isn't true. Only one migrant in six naturalized in Spain between 2003 and 2013, and of these one quarter did so in 2013.

economists admit in their paper - "the largely permanent departure of the younger and more educated workers may indeed be costly for those who stay". So the question they implicitly pose - could things be done differently? - remains, at least from the demographic point of view, unanswered.

The depth of ignorance which exists on the challenges these countries face was revealed last year when Prime Minister Pedro Passos Coelho actually said that the best solution to youth unemployment problem was for young people to emigrate. At best we are trying to handle the new and complex problems presented by the 21st century with the aid of simplistic formulas derived from 20th century textbook economics. It's time for someone somewhere to wake up to the fact that the old models don't work, because there are growing number of key factors they simply don't capture. The poor performance of economists using such models is increasingly getting the profession itself a bad name among the public at large. Mr Draghi's outright monetary transactions programme may have done a marvelous job of addressing the issue of financial capital flight but it offered few solutions to the human capital one. In the absence of policies which acknowledge these issues exist in order to then address them none of the sustainability analyses – debt, financial sector, whatever – are worth the paper they have been written on.

Portugal Hollowing-out?

As Portuguese President Aníbal Cavaco Silva once put it, "A country without children is a nation without a future." He was, of course, referring to his country's ultra-low birth rate, which is just over 1.3 (Tfr) and has been below replacement level (2.1Tfr) since the early 1980s. In 2012 only just over 90,000 children were born in the country, the lowest number in more than a century – you need to go back to the nineteenth century to find numbers like the ones we have been seeing since the crisis really took hold.

But added to this longstanding, yet unaddressed, problem there is now another, just as dangerous, one. High unemployment levels and the lack of job opportunities are leading an ever increasing number of young Portuguese to emigrate. The numbers are large, possibly a million over the last decade, victims of the country's ridiculously low growth rate – under 1% a year. And the departures are accelerating. Jose Cesario, secretary of state for emigrant communities, estimated recently that up to 240,000 people may have left since the start of 2011.

Now Portugal isn't Latvia, but it does have a very serious demographic problem. In Latvia the total population declined by about 14 percent (340 thousand people) between 2000 and 2011. Emigration was responsible for about two thirds of this decline while low fertility accounted for the remainder.

Portugal's case is not so severe, but the pattern is similar. Between 1998 and 2008 about 700,000 Portuguese nationals left their home country according to research carried out by the former Economy and Employment Minister Álvaro Santos Pereira. In the pre-crisis years the outpouring was to some extent offset by an inflow of immigrants from other countries, but now the migrants are leaving too so the country's working age and total population are both declining.

Naturally this is one of the reasons why Portuguese unemployment numbers haven't hit the Spanish or Greek heights. According to data from the Portuguese Institute of Employment and Professional Training, during the first nine months of 2012 24,689 people cancelled their unemployment registration due to a decision to emigrate. This compares with 16,977 in the first nine months of 2011. In September 2012 alone, 2,766 people signed off for the same reason, a 49% increase on September of 2011. Yet between January and September Portugal's EU harmonized unemployment rate rose from 14.7% to 16.3%, suggesting that without so many people packing their bags and leaving the figure would have been significantly higher, and offering some explanation as to why government officials don't do more to try and stop the flow.

Nobel economist Paul Krugman recently suggested that among the ailments Japan was suffering from was a shortage of Japanese[106]. Put another way Japan's slow GDP growth is partly a by-product of the country's ageing and shrinking workforce. Looking at the country's population dynamics Portugal certainly seems to be a likely candidate to have also caught this most modern of modern diseases. Not only does Portugal have the key ingredient behind the Japanese workforce shrinkage – long term ultra-low fertility – it has some added issues to boot. Japan may be immigration averse, but its inhabitants aren't fleeing in droves.

Of course, a shortage is always relative to something. Many hold that the planet is overpopulated, and that energy constraints mean fewer people would be better. So shouldn't we be celebrating all these children who aren't getting born? Well, no, at least not if you want sustainable pension and health system. And don't forget, that is what the developed world sovereign debt crisis is all about, how to meet implicit liabilities for an ever older population. Maybe population needs to fall, but should it be doing

---

[106] Paul Krugman, The Japan Story, New York Times, 5 February 2013 http://krugman.blogs.nytimes.com/2013/02/05/the-japan-story/?_php=true&_type=blogs&_r=0

so at – in historic terms - breakneck speed?

On the other hand, one thing Portugal won't have a shortage of is old people, since the over-65 age group is projected to grow and grow, even as the working population shrinks and shrinks. No wonder the young are leaving, even if the youth unemployment rate wasn't 38.3%, just think of all the taxes and social security contributions the remaining young people are going to have to pay just to keep the welfare ship afloat. Patriotism at the end of the day has its limits.

According to the European Commission's 2012 Ageing Report[107], projections for the Portuguese population during the period 2010 - 2060 previously anticipated that it would start to decline in 2034, but the latest data show the population unexpectedly reached its peak in 2010. The fact that this turnaround comes as a surprise is clearly the result of over-optimistic assumptions on the net-migration front since natural population movements are well known and change little over time. Clearly the unexpected factor here is the severity of the recession from which the country has been suffering and the size of the exodus of young people who have been leaving.

Just to highlight even more the speed of the change here, in Japan the interval between the initiation of the decline of the working age population and the beginning of total population decline was a full decade. In Portugal this interval was only two years.

Even more relevant from the economic growth point of view is the decline in the working-age population. In Portugal this group,

---

[107] The 2012 Ageing Report, European Union, 2012
http://ec.europa.eu/economy_finance/publications/european_economy/2012/pdf/ee-2012-2_en.pdf

defined as the population with ages ranging from 15-64, started declining in Portugal after 2008. This isn't the first time Portugal's potential workforce has been hit by emigration. Between 1986 and 1991 the workforce also stagnated, mainly as a result of the increase in emigration that followed Portugal's entry into the European Union.

Indeed, during this early bout of EU oriented "labour mobility" Portugal's total population also decreased, but at the time the population in general was much younger, and many more young people were entering the age group, so the growth rate of the workforce remained in positive territory. In other words, there were still enough Portuguese entering the labour market to replace those who were leaving it (either to retire or to seek a future abroad). During the second period of strong emigration, 2003 - 2008, the large exit of Portuguese nationals (as we have seen an estimated 700,000 between 1998 and 2008) was largely offset by an inflow of immigrants, although given the strong outflow of Portuguese nationals these were barely sufficient to hold the workforce constant.

All this changed, however, after 2008 when the growth rate of working age population finally (and probably irrevocably) turned negative.

Data Opacity in Italy?

Another issue which arises is the quality of the data available. Official data on short term migratory movements often falls short of offering a comprehensive picture. Italy offers a good example. In 2013 some 16,000 Italians moved to the UK, according to official statistics from Italian Ministry of Interior[108]. These

---

[108] See: Renzi's hidden problem: the brain drain, Valentina Romei, Financial

numbers are based on the registry of Italians living abroad (AIRE). On the other hand data from the UK statistics office suggest the number of Italians requesting a National Insurance Number (NINo) in 2013 in order to be able to work in the UK was over 44,000 - nearly three times the Italian official figure.

Regardless of the anomaly in the data sources a trend is clear: the number of Italians moving out of their country is rising significantly. National Insurance numbers allocated to Italians in the UK last year were 66% higher than in 2012, the largest increase of any of the top 20 nationalities entering the country.

As with other cases, the Italians moving to the UK tend to be young and skilled. Over 80% of those allocated a NINo in 2013 were under 34 and 42% were aged between 18 and 24, a significant increase from pre-crisis levels of around 30%. But the Italian diaspora is much larger than these figures suggest. The UK is only the fifth largest European destination of emigrants after Germany, Switzerland, France and Belgium.

In fact Italy, like Portugal, has seen young educated nationals leaving in large numbers since the start of the century, but the proportions have been much lower, and the population rose by almost 3 million people over the first decade (from 57 to nearly 60 million) due to substantial immigration. Skilled young Italians would be an important resource for a country where the proportion of older people (over 65) is the third largest in the world after Japan and Germany and the proportion of the population who attained tertiary education is the second lowest among OECD countries after Turkey. While politicians ponder reforms, the most promising part of the workforce is moving to

---

Times Blog, 27 February 2014,http://blogs.ft.com/ftdata/2014/02/27/renzis-hidden-problem-the-brain-drain/?infernofullcomment=1&SID=google

other countries.

Ireland's Rapid Adjustment

The economic crisis which hit Ireland in 2008 drove hundreds of thousands of young Irish people from their homeland in search of work, starting talk of a new diaspora and leaving some rural areas with a dire shortage of young working-age people. Since the height of the financial crisis more than 200,000 Irish people have left the country in search of work according to estimates from Ireland's Central Statistics Office.

In fact, far from improving as the economy has started to recover, statistics suggest more Irish nationals are leaving than ever. In 2013 some 250 people a day, most of them their 20s and 30s, simply packed their bags and left - many are highly educated, cursing the country with the unflattering trophy of having the highest emigration rate of any country in the European Union.

The new Irish diaspora – as of July 2014 there is even a minister with this title – often follows paths previously travelled decades before by earlier generations of migrants. Official figures show that 26,500 people moved from Ireland to the US between 2008 and 2013, a number which pales in comparison with the almost 70,000 who moved to Australia and the 90,000 who have gone to Britain. But as we have seen in the Italian case, official figures can be deceptive, and the new Minister for the Diaspora[109] estimates

---

[109] Irish Prime Minister Enda Kenny announced a cabinet reshuffle in July 2014 and appointed former Arts Minister Jimmy Deenihan minister of state for the Diaspora, the first time such an office has existed.
http://www.irishcentral.com/news/politics/First-ever-Minister-for-Diaspora-appointed-in-Irish-government-reshuffle.html

that there are at least 50,000 undocumented migrants working in the United States.

One particularly dramatic example of the situation is to be found in one of the country's popular sports: football. In 2013 clubs wishing to participate in the annual All- Ireland Football Championship woke-up to the unpleasant reality they had up to two-thirds of their teams of just two years earlier living overseas. On the other hand, demand for tickets was sky-high driven by exiles who wanted to return home for the final match. Six members of the Carna-Caiseal team from Galway who contested the county final nine years ago are currently living outside of Ireland, and two more are in Dublin. Kerry has been one of the worst affected areas for emigration. In the Dún Chaoin and Castlegregory areas, the population fell by 71 per cent between the 2006 and the 2011 censuses.

And again we find the same education and skill pattern. According to a report[110] from the University College Dublin based Clinton Institute recent Irish emigrants are younger, more professional and more networked than any previous generation although many are still experiencing psychological difficulties, financial hardship and feelings of isolation abroad.

Winners and Losers?

Naturally when it comes to migration population loss in one

---

[110] Supporting the next generation of the Irish Diaspora, Liam Kennedy, Madeleine Lyes, Martin Russell, Clinton Institute, University College Dublin, April 2014
http://ucdclinton.ie/userfiles/file/Supporting%20the%20Next%20Generation%20of%20the%20Irish%20Diaspora.pdf

country means population growth in another. We have seen in Chapter 3 how economically driven population flows – what I call the "hot labour" phenomenon" – are becoming an increasingly important factor in the process of bubble and imbalance generation. As fast as people leave the stricken countries on the periphery they arrive elsewhere, in countries that at that point in time seem to be more prosperous, even if this apparent prosperity, as we have seen in the Spain case, could be illusory.

Germany was facing an acute demographic crisis before 2007, not only was population falling, but net migration was negative. Suddenly, on the back of the crisis in the south, all that has changed. In 2008 and 2009 in fact more people still left than arrived, even if size of the difference was lower than before. But since 2010 the number of those arriving (and the difference between those arriving and those leaving) has steadily increased. The result has been that the German population is now rising again. And since most of those arriving are in younger age groups the same is true of the working age population.

Provisional estimates from the German Statistics Office, suggest 1.226 million people emigrated to Germany in 2013, an increase of 146,000, or 13%, over 2012. The last time immigration on this scale was recorded in Germany was in 1993. On the other hand some 789,000 people left Germany in 2013, 77,000 (+11%) more than in the previous year. The result was net immigration of 437,000 – also the highest figure since 1993. Naturally such a large number of people entering is producing a pressure on property prices in some of the large cities in just the same way as in London or Geneva.

Naturally, in a currency union net migration balances, like net trade ones, are zero sum: one man's meat is another's poison.

Cross regional population movements may serve to make the Eurozone more "optimal" but when working age population is the scarce resource they do nothing to raise the potential long term growth rate. To achieve this the region needs to be a net attractor for migrants, and for this to happen labour markets in Greece, Portugal, Spain and Italy need to start to function again. Absent further measures this seems unlikely to become the case anytime in the near future.

One swallow, as they say, doesn't make a summer, and two or three years of population transfer don't make a permanent trend. But the current flows need watching, much more carefully than is currently the case, since the long run consequence of not addressing this issue will surely not be benign.

8

Is It All Germany's Fault?

"The problem is that Germany has continued to maintain highly competitive labor costs and run huge surpluses since the bubble burst — and in a depressed world economy, this makes Germany a significant part of the problem." – Paul Krugman, German Surpluses: This Time Is Different[111]

According to one fairly widespread theory about the Euro crisis Germany bears a large part of the responsibility for the current mess. This view is met with a variety of responses inside the country itself, ranging from horror to amazement. Naturally, if the argument behind the criticism were simply about the way Angela Merkel has handled the crisis – no Eurobonds, no debt forgiveness, systematic fiscal austerity – then possibly some of it could be understood. But no, things go beyond that, Germany has been too successful, too competitive, and this has presented a big problem for its partners who simply haven't been able to keep up.

This deeper "German bad" argument can take a variety of forms.

---

[111] Paul Krugman, German Surpluses: This Time Is Different, New York Times 3 November 2013 http://krugman.blogs.nytimes.com/2013/11/03/german-surpluses-this-time-is-different/

The country is said to be obsessed with austerity even though all its partners are struggling to find air, it is thought to be guilty of running excessively large current account surpluses, it is accused of not showing sufficient solidarity with its south European partners by being unwilling to run higher inflation: what is more it is said to have benefited from a kind of vendor financing procedure during the good years only later to complain when it turns out the customers can't pay. The list is a long one. The UK economist Simon Wren-Lewis even accuses them of having attained their hegemonic status simply by undercutting everyone else[112].

"Within the Eurozone," he argues,*" we have a problem created by Germany undercutting pretty well every other economy in the 2000-2007 period. I am not suggesting this was a deliberate policy, but the consequences were not appreciated by any Eurozone government at the time."*

The Financial Times' Martin Wolf, while being generally on board with the approach, takes a rather different tack[113]: *"Germany is reshaping the European economy in its own image. It is using its position as the largest economy and dominant creditor country to turn members of the Eurozone into small replicas of itself – and the Eurozone as a whole into a bigger one. This strategy will fail."*

The argument that Germany's labour costs are highly competitive is a strange one, since this is simply the reverse side of the idea that periphery economies got themselves into trouble by living on credit and not worrying too much if their unit labour costs headed north. Relative prices are, well, relative. If one group of people

---

[112] Simon Wren-Lewis, Lessons of the Great Depression for the Eurozone, 28 August 2014, http://mainlymacro.blogspot.com.es/2014/08/lessons-of-great-depression-for-eurozone.html
[113] Martin Wolf, The German Model Is Not For Export, Financial Times, 7 May 2013
http://www.ft.com/intl/cms/s/0/aacd1be0-b637-11e2-93ba-00144feabdc0.html#axzz3CSRmkCuM

become decadent and let their economies slide, naturally members of the other group look good in comparison.

So what is going on here? Are people trying to pursue a fair and balanced approach, allocating equal blame to both parties? Naturally the rescue agencies can be criticized if they don't make it in time to help a group of people trapped on Mont Blanc during a snow storm, but if those people didn't bother to check the weather before they started to climb who holds the ultimate responsibility? Martin Wolf admirably sums up the spirit of this argument in his "What was Spain supposed to have done?"[114] article. *"The Spanish property sector created a huge boom and a huge crash. The big question is what the Spanish authorities should (or could) have done about it."* And he concludes, *"In my view, Spain made only one big mistake: joining the euro. Without that, it would probably now look more like the UK: yes, the economy would be in serious trouble, but its exchange rate and its long-term interest rates would both be far lower."*

So Spain only made one mistake, the original sin of Euro membership. For anyone who has lived in Spain during the last decade this conclusion is so ridiculous it is simply laughable. Yes, Spain did make a mistake in joining the Euro: we all make bad decisions sometimes. But just a brief look at the performance of Spain's political and financial elites over the critical years – the number of corruption trials, the lack of supervision and control in the banking sector, the systematic attempts to ignore the problems while financing huge vote-winning construction projects with developer money - shows just how complicit the country's leaders were in their own undoing.

---

[114] Martin Wolf, What was Spain supposed to have done?, Financial Times, 25 June 2012
http://blogs.ft.com/martin-wolf-exchange/2012/06/25/what-was-spain-supposed-to-have-done/

Setting up the Euro as a way of anchoring periphery countries to a set of institutional "way of doing things" improvements (the structural reforms) was always a mistake – the reforms should have been carried out first, political union established and then the common currency introduced – but exonerating south European politicians for having squandered what was also a marvelous opportunity to put things straight is just as big a half-truth as the one which declares the Euro a wonderful success. Already, back in 2005, two OECD economists - Romain Duval and Jørgen Elmeskov – presented evidence[115] of systematic fiddling while Rome was catching fire at an ECB conference with the suggestive title "What effects is EMU having on the euro area and its member countries?"[116] The conclusion the authors drew was that monetary union was serving to delay, rather than accelerate, the structural reform process in a number of key countries.

This whole "German Bad" approach is fundamentally flawed in my opinion, since while the crisis has – far beyond Spain - revealed many failings in the south European economies – book cooking, corruption and conniving with money hungry developers, the presence of large and systematic extractive networks who were basically living off economic rents[117] – the finger pointing towards their German counterparts smells all too much like saying something like "why did they have to be so good at selling their products."

Even the idea that Germany has done better than its partners

---

[115] Romain Duval and Jørgen Elmeskov, The Effects of EMU on structural reform in labour and product markets,
https://www.ecb.europa.eu/events/pdf/conferences/emu/sessionIV_Elmeskov_Duval_Paper.pdf
[116] ECB, "What effects is EMU having on the euro area and its member countries?", Steigenberger Frankfurter Hof Hotel, Frankfurt am Main, 16-17 June 2005
https://www.ecb.europa.eu/events/conferences/html/emu.en.html
[117] See Darren Acemoglu and James Robinson, Why Nations Fail: The Origins of Power, Prosperity, and Poverty, Crown Business, 2012

simply by driving down wages doesn't fit the facts. According to Eurostat, average hourly wages in Germany in 2013 were 31.3 Euros. In Greece they were 13.6 Euros (and 16.7 Euros in 2008), in Spain they were 21.1Euros (and 19.4 Euros in 2008), while in Italy they were 28.1 Euros (and 25.2 Euros in 2008). In fact Germany came 8th in the Euro 18 league as far as hourly salaries goes. The conclusion you should draw from this data is that Germany's unit labour costs are low not because Germans aren't paid much, but because they are very productive, and at the end of the day, despite all the bleating about the current account this is the model other members of the Euro Area (including France) not only need to, but are indeed compelled to, follow: high pay and high productivity. Indeed Paul Krugman more or less admits this reality:

"So while it's impressive that Germany can run a surplus despite quite high labor costs, and that's a testimony to the quality of its stuff, ultimately the surplus reflects high savings relative to investment."[118]

High savings relative to investment, as we will see later, is exactly the argument Krugman uses to explain demographically driven secular stagnation: it is a symptom of something. Simply a quick examination of German growth rates – the trend is now down to around 1% - suggests that all if far from well, as do the constant relapses back towards recession. The country simply looks good because all its partners are doing so badly.

What southern Europe needs is a revolution in the mindset and more "better quality" stuff, and no amount of blaming Germany for the situation can get over that. As we will see later, the under-

---

[118] Paul Krugman, More Notes on Germany, New York Times, 1 November 2013
http://krugman.blogs.nytimes.com/2013/11/01/more-notes-on-germany/

investment over-saving phenomenon bears a remarkable similarity to what has been happening in Japan, but these days Japan is normally sympathized with and not blamed for all the world's ills.

Did Germany Get a Bad Deal?

Sometimes the "German problem" is looked at from a different angle. From time to time it is suggested that Germany has always been a reluctant party to the common currency, one which will eventually seek to leave, possibly along with a number of other "core" countries like the Netherlands and Finland. Lombard's Chief Economist Alexander Dumas, for example, tells us[119] that what we're "actually dealing with here... is a German population which has had a rotten deal – and that's why they're all so angry". On another occasion he even went so far as to say that "European Union membership has slowed the German economy and left Germans worse off".[120]

Now this view is interesting since it highlights two popular misconceptions. The first of these is that Germany has been a long suffering victim of the spendthrift policy of its Euro Area partners, and the second is that German household consumption is so weak due to a domestic policy of wage compression.

In fact the German economy made a substantial transition at the end of the 1990s from being a partially consumer-credit-driven economy with a small current account deficit to being an export driven one running a large current account surplus. This adjustment was almost entirely domestically driven. And as we

---

[119] Charles Dumas, Why Germans and Dutch will exit 'suicide pact' Eurozone, City Wire, 18 January 2012 http://www.citywire.co.uk/money/why-germans-and-dutch-will-exit-suicide-pact-eurozone/a559322?ref=citywire-money-latest-news-list

[120] Charles Dumas, An Independent German Currency Will Spur Growth, New York Times 23 January 2013 http://www.nytimes.com/roomfordebate/2012/11/12/should-germany-leave-the-euro-zone/an-independent-german-currency-will-spur-growth

have seen, the German wage compression is only relative, relative to what they were paying themselves before.

Far from belonging to the Euro having damaged Germany, in many ways the country has been a net beneficiary. Clearly since the crisis broke out the country has enjoyed the benefit of very low borrowing costs, a boon that was not shared with its hard pressed partners, and certainly German companies were the big beneficiaries of excessive spending in the south. But the issue goes beyond that, and extends to the whole "export boom" phenomenon.

In a couple of highly stimulating essays two Citi economists, Nathan Sheets and Robert Sockin[121], have argued that since the start of EMU German trade performance has been significantly boosted by the fact that it was using a currency which was valued significantly below the valuation it would have had had the country still been using the Deutsche Mark. As a result of this systematic undervaluation Germany's external surpluses widened significantly, led by rapid export growth.

Using a simple econometric procedure Sheets and Sockin estimate that participating in the European monetary union, in combination with the country's extraordinary wage restraint, resulted in a real effective exchange rate for Germany 15 to 20 percent lower than the one which would have prevailed had Germany had its own floating currency. And naturally the weaker real exchange rate has provided a significant windfall for Germany's export sector.

They thus found that the lower German real exchange rate lifted

---

[121] Nathan Sheets and Robert Sockin, Germany's 'Windfall' from Euro-Area membership and European Imbalances, Citigroup Global Markets, Empirical and Thematic perspectives, 27 January 2012
https://ir.citi.com/DkHnljPA17OJBCgYbBozk5GXsbpJTG9K2O7tG8tU2LUrX%2BP7wkUYWw%3D%3D
and;
Nathan Sheets and Robert Sockin, Alexander Hamilton and Germany's 'Windfall' from Euro-Area Membership, Citigroup Global Markets, Empirical and Thematic perspectives, 17 January 2011

the country's nominal trade surplus by roughly 4 percent of GDP (or €100 billion) annually and the real trade surplus by about 3 percent of GDP annually. In addition, during the recent debt crisis, Euro weakness meant that German exports were in an almost uniquely privileged position to benefit from strengthening global demand in the emerging market economies.

The comparison with Japan is significant in this case: at the end of 2011 Japanese exports were still running at 8% **below** their pre-crisis high point, while German exports were about 7% **above** it. Indeed it could be said that during these years Germany was the recipient of a mild version of the policy which was later to become known as Abenomics, a point to which we will return below.

Since the global financial crisis German exports to China have risen strongly, while before the recent Abe devaluation Japanese exports to China virtually stagnated. What could be the explanation for this strange phenomenon, since evidently Japan also efficiently produces technologically-advanced products to sell? Well, the relative values of the two currencies the countries use might offer us some part of the explanation. From the start of 2007 to mid-2008, the Japanese yen was trading in the range of 0.06 – 0.065 to the Euro. At the start of 2012 it was trading at all-time record levels of just over 0.1 to the Euro – that is the yen rose versus the Euro by over 60% in just three and a half years. What German policy makers might with good reason worry about is the possibility that should their country go back to the Deutsche Mark a similar fate might well await them.

Naturally in June 2008 Japan's currency was significantly under-valued, due to it being the "carry" funding currency of preference, while Germany's currency has been significantly under-valued in recent years (due first to the impact of the sovereign debt crisis, and now to the anti-deflation stance of the ECB). In July 2008 Japan's currency valuation spiked dramatically – rising by around 30% in 3 months – as the global financial crisis took its toll and the carry trade unwound, and something comparable would very likely happen to any currency Germany participated in should the Euro finally break up. The key point to take away from these comparisons is that in the age of the global financial accelerator currency movements have a strong non-linear component[122].

Mentioning Japan brings us to the second basic misunderstanding about Germany's long 1999-2005 transition, that it was simply a question of wage compression. In order to understand why there is something more than a common or garden variety of wage deflation behind the German competitiveness correction it is worth reflecting on what the term "export dependency" means.

Ageing Populations and Export Dependency

Put simply, mature economies become dependent on export expansion for growth either if they are in the aftermath of a credit driven consumer boom (and hence deleveraging, weakening domestic demand) or their population median age rises above a certain (yet to be adequately calibrated) point meaning that the demand for consumer credit no longer expands as the balance between savers and borrowers shifts across cohorts and across the life cycle[123]. In this context Germany's wage moderation adjustment is not something exceptional (the same phenomenon is observed in Japan), or even reversible, but forms part of a natural process of competitiveness reinforcement in the export sector of a society with a large and growing elderly population. For such an economy to be internationally competitive exports must grow strongly enough to drive the economy forward. It's as simple as that.

---

[122] See Chapter Three
[123] See Derek Anderson, Dennis P. J. Botman and Ben Hunt, Is Japan's Population Aging Deflationary?, IMF, Washington, August 2014
https://www.imf.org/external/pubs/cat/longres.aspx?sk=41812.0 and
Gauti Eggertsson & Neil Mehrotra, A Model of Secular Stagnation, Working Paper, July 2014
http://www.econ.brown.edu/fac/Gauti_Eggertsson/papers/Eggertsson_Mehrotra.pdf

At the start of this century, when wages were relatively higher in Germany, consumption was already lackluster, but GDP growth was also mediocre, and unemployment was high. Contrary to what Alexander Dumas seems to assume, after the wage-cost adjustment consumer demand has improved moderately, GDP growth has revived a little and unemployment has fallen significantly. It is hard to argue that this has been a "bad deal for the Germans".

Given that the international value of the Euro served during the pre-crisis years to keep the Euro Area trade balance near to zero, the counterparty to Germany's rising surplus were the mounting deficits in the peripheral countries, where growth in wages significantly outpaced that in productivity. This has put these economies in an unsustainable position, and it is this imbalance within the Euro Area itself which must now be remedied by finding some way to enable the peripheral economies to follow the same path as the German one. This is the case because they need to deleverage, but it also so because their working age populations are now falling[124].

Since the degree of distortion is much greater than in the 1990s German case, and the level of indebtedness much higher, then it is hard to see how the transition can be achieved without substantial deflation and ongoing debt restructuring. In this sense Paul Krugman is right when he says[125], "these days German inflation is only one percent, euro area inflation is lower, and the only way for Southern Europe to gain ground is to have zero or negative inflation." As he then goes on to note, the lack of German inflation only makes the periphery adjustment problem even more difficult, largely because outright deflation worsens

---

[124] Indeed this decline is being accelerated by the fact part of the "adjustment" is taking place through trans-national labour mobility. See Chapter Five.

[125] Paul Krugman, Germany's Sin, New York Times, 29 August 2014, http://krugman.blogs.nytimes.com/2014/08/29/germanys-sin/?module=BlogPost-Title&version=Blog%20Main&contentCollection=Opinion&action=Click&pgtype=Blogs&region=Body

the debt burden. But what this argument misses is that low inflation in Germany may not be any more of a choice than deflation is in Japan. Demographic dynamics may be limiting the ability of monetary policy to shift the German inflation level upwards.

On the other hand, if you add to low German inflation the fact that the Eurozone as a whole remains depressed then it is hard to disagree that "Germany is in effect demanding that Spain and others accomplish a task vastly harder than the Germans themselves had to achieve." It also follows that Germany could be more helpful on the side of its fiscal stance, as Mario Draghi has recently been arguing. In any event a simple comparison of Germany's earlier adjustment and the current Spanish one is not, at face value, complete.

Indeed the critics are not wrong when they point out that ECB monetary policy was kept at a relatively low level to help Germany carry through its adjustment, even though the price for this was an exaggerated property bubble in Spain, a point Krugman correctly draws attention to.[126]

"The Germans are very proud of their own adjustment between the late 1990s and 2007, during which they emerged from economic doldrums and became very competitive. But that adjustment, from a European point of view, looked like my first figure: German belt-tightening was accompanied by what amounted to a highly expansionary monetary policy, which led to fairly high inflation in Southern Europe. So when Germany asks why other countries can't do what it did, it isn't just forgetting that we can't all run trade surpluses; it's also insisting that other countries replicate its success while denying them the kind of external environment that made its success possible."

---

[126] Paul Krugman, Europe's Macro Muddle (Wonkish), New York Times, November 11 2013
http://krugman.blogs.nytimes.com/2013/11/11/europes-macro-muddle-wonkish/

The Export Lead "Model"

It is now widely agreed that having a rising population (and especially the working age component) has been a key factor in economic growth in most developed countries throughout what we have come to call the modern growth era. We are also seeing how it is precisely those parts of Europe where labour forces are now in decline that the risk of an eventual Japan style outcome is most elevated.

Nowhere is this situation clearer than it is in Spain. The Spanish economy sustained several years of what was clearly above-par growth by increasing labour inputs dramatically, while productivity growth remained between "low" and "nonexistent". In the Spanish case the labour force growth came not from natural population growth, but from labour migration from other parts of the globe, while the demand which supported the growth was also not organic, but fuelled by the very cheap and ample liquidity which had become available with the creation of the Euro-wide capital markets.

In order to see how this dynamic may have arisen, and what may now happen to domestic saving in Spain, a comparison between the recent history of the Spanish and German economies is pretty illuminating. As I will argue below, there are strong structural homologues to be observed in the evolution of the two economies, with a time delay of about a decade between the process in one country and that in the other. The most evident difference is one of scale: Spain's economy became much more distorted than Germany's did, so the size of the adjustment which is taking place is much bigger. And as is repeatedly being pointed out it is taking place in a much more hostile environment.

The first, perhaps rather surprising, discovery which anyone examining the recent historical data for Germany finds is that it simply is not true that the Germans are a group of "non-consumers", and inveterate savers. Back in the 1990s German private consumption enjoyed a substantial boom, a boom which ground itself to a halt towards the end of the century. So it is only since 2000 that German private consumption growth has been lackluster, and seemingly incapable of driving GDP growth. Turning to Spain for a moment, it becomes immediately evident that Spanish household consumption growth enjoyed a similar – if much more pronounced - expansionary cycle between 1999 and 2007, demonstrating the same kind of "blossoming" (if on a much larger scale) that German consumption had experienced in the mid-1990s.

What is rather surprising – and not too often noticed – about the German boom is that the country experienced very little inflation: between 1994 and 1999 the average rate was only 1.4%. To some extent this inflationless credit boom prefigured the US one which took place between 2001 and 2007.[127] It also offers us a pointer as to why it is so difficult to fire up German inflation today.

Looking beyond the phenomenon of the consumption boom in and of itself, the interesting question to ask is what it was that was driving it. Unsurprisingly perhaps, what we find when we

---

[127] In fact in his game-changing speech at the 2013 IMF research conference Larry Summers said the following: "If you go back and you study the economy prior to the crisis, there is something a little bit odd. Many people believe that monetary policy was too easy. Everybody agrees that there was a vast amount of imprudent lending going on. Almost everybody believes that wealth, as it was experienced by households, was in excess of its reality: too much easy money, too much borrowing, too much wealth. Was there a great boom? Capacity utilization wasn't under any great pressure. Unemployment wasn't at any remarkably low level. Inflation was entirely quiescent."

come to examine the data is that same old "usual suspect" – a very rapid increase in private sector credit. Examined carefully the figures belie the idea that Germans have always been a nation of meticulous savers who tend to live in rented properties: mortgage lending in 1998/99 was growing at a rate of around 15% a year. The Spanish history of mortgage growth, naturally, tells a very similar (but even more exaggerated) story to the German one: between 1999 and 2007 mortgage debt in Spain was increasing at over 20% a year.

And in Germany it wasn't only households who were doing the borrowing, corporates were rapidly increasing their leveraging too. As ever the only real difference in Spain was in the magnitude of the phenomenon. While German corporates at the height of their boom were increasing borrowing at a 5% annual rate, in Spain the annual increase didn't drop below 15% in any year between 1998 and 2007. So Spanish corporate indebtedness has become a much, much bigger issue than German corporate indebtedness ever was. Indeed, while total private sector debt in Germany around the turn of the century was not that different from Spanish private debt today, German GDP at the time was (in relative terms) around twice as large as current Spanish GDP. It is also worth noting that during the adjustment period neither consumer nor corporate credit rebounded in Germany, so it should not surprise us if we are seeing a similar pattern in Spain at the present time. Spain is becoming "German", and clawing its way towards more saving: current account surplus and all. Inter-annual lending in Spain simply isn't going to climb back up again towards its previous levels, and we should expect it to continue to trawl around the zero percent mark in the years to come, as Spain's private sector steadily, and somewhat painfully, deleverages itself.

But there is another aspect of the situation which should attract our attention, and that is the close association between ongoing lending booms and current account balances. In this case, just one more time, Germany was no exception to the general rule: all through its consumption boom far from those large surpluses to which we have become accustomed the country actually ran small current account deficits. Deficits which then became surpluses in the wake of the huge structural adjustment the country passed through during the transition from being a consumer-driven to being an export-driven economy.

This is the path that the Spanish economy will now surely have to follow – in fact Morgan Stanley analysts largely understood this when they published their "Spain the New Germany" market game-changing report.[128]

Going back to Paul Krugman's argument, however, as has been emphasized there is a very significant difference in scale between the two cases. In comparison with the process Germany was submitted to between 1999 and 2005 Spain's adjustment will need to be quite literally enormous[129].

One More Time Export Dependency

So why do we see this strong underlying structural relationship? What is going on here? Certainly the close similarity between the two adjustment processes is too striking to be merely coincidental, and they aren't the only cases. The economic literature is replete with examples of countries that experienced financial crises, and then dug themselves out of the hole they

---

[128] See Spain is the 'Next Germany': Morgan Stanley, CNBC, 13 February 2013 http://www.cnbc.com/id/100456964#.
[129] See discussion in Chapter Four on the unprecedented magnitude of the current account adjustment.

found themselves in by increasing their exports.[130]

The reason for this is obvious. Once the private sector gets itself into trouble by accumulating unsustainable debt, there are only two realistic possibilities: restructure the debt, or pay it down. There isn't a third possibility of getting into even more debt (via for example government fiscal deficit spending and bank bailouts) because that just transfers the debt from one sector of the economy to another – as they have discovered in Ireland. So given that the restructuring option isn't an especially attractive one, most countries ultimately solve their problem by a brisk recovery of international competitiveness and then exporting their way out of difficulty, in order to subsequently restart the credit cycle. Naturally, this adjustment is especially difficult (as we have seen in Chapter Four) for countries who don't have their own currency to devalue.

But the idea being advanced here goes beyond this, since what is being postulated is not that of economies which become temporarily export driven, as they conduct a 'classic' deleveraging[131], but of ones which are completely and permanently export dependent for growth. It is now becoming increasingly accepted by economists that demographic processes – via shifts in the population structure - affect patterns of national saving and borrowing[132]. If we also accept that ageing is (whatever the

---

[130] See Carmen M. Reinhart & Kenneth S. Rogoff, This Time is Different: A Panoramic View of Eight Centuries of Financial Crises, NBER Working Paper No. 13882, March 2008 http://www.nber.org/papers/w13882

[131] See Ray Dalio, An In-depth Look At Deleveragings, Bridgewater, 2012 http://www.bwater.com/Uploads/FileManager/research/deleveraging/an-in-depth-look-at-deleveragings--ray-dalio-bridgewater.pdf

[132] See, for example, Ralph C Bryant, *Cross-Border Macroeconomic Implications of Demographic Change*, Brookings Institute Working Paper, 2004, or Axel H Börsch-Supan, Ludwig Alexander and Dirk Krüger, *Demographic Change, Relative Factor Prices, International Capital Flows and their Differential Effects on the Welfare of Generations*, NBER WP W13185, 2007, and Melanie Lürhmann, *Demographic Change, Foresight and International Capital Flows*, Mannheim Research

drivers of the fertility declines we are seeing may be), as a matter of simple fact an irreversible process, and if we y careful attention to the recent historical experience of countries as they age, then the evidence does suggest that there is some sort of transition going on. What is less often noticed is that the economic reflex of this transition has at its heart a constant and systematic transformation in the current account balance.[133] From what we are seeing it appears that as societies age their economies transit from being consumption driven to export driven, and it would seem that the process is not merely random, a question of options or "growth models".

So despite all the criticisms, the Eurozone is now "condemned" (if that is the right word) to traverse the path which Germany itself went down. In this sense I could not disagree more with Martin Wolf, when he says:

"The implications of the attempt to force the Eurozone to mimic the path to adjustment taken by Germany in the 2000s are profound. For the Eurozone it makes prolonged stagnation, particularly in the crisis-hit countries, highly likely. Moreover, if it starts to work, the euro is likely to move upwards, so increasing risks of deflation."[134]

As we will see in other parts of this book the prolonged economic stagnation and looming deflation have other (secular stagnation

---

Institute for the Economics of Aging (MEA), University of Mannheim 2003

[133] See David M. Cutler, James M. Poterba, Louise M. Sheiner y Lawrence H. Summers, *An Aging Society: Opportunity or Challenge?*, Brookings Papers on Economic Activity, Economic Studies Program, The Brookings Institution, vol. 21(1), pages 1-74. 1990
http://www.brookings.edu/~/media/Projects/BPEA/1990%201/1990a_bpea_cutler_poterba_sheiner_summers_akerlof.PDF

[134] Martin Wolf, The German model is not for export, Financial Times, 7 May 2013
http://www.ft.com/intl/cms/s/0/aacd1be0-b637-11e2-93ba-00144feabdc0.html#axzz3CSRmkCuM

related) roots so if the endgame for what he calls "the strategy of real wage suppression and soaring external surpluses" is "a costly dead end,"[135] the roots of this outcome are not to be found in Teutonic stubbornness.

Europe's Demographic Transition

The shift from domestic demand to exports is neither a cultural one, nor a pure question of public policy. And the hypothesis is empirically testable: if Spain does not follow Germany down the same road, and can return to sustainable growth without running a significant current account surplus, then this will undoubtedly count as some kind of refutation of the thesis. The chances are however that this test will prove impossible to realize, since Spain will in all probability not be able to return to sustainable growth in this way.

What is involved in this transition is not a question of choice, or at least it is only in the most indirect sense that these societies "chose" to start having so few children several decades ago. There are deep underlying structural dynamics at work, ones which conform to some pretty straightforward economic intuitions, and the whole process seems to be intimately associated with the current stage of Europe's demographic transition. As Paul Krugman put it[136], "What's really happening fast is the demographic transition, with Europe very quickly turning Japanese."

The reason for the constant reference to Japan is obvious: in terms of the velocity of demographic change, Japan's situation is

---

[135] Martin Wolf, Why Exit Is An Option For Germany, Financial Times, 25 September 2012 http://www.ft.com/intl/cms/s/0/1e2f2cd0-064e-11e2-bd29-00144feabdc0.html#axzz3CSRmkCuM
[136] Paul Krugman: For Bonds, This Time is Different, New York Times, 2 June 2014

the most problematic on the planet, since the country is set to experience the steepest part of the climb in dependency ratios roughly 10-15 years before either the EU or the US. Of course, it is important to note that Japan has already started to react to the problem, and labour force participation rates among males in the 70 to 75 age range in Japan are currently not dis-similar to those to be found among males in the 63 to 65 age group in many European societies.

In one European country after another the number of children born has fallen to levels which are simply not high enough for generational replacement. In Germany, Italy and Spain, where fertility has been lowest, the population is declining between one generation and the next at a rate of around 35%. And this process goes on and on, without end in sight. As Gerhard Heilig - Chief of the Population Estimates and Projections Section at the United Nations Population Division till he retired in 2013 - points out,[137] immigration will only help slow the rate of increase in the proportion of elderly dependent population, it won't be able to eliminate the problem altogether for simple arithmetical reasons:

"If you crunch the numbers, you realize it would require a continuous massive stream of people entering the continent annually – and not just tens of thousands. For instance, in Germany, some 261 million net immigrants would be necessary over the next 90 years to stabilize the current old-age dependency ratio..... At current levels of fertility, Germany's population would have to increase to roughly 490 million people through immigration to prevent further population aging!"

---

[137] Gerhard K Heilig, Immigration no solution to German demographic crisis, Project M, November 2013 http://projectm-online.com/leading-thoughts/demographics/immigration-no-solution-to-german-demographic-crisis

It is important to realize that in most cases not only will populations get older, they also will get substantially smaller. Aside from extreme situations, like the Black Death or major wars, Western societies have no real experience of dealing with ongoing population ageing and sharp population decline.

In Germany, for example, the total population is expected to fall from its current level of 81 million to reach anything between 69 and 74 million by 2050, depending on the future course of life expectancy, immigration and fertility. The degree of uncertainty is large due to the size of potential change in the life expectancy and immigration parameters. Fertility is a lot less likely to undergo a sizeable shift. What's more the proportion of people aged 65 and older is projected to rise from just under 20% today to just over 33% by 2050, while the number of very elderly (those aged 80 and over) will nearly triple to as much as 15% of the total population.

So the ratio of young people in the overall population will continue to decrease, and that of elderly people to rise: in the early 1990s there were almost three people of employable age for every person over the age of 60 in Germany. In the early 21st century, the ratio was only 2.2 to 1 and it seems very probable that within the next decade the ratio will already be less than 2 to 1.

But if the dynamics of population decline are clear enough we still need to ask ourselves in what way this could be driving the transition we are witnessing in the structure of economic growth? Well, as the Danish economist Claus Vistesen and I have suggested on a number of occasions[138], the close association of

---

[138] See Claus Vistesen Debunking the Demographics Irrelevance Proposition, Global Economy Matters, 17 April 2011 http://globaleconomydoesmatter.blogspot.com.es/2011/04/debunking-demographics-irrelevance.html and
Claus Vistesen, Is Germany Dependent on Exports to Grow?, Demography Matters, 30 September

the export dependence phenomenon with shifting population structures, and the demographic transition which lies behind both of them, may well provide us with the key. By fusing Franco Modigliani's life cycle saving and borrowing idea[139], with the Swedish demographer Bo Malmberg's notion of classifying social evolution according to median population "ages"[140] (child, young adult, middle aged and elderly), Claus prepared the following chart which attempts to illustrate the kind of process which might be at work.

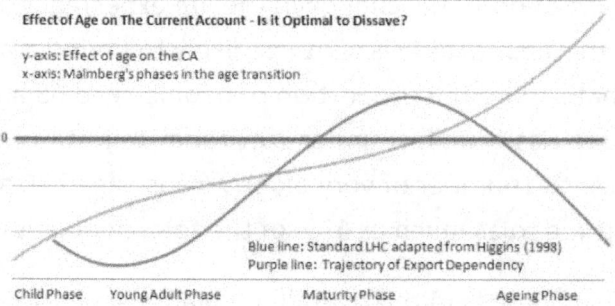

Under this view the current account balance is associated with the degree of dependence, or lack of it, of an economy on exports. Very young societies, such as those which are to be found in the African Sahel, or Uganda, or Pakistan, or Bolivia, have very low saving rates due to the very large percentage of children under the working age. As a result they are dependent on being able to finance current account deficits and imports to maintain a minimum standard of living for all. From an inter-temporal perspective these deficits are in fact more sustainable than

---

2009 http://globaleconomydoesmatter.blogspot.com.es/2009/09/is-germany-dependent-of-exports-to-grow.html
[139] See Gauti Eggertsson & Neil Mehrotra, A Model of Secular Stagnation, Working Paper, July 2014 http://www.econ.brown.edu/fac/Gauti_Eggertsson/papers/Eggertsson_Mehrotra.pdf
[140] Malmberg, Bo & Lena Sommestad. (2000). Four Phases in the Demographic Transition, Implications for Economic and Social Development in Sweden, 1820-2000. Arbetsrapport/Institutet för Framtidsstudier, Working Paper 2000:6

equivalent ones run in much older societies, since there is more future output to be brought forward to guarantee the borrowing needed[141]. Financing the demographic transition in young societies (frontier markets) is in fact a good investment if the moral hazard risk can be suitably hedged.

If markets were completely rational in this context, they would be prepared to finance these deficits conditional on policies to reduce fertility and raise female empowerment, which are sure ways to reduce the level of child dependence, in the same way they are prepared to finance elderly but highly indebted European societies conditional on policies to raise labour force participation rates and extend the working life via reform of the pension systems.

Once societies break out of the "high fertility" trap there follow two "ages" (the young adult and the maturity phase) where growth should be significantly domestic consumption based and the current account move slowly but steadily into positive balance. Then finally comes the ageing (or better put "elderly") stage, where export dependence continues to grow steadily even as the current account balance gradually deteriorates as countries (in theory) dis-save. Naturally this process is highly unstable, and is one of the reasons why we think permanent deflation beyond some critical tipping point (to be empirically determined) eventually becomes inevitable.

Of course, all of the above is highly stylized and remains for the time being at the level of hypothesis. What is beyond doubt is that Spain's boom-bust cycle followed Germany's by a decade, while the respective demographic profiles also reveal a ten year

---

[141] See ex-Bank Of Japan governor Shirakawa's comments cited at the end of Chapter Nine

lag between one country and the other. In terms of median population ages Spain was roughly at the same point in 2007 as Germany was at the turn of the century. And when we come to the percentage of the 25 to 40 age group in the total population, we find that this peaked in Germany at the end of the 1990s, while it peaked in Spain just at the end of the housing boom.

One of the clear macroeconomic conclusions that flows from this little excursus is that if the growing export dependency hypothesis is valid the Euro Area will maintain a stable and possibly growing current account surplus in the years to come (something which has been worrying Martin Wolf), enabling the region to self-finance itself in much the same way that Japan is able to finance for the time being. It also follows that a recovery in Euro Area domestic demand to the point of becoming a driver of growth is most unlikely: indeed, as I am suggesting, if it did there would be something fundamentally wrong with the hypothesis advanced above. On the other hand if this recovery isn't going to come we are wasting a lot of precious policy energy, time and breath on trying to make the impossible happen.

In fact the export dependency hypothesis is simply another variant of the domestic investment shortfall argument that Paul Krugman and others use in the context of Alvin Hansen's secular stagnation argument.[142]

"So while it's impressive that Germany can run a surplus despite quite high labor costs, and that's a testimony to the quality of its stuff, ultimately the surplus reflects high savings relative to investment."

---

[142] See Edward.Hugh.Blog, Paul Krugman's Bicycling Problem, 6 June 2014, http://edwardhughtoo.blogspot.com.es/2014/06/secular-stagnation-part-1-paul-krugmans.html

"Export surpluses do not reflect merely competitiveness but also an excess of output over spending. Surplus countries import the demand they do not generate internally."[143]

This doesn't mean that that the secular stagnation argument is valid, only empirical experience will establish that one way or the other. But it does mean that it is hard to maintain that secular stagnation is demographically driven, and keep arguing that "Germany is hurting growth and employment in the world at large."[144] The theoretical arithmetic just doesn't add up.

---

[143] Martin Wolf, Germany is a Weight on the World, Financial Times, 5 November 2013
[144] Paul Krugman, The Harm Germany Does, New York Times, 1 November 2013

9

Zero Bound and Then What?

"Can monetary policy committees, accustomed to describing their plans and actions in terms of the level of a short-term nominal interest rate, find effective means of conducting and communicating their policies when that rate is zero or close to zero?" This is the question US economists Ben Bernanke and Vincent Reinhardt asked in 2004 in what was to become a defining paper for the future of monetary policy. [145]

The answer they gave was that they most certainly can. As a first move the central bank can attempt to influence expectations over the duration of low short term interest rates and thus bring down longer term rates: a strategy which later came to be known as "forward guidance". As they say, "even with the overnight nominal interest rate at zero, a central bank can impart additional stimulus by offering some form of commitment to the public to

---

[145] Ben S. Bernanke and Vincent R. Reinhardt, Conducting Monetary Policy at Very Low Short-Term Interest Rates, Paper presented at the International Center for Monetary and Banking Studies Lecture, Geneva, Switzerland January 14, 2004

keep the short rate low for a longer period than previously expected. This commitment, if credible, should lower yields throughout the term structure and support other asset prices."

The second tool they identify is that of changing the composition of the central bank balance sheet, for example exchanging short term government bonds for longer term ones, or buying into other asset classes. This strategy has subsequently been called "qualitative easing".[146]

Finally they examine a third possibility, expanding the size of the central bank balance sheet through direct purchases of either public or private assets, a policy which has now come to be known as quantitative easing. They break down the mechanisms through which QE can work into three channels: i) a portfolio substitution channel; ii) an expectations channel, and; iii) a fiscal channel.

The first channel, which achieves its impact through what has now come to be known as the "portfolio rebalancing effect" was described by ECB Chief Economist Peter Praet as the "most powerful" component of the recent ECB programme.[147] Central bank purchases drive down interest rates across the term structure (from short term to long term), forcing investors to sell their holding and seek riskier assets to purchase if they want to maintain their income returns. The assets acquired may be such as to help finance domestic lending, or they may be overseas

---

[146] Qualitative easing; a policy that has been widely used by central banks during the financial crisis in an attempt to support private sector risk in extreme situations. It normally operated through purchases of privately held risky assets and their replacement with government debt, with a return guaranteed by the taxpayer.

[147] Praet Says QE Most Powerful Through Portfolio Rebalancing, Bloomberg News, 12 February 2015, http://www.bloomberg.com/news/articles/2015-02-12/ecb-s-praet-says-qe-most-powerful-through-portfolio-rebalancing

ones, in which case the currency will tend to depreciate. In the case of QE implemented to ward of a deflation threat this currency effect is considered to be particularly important. The second "expectations" channel "is equivalent to a commitment to keep interest rates at zero until the economic conditions are met, a type of policy we have already discussed": that is to say it is effectively another form of "forward guidance".

It is the third of the transmission channels mentioned – the fiscal one -that has subsequently attracted a lot of commentary and attention. As they say, "quantitative easing that is sufficiently aggressive and that is perceived to be long-lived may have expansionary fiscal effects. So long as market participants expect a positive short-term interest rate at some date in the future, the existence of government debt implies a current or future tax liability for the public. In expanding its balance sheet by open-market purchases, the central bank replaces public holdings of interest-bearing government debt with non-interest-bearing currency or reserves. If the open-market operation is not expected to be reversed too quickly, this exchange reduces the present and future interest costs of the government and the tax burden on the public."

This is the kind of transmission mechanism the ECB has set to work in initiating a programme of systematic sovereign bond purchases, bringing down interest charges to leave more room in government budgets for spending programmes.

A Brief History of QE

"It is not an exaggeration to say that almost all the policies adopted by other central banks after the Great Financial Crisis, though often described as "innovative", were policy measures which the Bank of Japan had "invented" much earlier, in uncharted waters, and without textbooks or precedents." Masaaki Shirakawa, ex-Governor of the Bank of Japan[148]

Quantitative easing, as we have seen is a form of unconventional monetary policy used by central banks to stimulate economies when standard interest rate policy has become ineffective. The policy has normally been introduced because interest rates are pushing up again the so called "zero bound" beyond which they cannot be moved with going into negative territory.

As we have also seen, the way central banks implement QE is by expanding their balance sheet through asset purchases. QE programmes tend to raise the value of financial assets - and lower - their yield, while at the same time increasing the monetary base. Such policies are called non-standard since they are not comparable to the normal monetary policy activity practiced by some central banks of buying or selling short-term government bonds in order to keep interbank interest rates at a specified target value. The objective of QE is to complement normal interest rate policy by addressing specific problems like financial instability or the risk of deflation. At this point an important distinction needs to be made between the QE policies introduced

---

[148] Masaaki Shirakawa, Is inflation (or deflation) "always and everywhere" a monetary phenomenon?, People's Bank of China-BIS Research Conference on "Globalisation and Inflation Dynamics in Asia and the Pacific ", 23-24 September 2013, Beijing, China
http://www.bis.org/events/gidap2013/home.htm

in the UK and the US – which were basically about ensuring financial stability – and those put in place in Japan and probably now in the Euro Area – which are about combatting deflation.

In practice, however, QE often increases the value of financial assets, and increases base money, without the effect passing through to the real economy and broader monetary indicators like credit growth. For this reason concerns have grown that QE (as it has been applied to date) is socially divisive since it largely benefits the holders of financial assets.

It is generally assumed that money printing "always and everywhere" generates inflation.[149] This may be true, but the inflation generated doesn't necessarily have to make itself felt in the real economy: it can be channeled off into the financial one, and then even via the so called "carry trade" exported abroad[150]. What is new about the recent problems in Japan and the Euro Area (as distinct from the US and the UK) is that the traditional transmission mechanism between money printing and the real economy has broken down. Unless the central banks by-pass the financial markets all together - and inject the money directly into people's pockets - they can't generate what is called "demand pull" inflation.

Japanese Origins

QE became a household expression in the UK and the US during the recent financial crisis, but in fact the origins of QE go back to Japan, and indeed the term itself was coined by a German

---

[149] For a reasonably exhaustive up to date assessment of the limitations of that view see the speech by former BoJ Governor Masaaki Shirakawa referenced in the previous footnote.
[150] See Investopedia definition of "currency carry trade" here http://www.investopedia.com/terms/c/currencycarrytrade.asp

economist who was working in Tokyo during the 1990s.[151]

Quantitative easing was first formally adopted as a monetary policy instrument by the Bank of Japan (BOJ) in an attempt to fight domestic deflation on 19 March 2001. Despite urging from a number of well-known US economists,[152] the Bank of Japan had for many years rejected the use of QE as being excessively risky. In similar fashion to the way some US economists expressed concerns about the Federal Reserve stocking inflation, Japanese economists with a classic monetary background feared the experiment might get out of hand. But since the BOJ had maintained short-term interest rates at close to zero since 1999, and was obviously getting nowhere in its attempt to shake off deflation, it gradually became the consensus view that something else had to be tried. Hence the BoJ decided to flood commercial banks with excess liquidity in an attempt to promote private lending, leaving them with large stocks of excess reserves and a large volume of liquidity. This objective was achieved by systematically buying large quantities of government bonds from the commercial banks. As the programme progressed the bank also bought asset-backed securities and equities and extended the terms of its commercial paper–purchasing operation.

In the four years that followed the central bank increased the

---

[151] The expression was first used in Japanese by Professor Richard Werner, a German academic who was working as an economist in Tokyo in the years after the housing bubble burst. See: UK QE has failed, says quantitative easing inventor, BBC Business News, 21 October 2013
http://www.bbc.com/news/business-24614016

[152] [152] See Ben S. Bernanke, Japanese Monetary Policy: A Case of Self-Induced Paralysis?, Princeton University, December 1999
https://www.princeton.edu/~pkrugman/bernanke_paralysis.pdf ; and Paul Krugman, Japan's Trap, MIT, 1998
http://web.mit.edu/krugman/www/japtrap.html

commercial bank current account balance by 700% - from ¥5 trillion to ¥35 trillion (approximately US$300 billion) – and tripled the quantity of monthly long-term Japan government bond purchases. But commercial banks simply held the majority of the new liquidity on deposit at the central bank: lending levels did not increase and deflation continued to linger. In the end this first Japanese experiment was terminated in 2005 as part of a G20 policy decision to raise interest rates and lower global liquidity in what would turn out to be an unsuccessful attempt to reduce the risk of bubbles. Foreshadowing criticisms that would be made later by Emerging Market central banks, the Japanese monetary expansion was held partly responsible for the high level of global liquidity prevailing, and the risk which this was perceived to pose to the global financial system.

The three building blocks of this first Japanese attempt at QE were thus; (i) ensuring ample liquidity provision; (ii) commitment to continue such liquidity provision, and; (iii) the use of various types of market operations, especially purchasing of long-term government bonds. In many ways these correspond to the three balance sheet expansion mechanisms identified by Bernanke, Reinhart and Sack[153] whereby a central bank can operate an expansionary monetary policy even at very low interest rates. While differences exist between the policies Bernanke & Reinhardt propose and those adopted by the BOJ, the basic ideas involved are essentially the same. Even at a zero short-term interest rate, they argue, it is possible to pursue further monetary easing and thus influence future short-term interest rate

---

[153] Ben S. Bernanke, Vincent Reinhardt & Brian P. Sack, Monetary Policy Alternatives at the Zero Bound: An Empirical Assessment, Federal Reserve Board, Washington, 2004
http://www.federalreserve.gov/pubs/feds/2004/200448/200448pap.pdf

expectations as well as long-term interest rates through a commitment to appropriate future monetary policy paths.

But the most notable feature of the first Japanese experiment with QE was that it did not obtain its objective: Japan did not manage to definitively exit deflation.

Some, like Paul Krugman, drew the conclusion[154] that it didn't work because those responsible for policy making lost their nerve in the final straight:

"I'd argue that an important source of failure was what I've taken to calling the timidity trap — the consistent tendency of policy makers who have the right ideas in principle to go for half-measures in practice, and the way this timidity ends up backfiring, politically and even economically."

Others, like me, and many more in Japan, drew the conclusion that it didn't work because it couldn't due to the fact that Japan's underlying problem is demographic and the liquidity trap is simply a reflection of this. In any event the Bank of Japan actually abandoned due to pressure from other central banks, and the debate continues about whether or not this sort of QE could, in some shape or form, really bring back stable and sustainable inflation.

Enter the Federal Reserve

Now let's fast forward to late November 2008, and the aftermath of the Lehman Brothers failure. In an attempt to stabilize the US financial system the US Federal Reserve took the decision to

---

[154] Paul Krugman, The Timidity Trap, New York Times, 20 March 2014 http://www.nytimes.com/2014/03/21/opinion/krugman-the-timidity-trap.html?_r=0

launch a QE programme which involved buying $600 billion in mortgage-backed securities. At the time this seemed to be a shockingly high figure, but in the end it was to turn out to have been only the first timid step.

By March 2009 the Fed had accumulated some $1.75 trillion of bank debt, mortgage-backed securities, and Treasury notes, an amount which later increased to $2.1 trillion in June 2010. Further purchases were halted at that point since the bank considered the economy was gradually improving, although the programme had to be resumed in August when the Federal Reserve decided the recovery was not sufficiently robust. After the June 2010 decision to stop purchases central bank holdings had been projected to fall to $1.7 trillion by 2012 as the assets gradually matured. But the Fed revised its goal upwards after the August restart, with the new objective of maintaining holdings at the $2.054 trillion level. The result was the Fed started to buy $30 billion in two- to ten-year Treasury notes every month.

Even so by November things still weren't going well enough, and the Fed announced a second round of quantitative easing (or QE2): this time the objective was to buy $600 billion in Treasury securities by the end of the second quarter of 2011.

Finally a third round of quantitative easing, known naturally enough as "QE3", was announced on 13 September 2012. In an 11–1 vote, the Federal Reserve decided to launch a new $40 billion per month, open-ended bond purchasing program of agency mortgage-backed securities. Additionally, the Federal Open Market Committee (FOMC) began the practice of forward guidance, and announced that" it would likely maintain the federal funds rate near zero "at least through 2015". Since even this did not prove to be enough to meet the bank's unemployment targets on 12 December 2012 it announced an increase in the amount of open-ended purchases from $40 billion to $85 billion per month.

This last ramp-up of the asset purchases was to be followed six months later - on 19 June 2013 – by Ben Bernanke's now famous "tapering" announcement, suggesting the Federal Reserve would gradually reduce the volume of bond purchases contingent upon continued positive economic data. Specifically, he said that the Fed might scale back its bond purchases from $85 billion to $65 billion a month at the upcoming September 2013 policy meeting. He also suggested that the bond-buying program could come to an end by mid-2014. While Bernanke did not announce an interest rate hike, he did suggest that if inflation achieved a 2% target rate and unemployment decreased to 6.5%, the Fed would initiate a programme of raising interest rates.

During the three days following this announcement the US stock markets dropped by approximately 4.3%. The Dow Jones fell 659 points between 19 and 24 June, leaving the index at 14,660. The months that followed were characterized by considerable uncertainty and volatility, especially in Emerging Markets, and on 18 September 2013 the Fed finally decided to put the decision to taper its bond-buying program on hold. Finally, at the end of the year tapering was actually implemented and at the time of writing the period of bond purchases is gradually coming to an end.

And On to the United Kingdom

The first attempts at QE in the UK – which came starting January 2009 - followed the path previously trodden by the US Federal Reserve. The Bank of England bought gilts from financial institutions, along with a smaller amount of relatively high-quality debt issued by private companies. These measures had the intended effect of depressing interest yields on government bonds and a number of broader assets, lowering long term interest rates and effectively making it cheaper for business to raise capital. As a side effect, once yields had "compressed" on government bonds investors started "rotating" towards other assets, such as shares, boosting their price and generating a wealth effect for those in the population who owned such instruments.

The Bank of England had purchased around £165 billion in assets as of September 2009 and around £175 billion in assets by the end of October 2010. At its meeting in November 2010, the Monetary Policy Committee (MPC) voted to increase total asset purchases to £200 billion. In October 2011, the Bank of England announced that it would undertake another round of QE, creating an additional £75 billion. In February 2012 it announced an additional £50 billion. In July 2012 it announced another £50 billion, bringing the total amount to £375 billion. Despite subsequent efforts by the Bank of England Governor Mervyn King the limit was not subsequently raised. The BoE have made a fairly positive estimation of the impact of QE on UK GDP, and there is no doubt that the purchases contributed to financial stability: the big point to notice that this kind of QE was not directed towards avoiding deflation since this is an issue which has not yet confronted the UK.

Second Round of QE In japan

Later, in response to the global financial crisis a second, relatively small, QE program was introduced in Japan in October 2010. From these quite humble beginnings the program then gradually morphed into a more aggressive intervention as a core component of the strategy that has become known as Abenomics that began in April 2013.

There is, however, a fundamental difference between the recent programmes of QE undertaken by the US Federal Reserve and the policies pursued by the BoJ between 2001 and 2006, and 2010 to 2014, and this difference concerns the objectives of the policy. While both initiatives have in common that they are strategies to get that "something extra" out of monetary policy in a very low interest rate environment, they differ in that the Federal Reserve's objective has been to underpin the financial system (and support longer term interest rates) in order to help sustain a recovery in economic activity in the United States. The principal objective of the BoJ, on the other hand, is and always was to provoke a rise in inflation expectations and shift the economy from a deflationary trajectory to an inflationary one.

Obviously the two processes - supporting growth and provoking inflation - are related, but there are also subtle differences in the way the respective banks have attempted to achieve their objectives. The Federal Reserve have been concerned about the liquidity question as part of an ongoing attempt to ease a credit crunch, which it is trying to do by bringing yield spreads (and in particular the so called TED spread) down. Few doubted that once this objective was achieved the Fed would start to slow its intervention and eventually wind down its balance sheet. The BoJ, on the other hand, was concerned to convince market participants that the excess balances would be maintained for a long time interval, beyond the point where the price index simply indicated it might move into positive territory. The BoJ had to convince market participants that they were serious about provoking inflation. That is, what they were really targeting weren't bank reserve balances as such - they were simply using their ability to influence the levels of these balances as an indirect tool for influencing inflation expectations. The Fed on the other hand has no explicit inflation target beyond its general objective of price stability and is not explicitly trying to steer inflation expectations upwards. Not yet, anyway. And with that caveat.....

10

Can the ECB Stop Deflation by Using QE?

Then There Was Abe and All Was Light

By now it should be clear that the monetary experiment being carried out in Japan (and known as "Abenomics") is fundamentally different from the kind of quantitative easing carried out to date in the United States and the United Kingdom. In particular it is hard not to draw the conclusion that something structural and more long-term is taking place in Japan, and that that something is only tangentially related to the recent global financial crisis. It is now more or less generally agreed that Japan's malaise is connected with the rapid population ageing the country has experienced. If this is the case then what is currently happening in Europe may have a lot more to do with the Japan experience than it does with what has been happening in the UK and the US, for the simple reason that Europe's population is the second oldest on the planet after Japan's. Certainly at first sight the similarity is striking.

Japan, as we have seen in the previous chapter, has applied QE programmes on a number of occasions, all of them without any kind of obvious success. What sets the Abenomics version of QE apart from all its predecessors is that while it fits comfortably on the normal austerity vs growth policy axis – leaning in fact very strongly towards the stimulus end - at the heart of the new approach lies not a strategy to directly create growth per se, but rather one to try to induce inflation. The idea, which may have some understandably scratching their heads in confusion, is to see whether by this rather circuitous route it is possible to tease the country back on to what advocates of the policy consider would be a more normal growth path.

The intention is to try to put the economy on the kind of trajectory from which it has been exiled for the best part of two decades now. The inflation-inducing monetary injection could be thought of as something like the kind of sharp jolt given to a twisted spine (or a dislocated shoulder) by the firm hand of an experienced osteopath. Once the shock has been administered, so the story goes, the patient should once more be able to walk - and develop - normally.

Naturally, the very existence of the this other, alternative, path for Japan remains a mere theoretical postulate since with so many bouts of fiscal and monetary stimulus having been administered over the years, just exactly what a normal growth pattern would be for the country, or even what exactly "normal" means in this context, is very difficult to discern. The fact that the population and workforce are now both ageing and shrinking in ways for which we have no historical precedent suggests that you wouldn't necessarily expect to see that much growth in the economy anyway. Indeed, in order to make allowance for this new phenomenon some have started to claim that Japan is not doing so badly after all,[155] since GDP per capita has been performing "tolerably well" in comparison with the US or Europe, so in some ways it is hard to see what all the fuss is about, except... except.....except for that nasty, nagging little detail of all the government debt that has been being run up in the meanwhile.

Enter Haruhiko Kuroda

Japan has been conducting one form of QE programme or another – almost uninterruptedly – since 2001. But what the Bank of Japan has gotten into now – at least in terms of its scale - is something entirely new. On 4 April 2013 bank governor Haruhiko Kuroda announced he was going to increase the money base by 1 percent of GDP per month every month for the next two years. That is to say Japan's monetary expansion was going to become incremental and continuous. In addition Kuroda went further, and stated he would continue to increase the money base beyond the initial 24 months if the targeted 2% inflation doesn't come. Right from the start it was clear to everyone concerned that Abenomics would involve a major yen devaluation, but despite growing worries about currency wars the issue was seen as being sufficiently important to make an exception, and the proposal was accepted unanimously and without criticism by the other members of the G20.

Now, for those who have not been following the Japan saga as it has developed over the last twenty odd years the debate

---

[155] See Paul Krugman, The Japan Story, New York Times, 5 February, 2013 http://krugman.blogs.nytimes.com/2013/02/05/the-japan-story/?_php=true&_type=blogs&_r=0 or Daniel Gros, The Japan Myth, Project Syndicate, 6 January 2011 http://www.project-syndicate.org/commentary/the-japan-myth

surrounding Abenomics may sound like a pretty strange way of thinking about things, after all isn't inflation supposed to be a bad thing, one central banks are supposed to combat? And how can a country become more competitive by force-feeding itself inflation? The fact of the matter is, however, that during more time than most care to remember the country and the Bank of Japan have been fighting and losing an ongoing battle with falling prices. And it is this battle with falling prices which means that the country's "tolerably good" economic performance becomes a serious problem, a serious debt problem.

Naturally, falling prices are not necessarily in-and-of themselves a bad thing - as any old consumer will tell you -since products get cheaper and cheaper with each passing day.[156] So the run of the mill consumer might find life in Japan quite a pleasing and even desirable thing, especially if that particular consumer happens to be retired and living on a fixed income from savings as many contemporary Japanese actually are. Falling prices only really become a problem in a more general macroeconomic sense if they lead people to postpone consumption, and if this postponement becomes self-perpetuating in a way which leads prices to continually fall, as the combination of constant productivity increases and stagnant demand produce perpetual oversupply. Falling prices also constitute a nasty headache for policymakers since while prices go down the value of accumulated debt doesn't, and herein lies the rub: additional fiscal "stimulus" which doesn't lead to increasing nominal GDP simply pushes the sovereign debt even farther along what was already an unsustainable path.

The problem Japan has is one of a perpetual shortfall in domestic

---

[156] See Chapter 4 on the "good deflation" argument.

consumer demand and the core issue is whether this shortfall is simply being generated by consumption postponement, or whether there are deeper structural factors at work.

Basically, in terms of our classical understanding of economic problems there are two straightforward solutions to the Japan debt problem: either the economy achieves more growth (which as we have seen will prove difficult given the shifting demographics) or it generates continuing inflation, since inflation pushes nominal GDP into positive territory and hence eases the scale of the debt burden. But, we need to ask ourselves, what if something important has changed and Japan now faces the worst of both worlds, getting virtually no growth while at the same time remaining stuck in deflation. While few are yet willing to contemplate either the possibility or the consequences of this eventuality this does not mean that it is an outcome which can't happen.

But before examining that possibility a bit further, let's dig a little deeper into the intellectual backdrop that lies behind Abenomics.

"Japan: what went wrong?" is the title of a 1998 article[157] by Nobel economist Paul Krugman. Krugman's work at this time has some significance for the current policy approach since in many ways he can rightly claim to be the intellectual father of the Japanese experiment. He was the first economist of note to see that something important was happening in the country, and the first to see that some sort of major initiative was going to be needed to address the emerging problems. In particular the whole idea of trying to correct the Japanese imbalance by targeting inflation can be traced, for good or ill, back to his door.

---

[157] You can find it on the "unofficial" Paul Krugman website in the "Japan" section.

The "what went wrong" article is useful, since there the Nobel economist tried to set out in simple layman's terms his version of the Japan story. For a number of reasons it is worth going back to these old arguments since they help make sense of recent events, and offer us the opportunity of glimpsing, in all its glory, the initial justification for the Bank of Japan policy initiative that many European leaders – like for example Spain's Prime Minister Mariano Rajoy[158] - find so interesting.

Krugman's starting point is population ageing. The details could be changed, and the argument fleshed out a lot, but this is basically the picture he paints to explain why the country fell into deflation - the Japanese don't spend more because, on aggregate, they are trying to hang onto their savings.

"Here's the story: Japan, like the United States only much more so, is an aging society. Thanks to a declining birth rate and negligible immigration, it faces a steady decline in its working-age population for at least the next several decades while retirees increase. Given this prospect, the country should save heavily to make provision for the future--and lacking the kind of pay-as-you-go Social Security system that allows Americans to ignore such realities, it does. But investment opportunities in Japan are limited, so that businesses will not invest all those savings even at a zero interest rate. And as anyone who has read John Maynard Keynes can tell you, when desired savings consistently exceed willing investment, the result is a permanent recession".

Actually more than saving, the problem is really that the Japanese won't commit to borrowing, or at least not sufficiently on

---

[158] Mariano Rajoy has often pronounced himself as being in favor of the ECB becoming more like the Bank of Japan. See, for example, ECB should get more powers, CNBC 8 April 2013, http://www.cnbc.com/id/100623712#.

aggregate. This is one of the reasons many people locate the problem as a monetary transmission mechanism one[159] - the normal credit cycle simply won't start because, they argue, the economy is suffering the after-effects of a "balance sheet recession".

But another approach to the problem would be to try and understand whether the failure of both Japanese households and corporates to harness themselves to what is considered to be a "normal" credit cycle might not be associated with the age structure of the country's population.[160] In fact the Japanese household saving rate has been falling steadily over recent years, and it is Japanese corporates who are doing the heavy lifting on saving, but the latter won't invest in the domestic market for the reason Krugman identified - the lack of consumer demand for end products - and indeed perhaps this reluctance is fortunate since with final demand limited more supply would only push prices down even further. The idea that further investment would in and off itself produce enough incremental demand to soak up the capacity expansion sounds very much like the Spanish housing and immigration story - Spain was, on this account, bringing in immigrants to build houses for which they themselves would be the customers. This kind of investment-lead demand simply doesn't work, as we are also seeing in China.

Investment has to some extent to be driven by autonomous demand, if it isn't imbalances are inevitably generated, even if in a well-oiled and functioning economic machine the investment generated by that autonomous demand is what drives the

---

[159] This was effectively the reasoning of the German economist who coined the expression "Quantitative Easing" in the 1990s.
[160] This is the conclusion a group of IMF economists have recently come to.

business cycle forward. But in Japan this kind of demand-lead investment process isn't working (outside the export sector) for reasons which have demographic roots. The lack of demand for credit is not simply the result of a malfunction in the monetary transmission mechanism (a liquidity trap). Thus the key difference between the world of contemporary Japan and the world Keynes contemplated is that the shortage of demand in his model was simply conjunctural (due to the presence of a debt-induced liquidity trap) and not structural and permanent, as in the case of demographic decline.

In fact the possibility of this kind of development had already been contemplated by economists in the 1930s. The Swedish Nobel prize winner Günar Myrdal, seeing what was happening in his own country, started to look into the impact of declining populations on economic growth[161] (fertility in Sweden had already dipped below the 2.1 child per woman replacement level during the great depression) as did Keynes himself in a brief lecture.[162] However the author of the General Theory didn't take the matter further and never really contemplated the kind of problem Japan is facing. One of his US followers, Alvin Hansen, known to some as the "American Keynes", did pursue the idea,[163] and developed a term – secular stagnation – to describe what could happen as the size of working age populations declined. Interestingly it was precisely this term that was reinserted in the

---

[161] Gunnar Myrdal: The Effects of Population Decline. Godkin Lectures, Lecture VI, 1938 http://edwardhughtoo.blogspot.com.es/2006/01/gunnar-myrdal-and-effects-of-population.html

[162] John Maynard Keynes: Some Economic Consequences of a Declining Population, Galton Lecture, 1937
http://www.ncbi.nlm.nih.gov/pmc/articles/PMC2985686/pdf/eugenrev00278-0023.pdf

[163] See: Secular Stagnation: Back to Alvin Hansen, Timothy Taylor, Conversable Economist Blog, 12 December 2013

modern macroeconomic debate by US economist Larry Summers at an IMF research seminar in the fall of 2013.[164]

The fact that Keynes never really adapted his general theory to encapsulate the population decline case – in effect people lost interest in the issue as the post WWII baby boom locked in - is a pity since it only really makes sense to use the expression "liquidity trap" if you are making the kind of assumption Keynes was: that there is some sort of "normality" (the normal credit cycle, for example) to return to, so that the damage that was being caused to the normal functioning of the economy could be put right (after a sharp nudge) by some kind of self-correcting mechanism. If what you are faced with is an economy that is becoming extremely dysfunctional following almost four decades of ultra-low fertility then it is not at all clear that this self-correcting solution is available. Hence Japan's dilemma.

As everyone now recognizes and accepts Japan has a rapidly ageing population and an ageing and shrinking workforce. This situation, which has really been obvious for years, has only lately come to be regarded as a significant component in the "Japan problem". This neglect has most probably been due to the influence of a deep seated predisposition among advocates of neoclassical growth theory to think that population dynamics don't fundamentally influence economic performance in the long run.

However, and I think this is now clear to all, one result of the "demographic transition" that is going on in Japan (and which will be replicated in one country after another as the century advances) is that while GDP per working Japanese continues to

---

[164] The video recording of Larry Summer's speech can be found at https://www.youtube.com/watch?v=KYpVzBbQIX0&feature=youtu.be

perform tolerably well, and, as I said, GDP per-capita growth bears comparison with many other countries in the developed world, government debt to GDP levels now bear no such comparison and have started to surge off the known register. Obviously something has to be done.

At the start of 2015 Japan gross government debt stood at close to 245% of GDP and naturally with falling nominal GDP the burden of the debt would still continue to rise even if there were no further fiscal deficits. But fiscal deficits there are and there will continue to be since without such "stimulus" it is apparent that even real GDP would be perpetually negative. The country has been running a fiscal deficit of close to 10% annually and Shinzo Abe has promised even more fiscal stimulus in 2014 as one of his three key "economic arrows".

You don't have to be an economic or mathematical genius to see that this can't simply go on and on. Japan has now passed some sort of tipping point. GDP per working Japanese may continue to rise nicely, but as the working population steadily shrinks as the 21st century advances then surely total GDP will eventually start to fall. If, in addition, prices continue to drop then government debt to GDP would start to rise almost asymptotically even without any more government borrowing. And naturally Japan is not a unique case, since during the course of the 20th century one country after another will be faced with the same sort of problem. That is why Japan is now so important.

But Does Abenomics Work?

According to one popular theory going the rounds, if this week's economics news exceeds consensus expectations then, then that is good, especially if you had been betting it would do. But if it's worse than expected then that's even better – always imagining you went against consensus - since there is lots more potential for things to improve next week. What's more the situation is asymmetric: bad news has the added advantage that it may be good since it could imply there will be even more reason for central banks to step in with more easing and push up asset prices even further, while good news could mean they take away the liquidity trough. Maybe all this sounds peculiar, even perverse, but it fits squarely with how many people working in financial markets are reasoning these days. The question is, does your average citizen have much in common with financial investors at this point? Sauce for the gander may be – in this case – a by-product of his counterparty getting "goosed".

This enigma is especially clear in the Japan case, where there is a lot of smart money riding on the continuation of the Abenomics experiment even while many Japanese are asking themselves the question: is this all working? The result of this is that there is an inbuilt tendency among analysts to overstate the upside and understate the downside in the country's economic performance.

Obviously the economy hasn't exactly responded well to this year's consumption tax hike. But that hasn't shaken the enthusiasts who have a permanent bias towards looking on the bright side of things. Takeshi Minami, chief economist at the Norinchukin Research Institute in Tokyo, for example, felt that Japan's April-June 2014 6.8% annualised fall in GDP wasn't a disaster, since – as he told Bloomberg[165] - despite the sharp fall, "the probability is high that the July-September quarter will see a rebound." Well, naturally, after a 19.2% annualised drop in

---

[165] Japan's Economy Shrinks the Most Since 2011 Quake on Tax, Bloomberg News, 13 August 2014

household consumption, and a 35.3% drop in residential investment doing better won't be hard, but really that is all a little beside the point if what you are interested in is sustainable growth in Japan.

Another line of argument you can find repeatedly in the financial press about Japan is that while the post tax-hike GDP number was undoubtedly a bad one, the silver lining is that this means the Bank of Japan is more likely to do additional QE. "The contraction was sharp. There is no argument about that," Toshihiro Nagahama, chief economist at Dai-Ichi Life Research Institute told the Wall Street Journal,[166] however he had "no doubt" the government and the Bank of Japan would come under pressure to act as a result. Pressure from whom? As we will see below, maybe not from the Japanese citizens these institutions are supposed to represent.

In fact the anticipated response from the BoJ was not long in coming. On 30 October 2014 Haruhiko Kuroda announced that he was putting in place a new, higher target for the increase in the monetary base, raising it from the previous JPY 60-7- trillion, to JPY 80 trillion.[167] At this pace, by the end of 2015 Japan's monetary base (money supply) would surpass JPY 350 trillion, not far from the JPY 450 trillion (approximately USD 4 trillion) level that the Fed reached in the United States after over five years and three waves of QE.

---

[166] 5 Takeaways From Japan GDP, Wall Street Journal, 12 August 2014 http://www.bloomberg.com/news/2014-08-12/japan-economy-shrinks-the-most-since-2011-quake-on-tax.html
http://blogs.wsj.com/briefly/2014/08/12/5-takeaways-from-japans-gdp-2/?KEYWORDS=toshihiro

[167] Kuroda Surprises With Stimulus Boost as Japan Struggles, Bloomberg News, 31 October 2014 http://www.bloomberg.com/news/articles/2014-10-31/boj-unexpectedly-boosts-easing-amid-weak-price-gains

A simple calculation suggests that when Kuroda achieves his target the BoJ balance sheet will have climbed to a level of over 70% of Japan's GDP (up from 30% when Kuroda assumed office). This compares with a level of some 25% of U.S. GDP which the US Federal Reserve has pledged not to exceed for the foreseeable future. In order to achieve its new objectives the BoJ will print money to buy JPY 80 trillion in Japanese government bonds a year. Japan specialist Richard Katz points out that "at this rate, the BoJ will be purchasing virtually all of the new Japan Government Bondss issued by the government....That means that the government can spend all it wants without raising the ratio of the privately-held JGBs to GDP."[168]

But even this renewal of the policy doesn't seem to be having the desired impact. The recovery continues to be weak, and consumer prices may well fall back into negative territory as early as April 2015. At the end of the day what matters isn't whether Japan's economy grows slightly (or not) in this quarter or that quarter, but whether the country is on a stable recovery path. And it is here where all the doubts continue to lie.

Furthermore, the expected boost to exports hasn't happened. In June 2014 exports were down 2% over a year earlier, and in volume terms they were down 2.5% from September 2012, just before the Abenomics-driven yen devaluation started. So if one of the objectives of Abenomics was to stimulate export growth it hasn't been a spectacular success. As Naohiko Baba, chief Japan economist at Goldman Sachs Group and former central bank employee explained to Bloomberg[169]: "The BOJ predicted that a

---

[168] Richard Katz, The Oriental Economist, 3 November 2014
[169] Japan Tallies Weak Yen as Prices Rise Without Export Gain, Bloomberg

weak yen would boost export volumes and spur spill-over effects by increasing domestic production and expanding the overall economy -- but that path isn't working. It raises the question of what the weak yen has done in terms of living standards of the general public."

The explanation for this "non-effect" is that Japanese manufacturers steadily moved production to lower-cost countries during the years of yen strength, thus reducing the effect of exchange rates on exports. Honda, for example, has more car production capacity in North America than its home market and last year exported more vehicles from its U.S. factories than it imported into the country from Japan. In addition many manufacturers have been simply happy to sit on the windfall profits that the devaluation has been bringing them when sales revenue is converted into yen.

And What About Inflation?

Reading the most of the statements that have come out of the Bank of Japan over the last six months, the speeches of Governor Haruhiko Kuroda or Finance Minister Taro Aso, you would get the impression that the days of deflation are now well and truly numbered. Martin Schulz, economist at Fujitsu Research Institute in Tokyo, went even further. "Deflation is over in Japan," he told Bloomberg Television First Up's Angie Lau in July 2014.[170] Even Japan's industrial leaders now believe inflation is here to stay: according to average forecasts in a Bank of Japan survey

---

News, 11 August 2014 http://www.bloomberg.com/news/2014-08-10/japan-tallies-weak-yen-as-prices-rise-without-export-gain.html

[170] Deflation Over in Japan: Fujitsu Research's Schulz, Bloomberg TV vídeo, 30 May 2014 http://www.bloomberg.com/video/deflation-over-in-japan-fujitsu-research-s-schulz-nqBYFX9KQT~n00O3koDeDQ.html

conducted in March 2014 the country's inflation rate will be 1.5 percent in the spring of 2015, and 1.7 percent in 2017,

But is such optimism – if that is what it can be called - justified? According to the Bank of Japan's favored price index, which includes energy but not the cost of fresh food, inflation stood at an annual 3.3% in April 2014. Sounds good if what you want to do is generate inflation.

But before getting too excited, it is worth bearing in mind that inflation one month earlier has stood at only 1.3% on the same measure. The difference between months is, naturally, a by-product of the 3% sales tax hike which came into force on 1 April. Without that, inflation would have been much lower since the base effect of the 20% yen devaluation was at that point starting to work its way out of the calculation. Indeed stripping out energy costs (which are the principal knock-on cost effect of the devalued yen), inflation was estimated to be only 2.3%, notably below the size of the tax hike. On another measure - the ex-tax rate as estimated by the Bank of Japan - inflation has been steadily weakening, and in January 2015 it was down to just 0.2%. So the question which should be being asked is what will the level of annual inflation be in April 2015, assuming that is there are no further yen devaluations or tax hikes to help push the number back up again? Will the country once more be facing the prospect of renewed deflation?

Leaving aside the sustainability issue, the **type** of inflation Japan has been experiencing since the advent of Abenomics – driven by rising energy costs and tax hikes – also constitutes a problem. It has been described by Bloomberg journalists Tsuyoshi Inajima and Brian Swint as the "wrong kind",[171] a way of putting things which highlights the amount of confusion that exists about just what it is that the BoJ is doing and what it is supposed to be achieving.

The Bloomberg journalists illustrated their point by citing Klaus Baader, chief Asia Pacific economist for Societe Generale in Hong Kong to the effect that "this isn't the kind of inflation we want in Japan to break the deflation mindset. We'd like inflation that is a reflection of higher wages, whereas this is pure cost inflation that decreases purchasing power." So at this point we start to understand that Japan doesn't need just any old inflation, it needs a very specific kind, which could be described as "demand pull", a realization which brings us straight back to the original problem we were struggling with. Domestic demand in Japan just isn't strong enough to generate this kind of inflation, and nudging up inflation expectations for a couple of years won't change anything substantial in this regard.

Possibly the type of cost push inflation Japan is experiencing is the "wrong kind" for adherents of the Abenomics approach, but it is more than likely the only kind they are going to get. If the structural lack of demand argument I have been advancing is valid, then this means there is permanent downward pressure on costs in an environment of constant oversupply making inflationary wage increases difficult to envision. Indeed, as reported by another group of Bloomberg journalists[172] (Masaki Kondo, Mariko Ishikawa and Yumi Ikeda), reality itself belies such expectations, since Japan's real wage index hit a post 1992 low at

---

[171] Japan Utilities Raising Prices Offer Abe Wrong Inflation, 1 May 2013
http://www.bloomberg.com/news/2013-04-30/japan-utilities-may-raise-prices-as-reactors-sit-idle.html

[172] Kuroda Stimulus Backfires as Mortgage Costs Rise: Japan Credit, 8 May 2013
http://www.bloomberg.com/news/2013-05-08/kuroda-stimulus-backfires-as-mortgage-costs-rise-japan-credit.html

the start of 2013. And the downward drift has continued. In April 2014 the average basic salary fell for the 23rd straight month, declining 0.2 percent to 243,989 yen, while average real, or inflation-adjusted, wages decreased 3.1 percent from a year earlier, marking the largest year-on-year fall in more than four years.

Rising inflation and falling wages don't seem like the sort of combination to make for a sustainable recovery. Indeed it all seems so off-mark as to make you wonder whether official sector economists really thought through what they were doing before embarking on this experiment.

As the Wall Street Journal put it[173]:

> *"The latest data, which exclude the effects of April's consumption-tax hike, suggest that Japan is slipping away from the 2% inflation target set by Mr. Abe's central banker, Haruhiko Kuroda. Price increases for imports, triggered by a yen-devaluation campaign, have now filtered through the economy. Since Abenomics hasn't included concrete economic reforms, Japan is sliding back into its status quo before Mr. Abe was elected in late 2012."*

Winners and Losers

Another problem which faces Abe is that the results of his policy have been very unevenly distributed. Those who gained from the yen devaluation or from the rise in Japanese equities, or those corporates who made windfall profits on their export sales have been the lucky ones, because the majority of Japanese have been

---

[173] The End of Japan's Inflation Affair, Wall Street Journal, 27 July 2014 http://online.wsj.com/articles/the-end-of-japans-inflation-affair-1406473045

facing falling living standards.

Not unnaturally under these circumstances many Japanese are starting to get fed up with Premier Abe and his economics revolution. What good to them is a policy which only helps the upper 10% of the population and the overseas investment community? Especially if it is all only an elaborate experiment to see if the economy can find a hypothetical trajectory which may not even exist. Isn't all this turning them into something like guinea pigs?

While many in the markets and in the academic community think the obvious response to the latest setback in the fight against deflation in Japan will be more BoJ easing, the Japanese themselves may not see it this way.

Part of the reason they might not see it in the same light as the central-bank-dependent investment community is that there is a solid body of opinion in Japan that now recognizes that a large part of the country's issue is demographic and that simply "jump starting" a bit of inflation won't make the problem go away.

So the question I would ask is this: given all the doubt which exists about the real roots of Japan's problem, and the fact that it may well be a permanent structural problem and not a temporary liquidity trap one, is it really justified to run such a high risk, all-or-nothing experiment? Even Paul Krugman seems to have changed his assessment various times since the problem started[174] and while he still fully supports the general approach being taken he now thinks the natural rate of interest may remain permanently

---

[174] Paul Krugman, Secular Stagnation in the Euro Area, NYT 17 May 2014 http://edwardhughtoo.blogspot.com.es/2014/06/secular-stagnation-part-1-paul-krugmans.html

negative and that fiscal stimulus might be necessary on a permanent basis (liquidity trap without end, amen). What makes people like me nervous is the thought that if the central bank can't deliver on its promise to deliver inflation, or if the Japanese voters decide they have had enough of the experiment, then a loss of confidence might ensue, and all those dubious risky asset positions might unwind suddenly, just like an earlier set did in 2008.

And there are plenty of people in Japan who have been pointing this out all along. Seki Obata, a Keio University business school professor for example, who in 2013 published a book "Reflation is Dangerous," argues exactly this, that "Abenomics" is exposing Japan to considerable risk without any clear sense of what it can accomplish. Obata also makes the extremely valid point that there is simply no way incomes can rise across the entire economy because the baby boomers are now retiring to be replaced by fewer young workers with post labour reform entry-level wages. Japan's overall consumer spending power will therefore fall, rather than rise as Abe hopes. "Individual companies may offer wage increases, but because of demographics it is simply impossible to increase the total amount that is paid out in wages," says Obata. "On the contrary, that amount will shrink." Simple logic you would have thought, but logic in the face of irrational exuberance scarcely stops people in their tracks.

As far as I can see, all of this points to one simple and evident conclusion: that Japan needs deep seated cultural changes, especially ones directed to greater female empowerment and more open-ness towards immigration. Hardly matters for central bank initiatives, and indeed ones for which Shinzo Abe, who naturally has given his name to this new economic trend, is singularly ill equipped to carry through. Japan needs a series of structural reforms – like those under discussion around the third arrow – but these would be to soften the blow of workforce and population decline, not an attempt to run away from it. Monetary policy has its limits. As Martin Wolf so aptly put it, "you can't print babies".

And if in Japan they can't get out of the deflation trap, what is the likelihood that a similar policy will work in Europe?

If Not Japan Then.......

Putting aside the Japan experience, let's go back to where we started this book, to Ray Dalio's September 2012 Bloomberg TV interview, and let's consider his best and strongest argument. Mario Draghi has vowed to do enough, and enough seems to have no limits: a conclusion which has only been reinforced by his most recent speech at the annual Jackson Hole meeting[175]. So what could the ECB do if we really put our imagination to work on the issue?

Well like Ray argues, they could print money, lots of it, even to the point of doing it helicopter style.[176] Which means that those people who erroneously think the ECB is already printing money haven't seen anything yet. That's what the "it will be enough" promise means. Certainly Japan style QE could, and most probably will, happen. When you're crossing a rope bridge and it starts to

---

[175] Speech by Mario Draghi, President of the ECB, Annual central bank symposium in Jackson Hole, 22 August 2014
http://www.ecb.europa.eu/press/key/date/2014/html/sp140822.en.html
[176] See, for example, Willem H. Buiter The Simple Analytics of Helicopter Money: Why It Works — Always, Economics: The Open-Access, Open-Assessment E-Journal, 8 (2014-28): 1—51. http://www.economics-ejournal.org/economics/journalarticles/2014-28

creak and sway then you just have no alternative but to continue moving towards the other side. We have all seen far too many movies about what happens to the people who try to turn back.

As the US saw in Vietnam, the deeper you get in the harder it is to get out, since you keep committing ever more resources simply to go the course. The losses you would have to accept to stop doing more keep growing and growing, so you keep deciding to continue doing whatever it takes. Really you are left with little choice.

So let's imagine this is what happens, and the ECB really goes to the imaginable limits and even beyond. Will it work? Will it be enough? Well this is where I think I find a flaw in Dalio's argument, and it is a very common flaw to be found in the thinking of those educated in the US monetary tradition.

Ray Dalio is assuming the ECB's eventual "money printing" will produce inflation, and that this inflation will help burn down the accumulated debt (often today this process is termed "financial repression"). Whatever the pain this entails for bondholders who see the yield on their investment turn negative, if the process produces deleveraging and an eventual return to stable growth you could say it is worth it. In any event, in cases of large scale Japan-style QE it is the central bank that is going to be the main bondholder, so the outcome may not seem so objectionable from an investor perspective. After all, there are plenty of other assets they can get into.

Inflation, always and everywhere, so the argument goes, requires money printing to happen (whether via private or public debt), and in fact it seems to be the case of so far so good, the truth of the expression is almost self-evident.

But is the argument symmetrical? That is, does it work the other way round? This is the question which was asked by former Bank of Japan Governor Masaaki Shirakawa in a speech given at the 2013 People's Bank of China-BIS Research Conference in Beijing[177]. Can we also say, he asks, that "Deflation is always and everywhere a monetary phenomenon"? As he notes, this reverse formulation of the question - replacing inflation with deflation - has been asked quite often in Japan over the past 15 years. "If we take the episode of hyperinflation in the early 1920s or deflation in the 1930s", he argues, "the answer to both questions appears rather straightforward". But what about the past quarter century? "To what extent," asks Shirakawa, "do these propositions describe price and economic developments and serve as useful guiding principles for policy conduct by central bankers?" Not a great deal is his conclusion.

In particular he stresses, the effectiveness of unconventional monetary policy also depends critically on real factors. "More specifically, it depends on the ability to create a gap between the natural rate of interest and the market interest rate." If, after the collapse of a bubble, the natural rate of interest declines and remains depressed for an extended period of time the effectiveness of unconventional monetary policy is diminished, compared to its effectiveness in a world without such declines in the natural rate. And Japan's experience highlights the difficulty presented by a decline in the natural rate of interest which is secular in nature.[178] As we have seen, the rationale for

---

[177] Masaaki Shirakawa, Is inflation (or deflation) "always and everywhere" a monetary phenomenon? Paper presented at the People's Bank of China-BIS Research Conference on "Globalization and Inflation Dynamics in Asia and the Pacific ", September 2013 http://www.bis.org/events/gidap2013/home.htm
[178] Gauti Eggertsson & Neil Mehrotra: A Model of Secular Stagnation, 2014, http://www.econ.brown.edu/fac/Gauti_Eggertsson/papers/Eggertsson_Mehro

unconventional monetary policy is that if we can just succeed in lowering the long-term real interest rate, we will stimulate demand and thus return the path of economy to full employment. But the implicit assumption here is that the economy has only been hit by a temporary demand shock or is in a Keynesian situation of demand deficiency. In this case, unconventional monetary policy at least in theory should be effective by bringing future demand to the present. "On the other hand", he says, "what if the economy is faced with a secular decline in the natural rate of interest? In this alternative case, the longer we rely on this mechanism, the less demand to be brought forward from the future there is and the less effective the inter-temporal substitution mechanism will be."

So the situation may be asymmetrical. Maybe you need money printing as a condition for getting inflation, but maybe in conditions of a secular decline in the natural rate of interest simple money-printing won't generate inflation. Let's give an example. If I want to suffocate myself I need to deprive myself of air. If I don't deprive myself of air I won't suffocate. Fine. And if I deprive myself of air, does that mean I will suffocate? The answer is it depends; the absence of air is a necessary but not a sufficient condition. I need more information to be able answer the question adequately, even though I find it impossible to imagine myself suffocating without a lack of air. Something similar happens with the inflation and money printing argument. It is unthinkable to have sustained inflation unless someone somewhere is printing money, but does that mean that printing money always and everywhere leads to inflation? No it doesn't.

Worse, in one developed country after another across the globe a lot of money printing is going on, we just aren't seeing the inflation. Why could this be?

The Black Swan Issue

According to Ray Dalio,[179] "Since everyone eventually gets through the deleveraging process, the only question is how much pain they endure in the process. Because there have been many deleveragings throughout history to learn from, and because the economic machine is a relatively simple thing, a lot of pain can be avoided if they understand how this process works and how it has played out in past times."

Those who do not conceptualize what is happening in Japan in demographic terms normally explain the phenomena we are seeing by resorting to some variant the "balance sheet recessions" idea. At the heart of the balance sheet recessions hypothesis (which is often associated with the name of Nomura economist Richard Koo[180]) is the idea that economies like the Japanese one are essentially deleveraging following a bubble-related unsustainable expansion of credit and debt. The demand side deficit that is observed can thus be thought of as being produced by this deleveraging process on the part of both households and corporates. Most financial market analysts assume that some such deleveraging process is what currently ails the economies of the developed world.

---

[179] Ray Dalio, An In-depth Look At Deleveragings, Bridgewater, 2012
http://www.bwater.com/Uploads/FileManager/research/deleveraging/an-in-depth-look-at-deleveragings--ray-dalio-bridgewater.pdf

[180] Richard Koo, The World in a Balance Sheet Recession: Causes Cure and Politics, Nomura Research Institute, Tokyo, 2011
http://www.paecon.net/PAEReview/issue58/Koo58.pdf

But this view is short sighted and over-simplified. There is no doubt that many economies are still laboring under a very heavy debt burden, even if this burden may be increasingly becoming a sovereign debt one. Yet it is hard to believe that – 20 years after the original bubble burst - the main reason Japanese households are not borrowing more on aggregate is that they are still deleveraging from earlier excesses, or that corporates are neglecting to invest more in domestic Japanese activities for similar reasons. Rather, it seems more plausible to assume that consumers are now borrowing less and less as the age profile and size of the entire consuming community steadily shifts while corporates are hoarding cash as investing in capacity without the necessary expansion in demand makes no economic sense. The structural deficiency in demand which produces the deflation is not an "accidental by-product" of "swings in the birth rate" but an absolutely comprehensible and systematic outcome of fertility dropping well beyond replacement levels and staying there over several decades.

This is not the conclusion drawn by legendary Hedge Fund manager Ray Dalio, who decided after studying a large number of deleveraging processes that "everyone eventually gets through the deleveraging process" the only real difference being in how much pain is inflicted on participants in executing the operation. Which brings us to the strange expression "rara avis in terris nigroque simillima cygno". The phrase, which comes from the Latin poet Juvenal, was in fact brought into the headlines during the global crisis by financial affairs writer Nassim Nicholas Taleb. Roughly translated it means "a rare bird in the lands, very much like a black swan". It was assumed – despite appearances – that it was not a black swan since such a bird was long thought not to exist. Hence the conclusion: all swans are white.

In fact, the issue of black swans is not exclusively associated with the problem made famous in Taleb's book on the subject[181] (the question of random tail-events), but has its origins in a basic flaw in inductive reasoning, long ago highlighted by the philosopher of science Karl Poppper: you simply can't assume something doesn't exist because you have never seen one. Ray Dalio falls into this very trap in the excerpt from his study cited above when he asserts that everyone eventually gets through the deleveraging process. It would be more correct to say that everyone had gotten through the process, and then Japan came along.

Two decades after the bubble burst, according to the balance sheet recession argument, the country has still not gotten through its process, and if the arguments I am presenting here have any validity then it is highly unlikely it ever will do. In which case the existence of a black swan in the first (simply epistemological) sense of the term may serve to bring into existence one which better conforms to the second use: in the shape of a very nasty unexpected tail event as expectations are forced to swerve violently from one direction to another.

The problem is that almost all investors at this point are assuming that both Japan and Europe will eventually overcome their deflation problem, and that the secular negative interest rate won't always be secular.

Indeed in both Japan and the Euro Area markets now positioning as if it were inevitable that, if only QE gets big enough, one day deflation will be a thing of the past. In the process they are producing large and systematic distortions in the price of financial assets.

---

[181] Nassim Nicholas Taleb, The Black Swan: The Impact of the Highly Improbable, Penguin, London, 2008

My conclusion then is that there is little evidence or possibility that systematic QE will work as advertised – either in Europe or Japan - largely because it is based on a misunderstanding. It might work if the two of them were in a simple liquidity trap as described by Keynes, or a balance sheet recession deleveraging process of the kind Richard Koo talks about. Once you introduce demography into the picture, however, the game gets changed and the water incredibly muddied.

So if even Japan itself finally discovers it cannot go fully "Japanese" in the sense of generating the anticipated inflation (nor even the expectation of it) then the implication will be that neither can anyone else who gets pinned down in a similar quandary. Black swans may indeed be very rare birds, but that doesn't mean you may not be able to sight one flying past the bottom of your garden at some point in the not too distant future

11

The Expectations Fairy

"You can fool some of the people all of the time, and all of the people some of the time, but you can not fool all of the people all of the time – Abraham Lincoln

Exiting a Liquidity Trap

The classic solution to the problem posed by a demand slump when monetary policy becomes ineffective due to the operation of a liquidity trap is a credible commitment to future inflation[182]. This commitment reduces the real interest rate despite the presence of a zero bound and thus stimulates spending, and it does so through the impact of the commitment on expectations about future inflation. At least that's the theory. In a later blog post[183] Nobel economist Paul Krugman who was behind the

---

[182] see for example Paul Krugman's 1998 Japan's Trap http://www.princeton.edu/~pkrugman/japans_trap.pdf
[183] Paul Krugman, Monetary Policy In A Liquidity Trap. New York Times, 11 April

escaping liquidity traps 1.0 version puts it like this:

"*Here's the thing, however: the economy won't always be in a liquidity trap, or at least it might not always be there. And while investors shouldn't care about what the central bank does now, they should care about what it will do in the future. If investors believe that the central bank will keep the pedal to the metal even as the economy begins to recover, this will imply higher inflation than if it hikes rates at the first hint of good news – and higher expected inflation means a lower real interest rate, and therefore a stronger economy. So the central bank can still get traction if it can change expectations about future policy.*"

So what you need to do is convince investors that it's going to rain inflation tomorrow. The tricky part is, as he goes on to note, this commitment won't convince if investors fear that at the first sign of good news the normally staid and serious central bankers revert to type and snatch away the punch bowl. An old Greek fable catches the feel of the situation remarkably well:

"*A lion is trapped in a deep hole. A fox passes by and the lion asks it to pass down a tree branch. The lion makes many promises about the reward it will give the fox if it escapes from the trap. The fox understands that the lion is hungry and that once escapes the trap it will simply eat it. Once the lion is free from the trap it has no incentive to fulfill its promise but has every reason to make the fox its meal.*"

So the central bank has to commit to future inflation in a way which credibly convinces investors that they are not going to be turkey's participating in a Christmas promotion campaign. In an

---

2013 http://krugman.blogs.nytimes.com/2013/04/11/monetary-policy-in-a-liquidity-trap/?_php=true&_type=blogs&_php=true&_type=blogs&_r=1

attempt to get over this difficulty the Icelandic economist Gauti Eggertsson came up with an additional set of proposals - in a paper entitled Committing to Being Irresponsible[184] - where the core idea was that removing central bank independence would make the commitment more credible, presumably because politicians are known to have a lower anti-inflation bias than central bankers. Eggertsson puts it like this:

"In this paper the zero bound is binding because of large shocks that make the Central bank unable to lower the nominal interest rate enough to prevent deflation and a deleterious decline in output. We show that in the presence of these shocks there is instead a deflation bias of a discretionary independent Central Bank."

"In a liquidity trap the Central Bank would best achieve its goals if it could commit to moderate future inflation in order to maintain price stability and keep employment close to potential. If it is a discretionary maximizer it cannot, however, do this because its announcements are not credible. The result is a liquidity trap characterized by excessive deflation and undesirably low output."

Paul Krugman uses exactly the same expression at the end of the post I cite above: "The hope now is that things have changed enough at the Bank of Japan that this time it can, as I put it all those years ago, 'credibly promise to be irresponsible'". So the question is, why isn't this short term irresponsibility - I presume the idea is that they don't go on being irresponsible forever (although see below) - some variant of what Washington Post journalist Matt O'brien calls the Jedi mind trick?[185]

---

[184] Gauti Eggertsson & Neil Mehrotra: A Model of Secular Stagnation, 2014
http://www.econ.brown.edu/fac/Gauti_Eggertsson/papers/Eggertsson_Mehrotra.pdf
[185] Matt O'brien, "Abenomics has only worked because foreigners think it will", Washington Post

"*So what's going on here?*" he asks us, "*Well, it might sound like a hokey religion, but central banking is really a Jedi mind trick. Just saying something can be enough to make it happen. That's because the power of the printing press gives their words a distinct power. Well, that and the fact that the economy is already one big self-fulfilling prophecy.*"

At the heart of the problem lies the issue of expectations, and what you can get people to credibly believe. Baron von Munchhausen was reputedly able to pull himself up by his own bootstraps, I advise my readers to try it and see if it works for them.

What's the Difference Between the "Confidence Fairy" and the "Expectations Imp"?

The issue of expectations is important, and central to the fiscal expansionary approach, since if the theory here isn't quite right then Abenomics simply can't work. Nor will QE at the ECB. This importance attached to the evolution of expectations contrasts sharply with the way some macro-economists ridicule those who suggest that all you need to get people to spend their way out of a demand slump is make them feel more confident.

But not everyone is comfortable with this rather forced contrast. As the US economist Brad DeLong says[186], "It is unfair for Keynesians to be making fun of the people who call for austerity by saying "confidence fairy" when they are making similar

---

Wonk Blog, 13 August 2014
[186] Brad DeLong, Confusion: High Public Debt Levels and Other Sources of Risk in Today's Macroeconomic Environment, 9 June 2013
http://delong.typepad.com/sdj/2013/06/confusion.html

expectational-shift arguments themselves." This comment has some force, since Brad himself is a high profile Keynesian.

The thing is, in the latest generation of theories about how to escape from a liquidity trap don't expectations play a role in some way equivalent to that of confidence in austerian ones? At least this is the point Brad DeLong seems to be making. To be able to behave as if inflation was looming just over the horizon you need to believe the central bank is both willing **and** able to create it, and to keep doing so. So what is the difference between confidence and expectations? Why should I not believe central bankers' (confidence raising) growth forecasts yet believe their inflation ones? Well, according to Paul Krugman in one of his most explicit attempts to date to address just this point:[187]

"The expansionary austerity types.........are (or were) actually counting on the supposed rise in confidence to avoid what would otherwise be nasty recessions, which have in fact materialized.......those of us hoping to summon the expectations imp want to do so with policies that are at worst harmless, such as expanding the monetary base under conditions where this has no direct inflationary impact."

Doesn't sound very convincing as an explanation, does it? Confidence arguments are used by those who try to avoid an unpleasant truth, expectations ones by people who believe you can change things. While generally agreeing with Krugman that deep seated economic imbalances are normally not resolved by simply improving confidence, I'm not sure he quite does the

---

[187] Paul Krugman,
The Confidence Fairy, The Expectations Imp, and the Rate-Hike Obsession, New York Times 9 June 2013 http://krugman.blogs.nytimes.com/2013/06/09/the-confidence-fairy-the-expectations-imp-and-the-rate-hike-obsession/

expansionary austerity argument justice here by saying that those advocating the view do so simply because they think in this way they can postpone a deep and nasty recession. Sounds more like "good" vs "evil" polemical stuff.

In fact, not unsurprisingly, the "expansionary austerity" proponents do have some stronger arguments than those Krugman saw fit to deal with. The first reference to this kind of argument I personally came across in the context of the current crisis was in the IMF Hungary Standby Loan Report.[188] Certainly in the reference I cite below the IMF economists who used it do not seem to be basing themselves on the kind of argument the Nobel economist suggests they do:

"In emerging market countries with debt overhangs, the "Keynesian" effect of fiscal adjustment is likely to be outweighed by "non-Keynesian" effects related to expectations and credibility. Non- Keynesian effects have to do with the offsetting response of private saving to policy-related changes in public saving. In particular, if fiscal adjustment credibly signals improved public sector solvency, a fiscal contraction could turn out to be expansionary, as private consumption rises based on the view that future tax hikes will be smaller than previously envisaged."

So as far as I can see the argument in its current form first emerged on the eastern European periphery and then headed south. I didn't agree with the argument at the time,[189] and I don't now, but hey, guess what: the argument is based on an

---

[188] Hungary, Request for Stand-By Arrangement, IMF, Washington, 4 November 2008
[189] The New Orthodoxy Is Upon Us, Hungary Economy Watch, 26 May 2009 http://hungaryeconomywatch.blogspot.com.es/2009/05/new-orthodoxy-is-upon-us.html

expectations mechanism. Private consumption is expected to rise on the basis of an anticipated lower future tax burden: pure Robert Lucas.

Now lets' leave aside for the moment the idea that fiscal stimulus policies are "at worst harmless" (or that Japan's rising debt level has no obvious ill-effects), these are after all polemical blog posts (even if in some cases "extremely wonkish" ones[190]) so we shouldn't be too harsh. But, as illustrated above, even a high profile Keynesian like Brad DeLong has trouble going to the line with some of the argument.

The core of the problem is that the "non-Keynesian effects" argument isn't wrong because it postulates you can avoid nasty recessions (don't Austrians and Schumpeter even think recessions are much needed, "cleansing" mechanisms, to purge out imbalances??), it's "wrong" (if that is the appropriate word here) since it is based on implausible assumptions about how people work (rational expectations) and as a result doesn't offer an adequate account of decision making dynamics. More especially it's wrong because it confuses the mechanics behind financial crises (collapse in confidence, self-fulfilling expectations, etc.) with the dynamics of crises which have deep roots in the real economy (more on this below).

In this sense, when Krugman said about Estonia's weak recovery, "Better than no recovery at all, obviously — but this is what passes for economic triumph?" he was basically right, increased investor confidence - of which there certainly was a lot - didn't do

---

[190] Paul Krugman, PPP and Japanese Inflation Expectations (Extremely Wonkish), New York Times, 27 October 2013
http://krugman.blogs.nytimes.com/2013/10/27/ppp-and-japanese-inflation-expectations-extremely-wonkish/?_php=true&_type=blogs&_r=0

the trick, and the economy continues to languish in limboland.

A Quick Look at Robert Lucas

"Lucas thought he could do better. His major innovation in his seminal 1972 article was to get rid of the assumption (implicit and often explicit in virtually every previous macro model) that government policymakers could persistently fool people." - The Concise Encyclopedia of Economics, "Robert Lucas"[191].

"Of course, if we knew - really knew - that one got much more reliable results by doing the things that ad-hoc macro does not, it would be a tool to be used only for the most preliminary examination of issues. But do we know that?" - Paul Krugman, How Complicated Does the Model Have to Be?[192]

A central role in the "expectations" tradition in modern macro is played, as Paul Krugman notes,[193] by another economics Nobel, Robert Lucas. Lucas came online professionally in a world where large-scale Keynesian models were hegemonic when it came to forecasting and policy evaluation. He erupted onto this stage by making one very simple point: the economic models then in vogue were not reflexive enough, in that the observed empirical relationships between variables tended to be "regime specific" and thus of limited value in situations of regime change. The regime Lucas was talking about was the government policy one - a relationship (between say interest rates and inflation) which is

---

[191] Robert E. Lucas Jr., The Concise Encyclopedia of Economics http://www.econlib.org/library/Enc/bios/Lucas.html
[192] Paul Krugman, How Complicated Does the Model Have to Be?, Oxford Review of Economic Policy, Vol 16, No IV, 2000 http://www.princeton.edu/~pkrugman/oxrep.pdf
[193] Paul Krugman, Lucas In Context (Wonkish), New York Times, 26 September 2011 http://krugman.blogs.nytimes.com/2011/09/26/lucas-in-context-wonkish/

observed under one policy regime may not be under another, different, one. In fact the argument could be used to question virtually any model based on the extrapolation of patterns from historical time series under conditions of rapid change, and hence has as much validity today as it did in the 1970s. It may, for just this reason, be less than helpful, for example, to compare what happened when Paul Volker to the helm at the Federal Reserve in the 1980s with the situation facing Janet Yellen today.

The so called "Lucas critique" focused on the role played by expectations in determining movements in large economic aggregates. The conclusion he came to was that generalizations about policy impacts are difficult, since the impact and effectiveness of a given policy in given circumstances may be critically determined by how that policy alters the expectations of the various economic agents involved. Regime change in a central bank and inflation is a typical example. A bank which convincingly commits to doing whatever is necessary to maintain inflation at or around 2% may change actor reaction functions rapidly if a previous regime had been seen to be having a "live and let live" relation with regards to inflation. Equally, a regime committed to doing whatever it takes to generate inflation could influence the behaviour of economic agents by changing their expectations - if that is they have the capacity to do so (see below): if not, they are just another version of Baron Munchhausen.

There is no doubt that the influence of new-generation neoclassical theorists like Robert Lucas gave macroeconomics the appearance of being an increasingly rigorous discipline, in particular in its recourse to ever more sophisticated mathematical techniques - techniques which were so rigorous that the subject came to look as if it were more amenable to theoretical physicists than to those with basic economic intuitions. There was also a systematic attempt to integrate the models used more closely with basic macroeconomic foundations.

But what **was** in doubt from the start - and still remains without an adequate answer today - was whether all that extra rigour and all the mathematical sophistication did not come at a price: that of substituting theoretical sophistication for realism and plausibility. There seemed to be a growing distanciation between the theoretical models being developed and everyday economic reality. Long before the recent global economic crisis brought the fact to everyone's attention it had been evident that the new theoretical economics had still to develop testable - and easily falsifiable - models that would enable practitioners to predict and foresee interesting, unexpected and surprising phenomena in the domain of real world economies: and this surely is where the simple dividing line between science and "doxa" (or mere opinion) has to lie.

And it's evident you don't need a whole lot of math to decide the issue we are looking at in this book - the ability of central banks to "always and everywhere" generate inflation - since whether or not they can is, at the end of the day, an empirical question. All you need is a dictionary to help you understand the meaning of words like "always", "everywhere" and "inflation" and sufficient curiosity to go take a look at the data. In this sort of environment one simple counter example can bring a whole mountain of math tumbling down like a pack of cards.

These points are far from new, 30 years ago Nobel economists were already conducting a "battle of the titans" over exactly these kinds of topic. Most notably the two Roberts – Solow and Lucas - were already clashing over them the best part of thirty years ago.

To Lucas's lament; "I don't think that Solow, in particular, has ever tried to come to grips with any of these issues except by making jokes," Solow retorted: "Suppose someone sits down where you are sitting right now and announces to me that he is Napoleon Bonaparte. The last thing I want to do with him is to get involved in a technical discussion of cavalry tactics at the Battle of Austerlitz. If I do that, I'm getting tacitly drawn into the game that he is Napoleon Bonaparte."[194] As Gregg Mankiw observes: "Lucas seems to be complaining that Solow does not appreciate the greater analytic rigor that new classical macroeconomics can offer. Solow seems to be complaining the Lucas does not appreciate the patent lack of reality of his market-clearing assumptions."

Although economists like Thomas Sargent and Robert Lucas viewed Keynesian modelling and forecasting as based on flawed science - even going so far at one point as to say, "For policy, the central fact is that Keynesian policy recommendations have no sounder basis, in a scientific sense, than recommendations of non-Keynesian economists or, for that matter, non-economists."[195] - they also knew that simply knocking down one edifice isn't equivalent to building another. This would require new, more plausible and more effective models. In this sense although much was promised little actually materialized. "We consider the best currently existing equilibrium models as prototypes of better, future models which will, we hope, prove of practical use in the formulation of policy," they declared in 1979. They even went so far as to suggest that such models would be available "in ten years if we get lucky." They obviously didn't get lucky, since 35

---

[194] See Mankiw's extremely interesting The Macroeconomist as Scientist and Engineer http://old.ccer.edu.cn/download/7432-1.pdf
[195] Ibid

years later the world is still waiting.

Naturally this has harmed perceptions of their project since macroeconomics is not, in principle, a discipline which seeks to determine how many angels you can balance on the head of a pin. As Paul Krugman[196] caustically commented: "One can now explain how price stickiness could happen. But useful predictions about when it happens and when it does not, or models that build from menu costs to a realistic Phillips curve, just don't seem to be forthcoming." "Even as a proponent of this line of work", Gregg Mankiw tells us, "I have to admit that there is some truth to that assessment."

Beyond the difficulties involved in understanding the dynamics of expectations, tying macroeconomics down to micro foundations was always going to be a problematic exercise. The subject is inherently about trying to identify patterns which are to be found in the economic system as a whole (relationships between large aggregates)and studying the systemic properties revealed by those patterns. These properties are often discrete and distinguishable from the properties and relationships of the component elements observed at the micro level.

Confidence versus Expectations

As I say above, in the context of financial crises confidence is an extremely important factor - surely it is obvious to everyone that banks runs are always bad. In that sense the large central banks did a sterling job during the global financial crisis by maintaining confidence in the respective banking systems. During so-called "balance of payments crises" sustaining confidence is also vital,

---

[196] Paul Krugman, How Complicated Does the Model Have to Be?, Oxford Review of Economic Policy, Vol 16, No IV, 2000 http://www.princeton.edu/~pkrugman/oxrep.pdf

since sudden fund outflows can lead to self-fulfilling expectations whereby a country which has only a transient liquidity problem can be driven to insolvency. Again, there is consensus on this, so when Jean Claude Trichet declares "Confidence-inspiring policies will foster and not hamper economic recovery,"[197] perhaps it's worth remembering he is a banker, and that he thought the Euro Crisis was based on balance of payments (liquidity) problems in a number of periphery countries.

If the problem is more a question of deep seated competitiveness issues, coupled with potential solvency problems then simple confidence raising won't do that much. To move towards a solution in these - real economy - cases you need to do much more than raise confidence, you need to generate the expectation that the problems are being addressed and resolved. And you generate this confidence by addressing and resolving them. And here Krugman is surely right, fiscal austerity measures don't help at all during adjustments which are carried out in these cases: au contraire, and the IMF effectively admit as much in their mea culpa over Greece.[198] If Greek debt had been restructured from the start and the country had entered a longer term (Extended Fund Facility) programme the fiscal adjustment wouldn't have been so sharp and the outcome would have been better.

So the really important issue is what role can/do expectations play in economic processes? The answer is evidently a significant one. If people who were expecting inflation come to the conclusion that there's going to be a lot less of it, then they probably change their behaviour. It's the mechanism through

---

[197] Paul Krugman, Death of a Fairy Tale, New York Times, 26 April 2012
http://www.nytimes.com/2012/04/27/opinion/krugman-death-of-a-fairy-tale.html
[198] Greece: Ex Post Evaluation of Exceptional Access Under the 2010 Stand-By Arrangement, IMF, Washington, 5 June 2013 http://www.imf.org/external/pubs/cat/longres.aspx?sk=40639.0

which this process works - that of the central bank having a regime change and the person in the street changing their behaviour - that I would say isn't very clear. The "young" Lucas would obviously have said that they hear the message coming out of the central bank and then, if it is credible, start to adapt accordingly. This all sounds horribly simplistic, and as Krugman notes,[199] the "elder" Lucas moved over talking about "price signals" which sounds more plausible (and is completely compatible with a kind of restricted behaviorism which doesn't need to assume fully rational agents). So as people note that prices aren't going up, they may start feeling that inflation is coming down, and start adjusting their behaviour to the expectation of lower inflation, which in and of itself lowers future inflation, and so on.

This adaptation (and self-fulfilling behaviour) obviously works with a lag - and what that lag is an empirical matter which may change from case to case - so expectations generally change after, and not before, the fact. Perhaps the best example of this comes from the Bank of Japan in the 1990s (or the ECB now) where expectations – those of the central bank, investors and consumers - structurally exceeded outcomes all the way down the price curve till the country ended up in deflation. So the deflation was not produced by self-fulfilling behaviour, the latter comes as a result of the fall into deflation and the feeling the central bank is powerless to stop it (Mr Draghi take note!).

The reasonable conclusion to draw is that expectations really are constantly at work in day to day economic processes, even if we don't fully understand the mechanisms through which they work,

---

[199] Paul Krugman, Lucas In Context (Wonkish), New York Times, 26 September 2011
http://krugman.blogs.nytimes.com/2011/09/26/lucas-in-context-wonkish/

and it is a perfectly plausible approach - and not simply a Jedi mind trick - to adopt a policy aimed at changing people's expectations. Especially if the problem you are trying to deal with is deflation rather than inflation. As Mario Draghi says in his standard definition of deflation: "Deflation is a protracted fall in prices across different commodities, sectors and countries. In other words, it is a generalised protracted fall in prices, with self-fulfilling expectations." So obviously to break out of deflation you have to change expectations.

But the question arises: in the case of the deflation we are seeing in Europe and Japan is that possible?

Maybe it would be a good economic outcome for us all to practice levitation. But - despite what some may think - we won't become able to do so simply because some government agency or other works hard to try to convince us that we all can. We need to think to some extent about the mechanics of flight.

Something similar is evidently the case with deflation. We need to think about the causes, and whether or not the proposed solutions work before we can decide whether or not the attempt to generate (at the central bank or elsewhere) the appropriate expectation is achievable. If we think the current deflation is just an expectations issue – and not a phenomenon with deep roots in the real economy – we may well end up leading ourselves totally astray.

Just to help the argument along, let's accept the basic definition Paul Krugman gives as to why there is deflation in Japan.

"To have more or less full employment, we need sufficient spending to make use of the economy's potential. But one important component of spending, investment, is subject to the

accelerator effect: the demand for new capital depends on the economy's rate of growth, rather than the current level of output. So if growth slows due to a falloff in population growth, investment demand falls — potentially pushing the economy into a semi-permanent slump."

Well, that's pretty straight forward, isn't it? An easy to understand explanation about how a society with long term very low fertility gets stuck in a semi-permanent slump, which is what, of course, leads to the deflation. Nothing about expectations here. So if the slump is semi-permanent and demographically produced why should people believe the central bank when they say inflation and recovery (the ending of the semi-permanent slum) are just around the corner and about to arrive? This does sound like some sort of Jedi mind trick to me.

Of course, no one doubts that - in extremis - the central bank could produce inflation. It could practice a literal version of the Willem Buiter type helicopter drop[200], or some Steve Keen debt moratorium type direct transfers into people's bank accounts.[201] It would need to do lots of them, however, since otherwise people might just treat the added income as a windfall (Milton Friedman[202]) and hoard for the future. Naturally if the central bank continued with the helicopter drops, and managed to convince everyone that they really were being irresponsible (and not a lion asking a fox for help), then expectations would certainly

---

[200] Willem H. Buiter, The Simple Analytics of Helicopter Money: Why It Works – Always, Economics e-journal, No 2014-24, 13 June 2014
http://www.economics-ejournal.org/economics/discussionpapers/2014-24
[201] See Masaaki Shirakawa, Is inflation (or deflation) "always and everywhere" a monetary phenomenon?, Paper presented at the People's Bank of China-BIS Research Conference on "Globalization and Inflation Dynamics in Asia and the Pacific ", September 2013 http://www.bis.org/events/gidap2013/home.htm
[202] See ibid

shift, and maybe the accompanying shock to confidence would be so great these could even produce panic and hyperinflation, but if the problem is a demographically driven one who's to say that after the chaos settled what was left of the country wouldn't be right back into deflation again?

The sad truth is that over the last 15 years, and despite all the monetary promises, the only thing people have seen in Japan is deflation. There isn't deflation in Japan because people have built-in, self-fulfilling, expectations: there is deflation because they have had nearly 40 years of ultra-low fertility. And many people can sense that, and see that this isn't something that monetary policy can fix. To repeat the Martin Wolf phrase, "you can't print babies".

To close this chapter, I would like to quote the ex-Governor of the Bank of Japan, Masaaki Shirakawa, and the conclusions which he has drawn after many years of trying to battle with this problem:

"If, after the collapse of a bubble, the natural rate of interest declines and remains depressed for an extended period of time, the effectiveness of unconventional monetary policy is diminished, compared to its effectiveness in a world without such declines in the natural rate. Particularly relevant in the light of Japan's experience is the implication of a decline in the natural rate of interest which is secular in nature. The rationale for unconventional monetary policy is that if we can just succeed in lowering the long term real interest rate, we will stimulate demand and thus return the path of economy to full employment."

"But the implicit assumption here is that the economy has only been hit by a temporary demand shock or is in a Keynesian situation of demand deficiency. In this case, unconventional

monetary policy at least in theory should be effective by bringing future demand to the present. On the other hand, what if the economy is faced with a secular decline in the natural rate of interest? In this alternative case, the longer we rely on this mechanism, the less demand to be brought forward from the future there is and the less effective the inter-temporal substitution mechanism will be."

12

Give Me the Facts, All the Facts, and Only the Facts?

"The "beautiful soul," lacking an actual existence, entangled in the contradiction between its pure self and the necessity of that self to externalize itself and change itself into an actual existence, and dwelling in the immediacy of this firmly held antithesis—an immediacy which alone is the middle term reconciling the antithesis, which has been intensified to its pure abstraction, and is pure being or empty nothingness—this "beautiful soul," then, being conscious of this contradiction in its unreconciled immediacy, is disordered to the point of madness, wastes itself in yearning and pines away in consumption." -- GWF Hegel, the Phenomenology of Spirit

"The problem which troubled me at the time was neither, "When is a theory true?" nor, "When is a theory acceptable?" My problem was different. I wished to distinguish between science and pseudo-science; knowing very well that science often errs, and that pseudo-science may happen to stumble on the truth." -- Karl Popper, Conjectures and Refutations

There's an interesting question about economic "analysis" which confronts anyone who seriously wants to engage in it: do you focus on what you think should happen, indeed what you think absolutely needs to happen? Or do you try to come up with a practical policy, something which has a "what is doable" label pasted all over it? Or, there is a third alternative, do you give both these up as either impossible or unsatisfactory, and instead concentrate your efforts on detailing and outlining what you think will happen given the expectations and beliefs of others?

The third alternative certainly makes for the most interesting reading, especially if you have a strong sense of humour, and a taste for the ironic. But it has an important consequence, since it means the analyst/theorist is relegated to standing on the sidelines as a mere observer, simply chronicling what happens. Chroniclers may be useful for future historians, but they are not exactly men (or women) of action. This is the dilemma facing what the German philosopher Hegel termed the "beautiful soul", as described in the above quote. Such a person suffers the plight of the analyst or thinker who, possessed of what they consider to be the "best among the available theories" guards their purity by limiting themselves to simply expounding it and standing apart from the policy proposals fray. This approach certainly avoids contamination and conflict, but at the same time it involves, as Hegel indicates, a deep sense of frustration since the exponent fails to achieve interaction or self-realization as a valid actor within the only world that matters, the real one. They risk becoming a person whose work only influences things after they are dead, and only then if they are lucky. We could call this the Vincent Van Gough syndrome.

In some senses the dilemma I am trying to identify resembles a classic problem in economic theory: the relationship between positive and normative economics. Traditionally this dichotomy has been structured around an apparent distinction between what "is" and "what ought to be". Thus Milton Friedman, writing in 1955, suggested that:

"in the Western world, and especially in the United States, differences about economic policy among disinterested citizens derive predominantly from different predictions about the economic consequences of taking action—differences that in principle can be eliminated by the progress of positive economics—rather than from fundamental differences in basic values, differences about which men can ultimately only fight."[203]

Leaving aside the thorny issue about whether the assertion that differences about policy among disinterested citizens *"derive predominantly from different predictions about the economic consequences of taking action,"* is **a valid one** (it appears it may well not be, not even among economists[204]), what Milton Friedman neglects (as a good positivist he would do) is that there may well not even be basic agreement about the relevant "facts" which serve to test the consequences of action.

Take a good example, Friedman's most famous popular phrase: "inflation is always and everywhere a monetary phenomenon,"[205]

[203] Milton Friedman, The methodology of positive economics. In M. Friedman (Ed.), Essays in positive economics (p5). Chicago: University of Chicago Press
[204] Bryan Caplan and Stephen C. Miller, Positive versus normative economics: what's the connection? Evidence from the Survey of Americans and Economists on the Economy and the General Social Survey, Public Choice January 2012, Volume 150, Issue 1-2, pp 241-261
[205] Milton Friedman, Inflation Causes and Consequences, Asian Publishing House, 1963.

For many years this "truth" was widely and uncritically accepted by economists. Simply put, it was assumed that if you printed money you would get inflation, either in the short or the long run. Then along came 15 years of deflation in Japan, and experiments in QE. Now things are not so obvious, it is not so clear that money printing can "always and everywhere" generate self-sustaining inflation and some economists are beginning to question whether or not Friedman was as right as he thought he was about this. [206]

Nonetheless the belief that it can continues to dominate contemporary economic discourse. The consequence of money printing is assumed to be inflation, and the predicted Japanese inflation is normally assumed to be about to arrive. Interest in formulating an agreed methodology which could really put to the test whether Friedman's description of the situation is in fact a "universal truth" is not exactly making its presence felt.

Economics is just not an empirical science in this sense, in large part because it is not even a science in terms of having a shared consensual paradigm. Rather, as a discipline it is characterised by constant disputes between rival theories, a state of affairs that would have been regarded by theorists of science like Karl Popper and Thomas Kuhn as "pre-paradigm".

It's worth remembering that Popper was particularly critical of systems of ideas like Marxism and Psychoanalysis which seemed to be hermetically sealed, in the sense that there were no identifiable "facts in the world" that could test their core theories.

See Masaaki Shirakawa, Is inflation (or deflation) "always and everywhere" a monetary phenomenon?, People's Bank of China-BIS Research Conference on "Globalisation and Inflation Dynamics in Asia and the Pacific ", 23-24 September 2013, Beijing, China
http://www.bis.org/events/gidap2013/home.htm

Psychoanalysis, he thought, was "simply non-testable, irrefutable. There was no conceivable human behaviour which would contradict it."[207]

He also pointed out that what he termed "pseudosciences", ways of seeing things like, for example, astrology, make plenty of appeals to observational evidence. There is no shortage of attempts to measure things. So simple recourse to empirical data isn't sufficient, given that data selection is often another name for interpretation of experience in terms of one's own theory. The theory configures and selects the choice of facts. Freud and Adler don't exclude any particular person acting in any particular way, whatever the outward circumstances. "Whether a man sacrificed his life to rescue a drowning child (a case of sublimation) or whether he murdered the child by drowning him (a case of repression) could not possibly be predicted or excluded by Freud's theory; the theory was compatible with everything that could happen."[208] Or as he put it elsewhere:

"I found that those of my friends who were admirers of Marx, Freud, and Adler, were impressed by a number of points common to these theories, and especially by their apparent explanatory power. These theories appeared to be able to explain practically everything that happened within the fields to which they referred. The study of any of them seemed to have the effect of an intellectual conversion or revelation, opening your eyes to a new truth hidden from those not yet initiated. Once your eyes were thus opened you saw confirming instances everywhere: the world was full of verifications of the theory. Whatever happened always

[207] Karl Popper, *Conjectures and Refutations*, Routledge, Kegan and Paul, London, 1963, p37

[208] Karl Popper, "Replies to My Critics," in The Philosophy of Karl Popper, vol. 2, Paul Arthur Schilpp, ed. (La Salle, Ill., 1974), p. 985.

confirmed it."[209]

So what I am not taking about is the simple distinction between normative and positive economics, but rather the problem of practicing positive economics in an effective way, in a situation frequently characterised by a lack of agreement about what the salient "facts" are. As Popper pointed out, you cannot simply "observe". Prior to observation you need a hypothesis which structures what you observe (and logically, what you don't). So any screening-in, is also a screening-out. The case of inter-country current account balances between members of European Monetary Union during the pre-crisis years would be a good case in point: they were not monitored (or even observed) since the prevailing theoretical assumptions were that they didn't matter. And no matter how often you drew attention to them no one would take any notice. Migrant flows between member states (Spain-France, Greece-Germany) suffer the same neglect at the present time. They are just not seen as important, not because of any difference in values (normative bias) but because demographic shifts aren't conceptualized as being important.

Evidently this is not a trivial question, even in an economic-theory context where creativity is hardly overvalued. A great deal of what passes for analysis these days restricts itself to discussing the mundane, even the trivial, and the short term bias is almost absolute. Topics typically become issues like will this or that central bank raise or lower interest rates next month, or possibly early next year? When will the ECB start implementing QE, and when will the Bank of Japan stop? The question why interest rates have been so low for so long in so many developed countries is

[209] Karl Popper, Conjectures and Refutations, Routledge, Kegan and Paul, London, 1963, p37

seldom discussed, it is simply assumed that one day or another they will "normalize", that is to say rise to levels typically seen during economic expansions in the pre-crisis world. I often think economic practice has an inbuilt backward looking bias. Economists scour the past looking for something resembling what they see around them, while they devote relatively little time to asking what may be new, or how the future will differ from the past. This bias towards the past is naturally built in to popular concepts like NAIRU, "output gap", "potential growth" or "trend growth".

But what, to take a contemporary example, if interest rates aren't going back up? At least to anything like the level they were at before the crisis. What if the world around us experienced a sea change at the time of the global crisis? What if what we will see as the years pass will be increasingly different from anything we have seen before (this is my baseline hypothesis). What if, to take matters to an extreme, what we have now is now longer a mixed market economy, with substantial state sectors, within which the majority of prices are set in free market interactions? What if the growing role of central banks in setting asset prices means we are seeing the emergence of something new? A world which is different from the old, soviet-type economies, insofar as it is the central bank, which is in theory politically independent, which tries to set relative prices through its massive and continuing financial market interventions.

These are the sort of questions which arise in a world where interest rates hover around zero and central banks practice monetary policy by having recourse to non-conventional policies largely associated with expanding or contracting their balance sheets.

What should we do if we constantly find ourselves in a world were the improbable or unexpected scenario is the one which actually materializes – a situation often referred to by market participants as "tail risk"? The difficulty is that it is virtually impossible to open up the relevant discussion as long as the great majority of observers and policymakers just don't see it, and continue to believe that economies are recovering from a "one off" financial crisis, and that interest rates will one day "normalize". Since we know that what people expect to happen constitutes an important input in determining what actually happens (even if that may not be what those having the expectations are expecting) this becomes a crucial question.

So before a broader debate on fundamental long term issues can take place there needs to be a shift in expectations, towards ones which make such a debate more comprehensible to current-discourse insiders. Such a shift becomes a precondition of self-realization for an actor who finds him or herself in perpetual "beautiful soul" mode. The result is that instead of writing about what he or she really wants to write about, the person involved ends up tailoring their work around arguments they think will help change the expectations climate so that the real, and much needed, debate can happen. This could be called Popperian "falsification" in reverse, since the process could be seen as trying to help others put their own assumptions to a falsifiability test, or taking a reluctant horse to water to see whether it can be encouraged to drink.

The contemporary debate about how to respond to deflation offers us perhaps one of the clearest contemporary examples of the phenomenon I am trying to draw attention to. If the roots of Japan's (and now the Euro Area's) deflation are in reality demographic then Quantitative Easing will do little to bring the deflationary trend to a permanent halt. Yet most observers continue to think that monetary policy can serve this purpose, simply because of the simple causal connection they make between money printing and inflation. That is to say they hold was it perceived to be a universal hypothesis as true, when in fact its applicability may be far more limited. Some would claim indeed that this earlier universal belief is now contradicted by fact, but as we have seen there is no agreement on what would count as a telling fact. Even if Japan is falling back into deflation as I write, this must be for some other reason than the theory being wrong, possibly the monetary experiment hasn't been daring enough, for example.

As a result the idea that money printing won't work just doesn't enter the discourse and most attention is centered on issues surrounding standard QE topics like "when will it start", "how big will it be", "when will it stop", "will they do more of it", etc.

Meanwhile it is very difficult to open up a serious "will QE work" debate, let alone a "how do we learn to live with deflation" one. As we can see in Japan, even two years after the initiation of massive bond purchases at the BoJ such discussion remains difficult, even though all the evidence points to the likelihood that the country will soon fall back into deflation again.

Naturally the closer you are to having an ideological discourse (of the Marxism/Psychoanalysis kind) the harder the sort of distinction I am trying to make is to either see or maintain. But even for "non-ideological" thinking the issue is far from being an easy one. Whether or not there is any such thing as "objectivity" is a complex philosophical question and attempts to achieve it fraught with all manner of difficulty, but surely we at least have to continue to try? In the meantime the non-ideological thinker is trapped in an economic discourse which is polarized between Austrian thinking and Keynesianism where reaching consensual procedures for putting hypotheses to empirical tests seems to be the last thing people are interested in.

The issue becomes even more complex when you consider just how major multilateral institutions like the EU Commission and the IMF have steadily shifted their role since the start of the financial crisis, away from independent criticism and towards "talking up" troubled economies who are under their guidance. I think Larry Summers presented this issue nicely in his IMF research conference speech[210] when he said:

"I agree with the vast majority of what has just been said [by Ben Bernanke, Stan Fischer and Ken Rogoff] – the importance of moving rapidly; the importance of providing liquidity decisively; the importance of not allowing financial problems to languish; the importance of erecting sound and comprehensive frameworks to prevent future crises. Were I a member of the official sector, I would discourse at some length on each of those themes in a sound way, or in what I would hope would be a sound way. But, I'm not part of the official sector, so I'm not going to talk about any of that."

Summers then went on to advance his secular stagnation hypothesis, which actually reconfigured debate among economists in a way no one would have anticipated. Evidently beyond what is being said, what also matters is who is saying it
IMF 14th Annual Research Conference in Honor of Stanley Fischer, International Monetary Fund, November 8, 2013
http://larrysummers.com/imf-fourteenth-annual-research-conference-in-honor-of-stanley-fischer/

(Foucault), when and where. Even such high profile thinkers as Nobel Economist Paul Krugman can find himself wrong-footed in this context[211], as the following extract illustrates:

"I'm pretty annoyed with Larry Summers right now. His presentation at the IMF Research Conference is, justifiably, getting a lot of attention. And here's the thing: I've been thinking along the same lines, and have, I think, hinted at this analysis in various writings. But Larry's formulation is much clearer and more forceful, and altogether better, than anything I've done. Curse you, Red Baron Larry Summers!"

In fact, it isn't clear that Summers formulation is much clearer and more forceful, indeed it isn't even clear that his argument is exactly the same as the one Krugman himself had been advancing, but nonetheless The Nobel economist's frustration is entirely comprehensible. This inbuilt bias of institutional economists having significant resistance to giving due consideration to alternative scenarios came to the fore at the time of the global financial crisis. As part of its review of why the IMF had failed to see the crisis coming the Independent Evaluation Office report[212] came to the following conclusion:

"Part of the problem was the similar mindset of many mainstream economists working at the Fund, with similar background and training and who were not open to dissenting views. Both in and outside the Fund, there were other economists and policymakers with contrarian views. But their views were not encouraged or

[211] Paul Krugman, Secular Stagnation, Coalmines, Bubbles, and Larry Summers, New York Times, 16 November 2013;
[212] Background Paper 1 - Summary of Views of the Advisory Group (Series Number: BP/10/01), IMF Performance in the Run-Up to the Financial and Economic Crisis: IMF Surveillance in 2004-07. Independent Evaluation Office, 2011

closely examined within the Fund."

Far from this situation having improved since, things have gotten worse, as my own personal experience confirms for me. Why should this be? Well, one part of the explanation would be the following: ever since Robert Lucas shifted attention in economic theory towards the role played by expectations, the artist has somehow been painted into the very picture he or she is painting. You can't talk about a topic without in some way changing the understanding (expectations around) the phenomenon in question. If you write, for example, that the Euro Area is stuck in deflation, doesn't that somehow add to the expectation that it may be? So naturally, if your opinion is that Greek debt is not sustainable, might that not help ensure that it isn't? Whatever the doubts, and whether we are talking about the first, or the second, rescue programme, the idea that Greece is on the path to recovery has to be maintained, since admitting it might not be could very easily ensure that it wasn't. Hence ranks are steadily closed into what ultimately becomes a kind of monolithic bloc, with dissension pushed to the sidelines, and the ability to critically evaluate current practice becoming ever more curtailed.

And then we see where Greece actually ends up. Should we be surprised? The methodology applied to studying the case almost guarantees a bad result.

But there is another issue, and it's not simply about objectivity or institutional bias, it's about communication, and about what others are prepared (or able) to think about (contemplate) at any particular point in time. I had my own personal issue with this recently, when I wrote on the so called "good deflation" phenomenon in Spain. I personally think - for reasons which will emerge below - that contemporary deflation is substantially different from the depression-related deflation we saw in the United States in the 1930's, the phenomenon around which much of modern economic theory on the topic cut its teeth. There is a very big difference between a 1% fall in prices every year for 15 years (the Japan experience) and a 15% fall in one year. Modern deflation seems more associated with shifting demographic dynamics than it is with ongoing debt deflation, although many would be inclined to dismiss this possibility outright.

But is the tendency to rule out such a possibility based on intensive empirical study of the modern deflation phenomenon, or is it driven by the fact that if the problem is largely demographic then it has no evident solution? This would be a clear example of how the need to **do** policy can frame analysis, since the objective (sound but doable policy) governs the analysis, indirectly making the practitioner more inclined toward one hypothesis rather than another.

At the end of the day none of the issues raised in this chapter have any easy solution, but it has been written in the hope that becoming more aware of the problems which exist may in some way help to lessen their impact.

14

Towards a Transfer Union Without Transfers?

That difficulty notwithstanding, what I want to look at in this chapter are the implications of having ongoing deflation and increasing QE at the ECB (both contingent but empirically verifiable conditions) for the balance of calculation about whether or not a given country is better off staying in the Eurozone or leaving it. In other words, it's a kind of thought experiment based on two plausible assumptions: i) that deflation is demographically driven; and (ii) that the ECB will continue to implement QE (or ~~QQE)[213] more or less indefin~~itely in a (forlorn) attempt to bring it

[213] Quantitative and Qualitative Easing. The name used for the Kuroda measure in Japan, where qualitative refers to the composition of the assets purchased,

to a halt. I think this kind of line of thought is worth pursuing since it will give us some idea of the kind of world we may be living in 10 years from now and this may help us understand better what it is we want to do now. In any event it moves us on a bit from scrutinizing every piece of communication to determine whether the list of reforms proposed by the Greek government will be acceptable to the German one. Or whether the Greek government will have to meet its short term financing needs by issuing T-bills, or indeed whether the ECB will agree to advance the 1.9 billion Euros interest rebate which is currently pending? Sometimes we need to look beyond the end of our noses.

What Greece Needs Is Its Own Currency?

Judging by what runs through my Twitter feed, I can't help getting the impression that most London-based investors still have an approach to debt, currencies and interest rate policy which hasn't evolved that much since the 1990s. The over-riding assumption is the Euro is overvalued for Greece's needs, yet undervalued for those of Germany. This leaves them to the conclusion that having your own currency and being able to implement your "own" monetary policy carries strong benefits, ones which far outweigh - for example - losing the anchor which is provided by an EU promoted structural reforms programme. Yet does anyone these days set the value of their own currency? Even, as Janet Yellen recently pointed out, the United States is not immune to contagion. The Chairwoman of the Federal Reserve made her first reference to the value of the currency at the bank's March 2015 meeting. "Export growth has weakened. Probably the strong dollar is one reason for that," she told the post meeting <u>news conference in Washington. "On the other hand, the strength</u>

which may change without any alteration to the quantity purchased.

of the dollar also in part reflects the strength of the U.S. economy."[214]

The reference was widely interpreted as meaning a first rate rise would come later rather than sooner, and that the main reason for this was a largely ECB/BoJ induced rapid surge in the dollar.

As Ralph Atkins put it in the Financial Times: *"In the 1980s international agreements ... [like the Plaza Accord] had a degree of success in smoothing economic adjustment processes. These days such an approach is unlikely, partly because in the post-2007 crises world the previously abnormal seems normal. More practically, massively expanded capital markets make intervention by central banks in the biggest foreign exchange markets much less likely to succeed, especially if their interests are not aligned."*[215]

That the Euro was set up with major - almost fatal - institutional deficiencies is obvious, possibly now to everyone. Ditto for the fact that for many of the countries who participated in the experiment the balance of the first decade is in all probability negative. Ditto too to the idea that the single size monetary policy was manifestly applied counter to the interests of a number of economies on the periphery, economies which subsequently got into a great deal of difficulty.

But the question that really is crying out to be asked is: "has anything relevant changed" since the Euro's creation? Is there no difference between the world of 1995 and that of 2015?

---

[214] Janet Yellen Says Strong Dollar Holding Down Exports and Inflation, But Reflects U.S. Economy's Strength, Wall Street Journal, 18 March 2015 | http://blogs.wsj.com/economics/2015/03/18/yellen-says-strong-dollar-holding-down-exports-and-inflation-but-reflects-u-s-economys-strength/
[215] Ralph Atkins, Yellen battles Draghi in euro-dollar drama, Financial Times, 19 March 2015

personally think there is, and that the changes that have occurred can alter how we think about the whole question of Euro Area membership. Possibly to the extent of being able to understand why it is very much not in the interest of the Greeks to exit the currency at this point.

There are a number of features of our current economic and financial environment which make the world a very different place now to the one we used to live in back in the 1990s. These would be: i) the rise of financial globalization, ii) the arrival of deflation in a number of developed economies and iii) the limitations placed on standard interest rate policy by the perceived presence of a Zero Bound and with this the rise of non-standard monetary policy measures, in particular QE.

There is a fourth and separate point - the existence of accumulated sunk costs - which also enter into any calculation about the difference between deciding to join and deciding to leave, but this one has been widely covered in earlier debates about Grexit, so can be treated to some extent as "shared knowledge".

The Arrival of QE at the ECB

January's decision by the Governing Council of the ECB to initiate a series of sovereign bond purchases as part of more general programme of quantitative easing is historic and its significance goes well beyond the immediate deflation concerns which prompted it.

The ECB's intention is to purchase 50 billion Euros in sovereign bonds every month from March 2015 to September 2016. To this will be added a further 10 billion Euros each month under an existing asset backed securities and covered bond programme.

This is a large programme, which will produce an increase of around a trillion Euros in the ECB balance sheet.

The decision to warehouse 80% of the bond purchases at the national central banks has attracted a lot of attention, since it is clear that this procedure falls well short of full financial integration. The other side of the coin, though, is that it makes the cost of leaving the Euro much higher, since the part of the debt which will be held at the national central bank will effectively remain virtually interest free as long as the country is in the Eurosystem (see below). Outside the Eurosystem framework this kind of QE programme would almost certainly be impossible to maintain, and the country would be faced with market based interest rates making the debt burden much more onerous.

If you are a country with no debt, then maybe life outside the Euro would be beneficial (maybe, there are other considerations), but if you have legacy debts (even restructured ones) then in the context of evolving QE (and there is a long, long way that the ECB can go with this over time) it can only be more expensive for you to find yourself outside. This is so whether you are looking at things from a purely debt sustainability point of view, or from an indebtedness as a drag on growth one. What makes the difference? The arrival of deflation is what makes the difference, since it is this that enables a central bank with deep pockets to increase its balance sheet almost indefinitely without generating inflation. And it is this deflation aspect which makes ECB QE so different from that practiced in the UK or the US, and so similar to what is going on in Japan.

Long Term Disinflationary Trend

Many argue that the current deflation in Europe is simply the result of a short term energy price shock, but as Larry Summers argues in support of his secular stagnation hypothesis, the trend towards ever lower interest rates and ever weaker inflation has been a long lasting one. As has the trend towards lower (and eventually negative) government bond yields.

So something is happening, and that something evidently isn't simply transitory and energy related. The deflation we are seeing in Europe is by and large the result of weak consumer demand, and the impact this has on investment. In addition, this "deflationary moment" coincides with the turning point in working age population dynamics, entailing the possibility that we will see long term deflation, Japanese style.

If what we are witnessing is the arrival of long term structural deflation, and with it the process known as secular stagnation (Larry Summer's hypothesis), then the policy of Quantitative Easing recently adopted by the ECB will not be short term in duration, nor will interest rates in Europe move far in the foreseeable future from what has become known as the Zero Bound.

Certainly the bank of Japan has not been shy in increasing its balance sheet.

Yet despite the extensive and ample use of QE and a 40% devaluation in the yen against the US dollar, ex-tax inflation in Japan has been steadily falling back and in January 2015 it was down to an annual 0.2%. So obvious is the failure of the policy to really produce sustainable inflation that Shinzo Abe policy adviser Koichi Hamada recently argued that the government could cut the inflation target in half (from 2% to 1%) without any major loss of credibility.[216]

So it is far from clear that the ECB's attempts to obtain its price stability target of near to 2% inflation will be successful, although the view you take on the issue will depend on what you think the underlying reason for the deflation really is. This inflation quandary is important since meeting its price stability objective is Mario Draghi's principal justification for introducing sovereign bond purchases under quantitative easing. Indeed Mr Draghi has even stated that far from such purchases not being within the banks mandate, not conducting such purchases (or similar policies) would be illegal under the mandate given its price stability objective.

So, since QE has – in principle (see next chapter) - been introduced until at least September 2016 the possibility exists that it will be continued beyond that point. Indeed it's hard to see how it won't be. And this difficulty in terminating QE will not only relate to inflation insufficiency, debt sustainability will also form part of the picture. Let's take an example.

The ECB has announced that 50 billion Euros in institutional bond purchases will be conducted monthly between March 2015 and September 2016. That means a total of around 900 billion Euros in bonds. Of these purchases 12% - i.e. around 100 billion Euros worth - will be purchases of EU institution instruments (not national government ones). So total sovereign bond purchases will be around 800 billion Euros. These will be bought by ECB (or national central banks) roughly in proportion to Euro Area GDP shares.

Now France accounts for around 20% of EA GDP. So we should

---

[226] Japan PM adviser Hamada says BOJ can halve inflation target, Reuters, 23 February 2015 http://uk.reuters.com/article/2015/02/23/uk-japan-economy-hamada-idUKKBN0LR0G620150223

expect about 160 billion Euros in French bond purchases during 2015/2016. At the same time, the French government deficit is around 4% of French GDP, or an annual 90 billion Euros a year. The conclusion is that the vast majority of this new deficit will be effectively bought by the ECB. Not only that, this debt will be essentially free of interest service charges, since under the seignorage principal, the French government will recover the interest paid to the ECB (or the national central bank). This is what I call "money for nothing and your debt for free".

So far, so good. The European Court of Justice gave the opinion in January that sovereign bond purchases in pursuit of monetary policy objectives don't amount to debt monetization as long as the purchases clearly take place in the secondary market. So that's OK, but let's think about the longer term implications of what's going on.

As is widely known, Japanese gross government debt currently constitutes around 245% of Japan GDP. About 30% of that (or 80% of Japan GDPs worth) is now in the hands of the Bank of Japan. This - as explained above - now effectively costs the Japanese government nothing more than the admin costs of handling so many bonds. The proportion of GDP the BoJ stock of bonds constitutes is rising by the month. The other part of the debt (in private hands) costs, thanks to Japanese QQE, very little to maintain as yields have been driven to a very low level (0.4% on 10 year at the time of writing).

Now let's imagine that at some point the Bank of Japan ends QQE. (This again is what is normally called a thought experiment, since if I am right it simply won't happen, basically because it can't). In the first place Japanese bond yields would start to rise on new debt issuance sold to the private sector, while the proportion of the debt which is "for free" would become less and less as BoJ holdings steadily mature. The debt, remember is very large. This move would constitute an ongoing fiscal tightening (over several years) for the Japanese economy since interest service debt costs rising would mean less revenue available for government spending, or less demand in the economy. Just a 1% rise in interest charges is a negative fiscal hit of around 2.5% of GDP. This tightening would almost certainly provoke a relapse of the fragile Japanese economy and most likely induce a return to deflation (if, that is, Japan had ever really managed to leave).

It seems clear to me at least that Japan can now never completely exit some form of QE, at least it can't do so without going through a major restructuring of its sovereign debt, and a major shake-up in its financial system

Goings On Behind the Veil of Financial Ignorance

Now let's turn to Europe, and Greece: the country with the second highest gross sovereign debt level globally (175% of GDP). Now the change in government in Greece has bought to the headlines the fact that this sort of debt level is not sustainable, unless someone else makes your debt effectively interest free. The Greek finance minister wanted to declare the country bankrupt, and accept the debt could not be paid. But the Euro Area partners rejected this, and preferred to maintain the fiction of sustainability. More money for nothing and your debt for free is the solution that has been found to maintain that fiction. The significance of the recent Greek draft deal is that things are essentially going to remain that way.

In a speech given in Athens last year[217], ECB Executive Board

[217] Investing in Europe: towards a new convergence process, Speech by Benoît

member Benoît Cœuré, referred to Rousseau's "veil of ignorance" initial condition for agreeing on a social or fiscal contract, but maybe more to the point would be the "veil of financial ignorance" which surrounds EU decision making, and effectively means the majority of citizens have little idea of what is really going on. Some even talk of "protecting taxpayers' money in Greece" in relation to the European Financial Stability Fund loans, as if some actual money -rather than debt instruments and guarantees - had changed hands. Greece isn't ever going to pay back its debt to the official sector, nor will Euro partners ever have to recognise losses on money they haven't actually lent: the ECB can buy EFSF bonds to the appropriate amount and the matter will rest there, possibly with the bonds being renewed every 20, 30 or even 50 years.

So then work down the queue, to Portugal and Italy with gross sovereign debt levels of around 130% of GDP and rising. These debt levels are not sustainable either, unless that is someone is going to relieve you of your interest service charges, in which case such debt becomes merely an accounting problem. Enter the ECB.

But for the same reason I mentioned in the Japanese case, once the central bank has bought sufficient quantities of this debt, I simply don't see how we can ever move back to the initial position, at least not without some serious debt restructuring. The respective economies simply couldn't stand it. Italy's long run trend growth rate is nearly negative, and Portugal's isn't much better.

Cœuré, Member of the Executive Board of the ECB, Panel "The big rethink for a stronger Europe", The Economist Roundtable with the Government of Greece, Athens, 9 July 2014
http://www.ecb.europa.eu/press/key/date/2014/html/sp140709.en.html

All of this will make policymakers in Portugal and Italy very wary of any kind of Euro exit, and increasingly so as debt levels and ECB bond purchases increase.

Favorable Winds Move All Boats

The Euro crisis has come a long way since the heady days of May 2010. A large part of the transition which has taken place has been the responsibility of one man: Mario Draghi. First through his "whatever it takes" speech of July 2012, which marked a watershed in the crisis, opening the period of declining sovereign bond yields. And secondly in a key speech made at the central bankers forum in Jackson Hole in August 2014.[218] This speech - which was actually rewritten during the gathering with the ECB having to amend the original version on its website - was historic in that it was the first time the ECB President explicitly recognized that Euro Area 5 year inflation expectations were not "well anchored". It thus paved the way for the eventual introduction of QE.

The speech was also important since he laid down a three point plan:

i) Monetary easing at the central bank

ii) Structural reforms by national governments

iii) Expansionary fiscal policy in those countries which had "fiscal space" - i.e. capacity to run higher deficits within the EU guidelines.

---

[218] Unemployment in the euro area, Speech by Mario Draghi, President of the ECB, Annual central bank symposium in Jackson Hole, 22 August 2014
https://www.ecb.europa.eu/press/key/date/2014/html/sp140822.en.html

This plan looks very much like a Euro-specific version of Abenomics "light". Progress has been made on the first two points, but so far the response from Germany on the third one has been less than negative. In fact the country is proudly paying down its debt. Without taking this situation into account it is impossible to understand what has happened in recent weeks with regard to the Greek bailout negotiations.

Billed widely in the press as a "great" victory for Germany, and a major humiliation for Syriza the outcome is in fact neither. The main victors (if such a name be relevant) have been - oh irony of ironies - the Troika (henceforth known as "the institutions"). In fact we are talking about the ECB (Mario Draghi), the IMF (Christine Lagarde) and the EU Commission (Jean Claude Juncker). There is basic agreement between the leaders of these three institutions that Greece was subjected to excessive austerity at the time of its first bailout programme (the IMF have even made self-criticism over this)[219], and that at a time of extended low inflation/deflation and worries about the settling in of long term deflation expectations further austerity is inappropriate.

Draghi's Jackson Hole plan is in reality the plan of Christine Lagarde and Jean Claude Juncker as well - indeed Draghi even explicitly mentions Junker's 300 billion Euro infrastructure plan in his August speech, so it would not completely surprise me to find that the ECB EU institutional purchases involved some related to the European Investment Bank and its financing of the project.

If you add to the Troika the "coalition of the willing" lead by François Hollande and Matteo Renzi (both of whom want some

[219] Greece: Ex Post Evaluation of Exceptional Access under the 2010 Stand-By Arrangement IMF Country Report No. 13/156, June 2013
http://www.imf.org/external/pubs/ft/scr/2013/cr13156.pdf

deficit relaxation in return for a commitment to structural reforms) it isn't hard to see that it was Germany, and in particular the country's finance minister Wolfgang Schaüble, who was isolated, and basically cornered in the Finmin EuroGroup where Germany effectively have a veto (something they don't have on the board of the ECB, which is why much of the current Euro "action" is centered on that institution).

So some sort of coherent policy is now being implemented in Europe in response to the regions long standing low growth issues. It's not clear that the measures being taken will serve to remedy the problems they were brought into being to address, but they will have long term consequences and they will make the currency union participants act more like one coherent whole, and in that sense they are to be welcomed. It may be that there is no real "solution" to the long term deflation issue, in which case other measures will eventually have to be found. But neither is having one weak country after another sliced off and savaged in the bond markets any more satisfactory as an outcome.

What we could be seeing is the birth of a transfer union with the specificity that there will be no actual inter-country transfers. If things are happening in this peculiar way then that will be because this is the EU, and this is how things are done here. It could be, of course, that the basic premise that contemporary deflation has demographic roots is false. In that case none of this will happen, and this argument can be relegated to idle speculation, a mere fantasy world which never has and never will exist. But are you really sure enough that **it is** false to be willing to do that?

15

Where Do We Go From Here?

In the latter part of this book I have talked a great deal about Japan. This should not strike the reader as strange, since the thesis here is that what the Euro Area is undergoing at the moment is a process of "Japanisation". The gut response of many is thus to push the Eurosystem steadily along the Japan path, but this as we have seen has its dangers. What is going on in Japan is a huge collective experiment on all our behalf's. But the outcome of the experiment is still unknown. Worse, the country has now passed some kind of tipping point, and if what Abe is doing doesn't work there is now no realistic possibility of turning back without accepting a lot of collateral damage.

Relative prices and values across the whole global economy are currently being so distorted by the substantial intervention from central bankers that any sudden loss of faith in the new style central banking experiment would surely have consequences which reached far afield and would be far from benign. Yet as we have seen, the Japanese government may be forced to turn back, precisely because voters stop believing in the policy.

Looking at Europe, the world seems to be constantly turning upside down. At the end of 2014 it was all "Europe bad, USA good" to the point that most observers were expecting an imminent rate rise from the Federal Reserve, even while the Euro was in such a bad state that ECB was being steadily pushed - kicking and screaming - towards a full blown programme of sovereign bond buying QE.

But now, only 3 months into 2015 everything is switching round, as investors become increasingly bullish on the Euro Area recovery outlook, even while doubts on prospects for the US continue to mount.

One of the most striking features of this turnaround is the way the trend in the Citigroup Economic Surprise Indexes has inverted. These indicators measure economic surprises for the US, Europe, Japan etc. in terms of whether data exceeds or falls short of consensus expectations. Such indexes are quite useful as they give some sort of "soft" reading on whether economies are accelerating or decelerating at any given moment in time. If surprises are tending to the upside this means that (by-and-large) data is coming in better than the economists models forecast, and vice versa if the opposite is happening. Models base their expectations on historic data, but each moment in time is unique, so deviations from model predictions do have some meaning. And if these deviations follow a pattern, then they can give you a reading on the state of play of the business cycle.

Euro-land is on a strong upswing, while the US economy is

congenitally under-performing (relative to expectations). Meanwhile monetary policy divergence is accelerating, but in what appears to be the wrong direction. The Federal reserve is widely expected to raise US interest rates sometime in the next six months (although doubts are growing), while the ECB has just launched QE to a barrage of claims that it has achieved most of its objectives before it even got started. Eurozone bond yields are down, even negative, inflation expectations have started to rise, the Euro has devalued sharply, and now even Mario Draghi has started to tell us the indicators suggest a sustained recovery is taking hold."

This being said, it is important not to get overexcited about things. There are obvious reasons why mainland Europe's economies may grow faster in the first six months of 2015 than in 2014: the cheaper Euro boosts exports, falling prices are encouraging consumer spending, fiscal policy remains supportive while interest rates are very cheap. At the same time due to the low underlying growth issue and weak inflation nominal Euro Area GDP may still only increase slowly over the next few of years, with the knock on consequence that sovereign debt levels in the most indebted countries will surely be jolted onwards and upwards. This is important since all official sector projections have these levels peaking either in 2014 or 2015, but now such estimates will surely need to be revisited.

"Europe is becoming Japanese"[220] is an expression that is being used more and more. People saying this normally point to the fact that German 10 year bund yields have now gone under 1% (and

[220] Paul Krugman, What's the Matter With Europe?, New York Times, 13 August 2014 http://krugman.blogs.nytimes.com/2014/08/13/whats-the-matter-with-europe/

hence have started to look like 10 year Japan Government Bonds).

But behind this argument lies some kind of "reverse causality". In Japan JGB yields have been driven to very low levels by central bank intervention, with the BoJ now buying a very large share of all new issue bonds. In Europe, on the other hand, the ECB isn't buying Euro Area sovereigns, the markets **are** in anticipation of QE. So to talk about the Japanification of Euro Area yields is a little misleading. Bond purchasers and their models have been **provoking** this downward lurch, not the central bank response to weak growth or deflation.

Another argument used to justify the "Japanisation" of the Euro Area idea carries much more clout, and that is the one being used by Paul Krugman based on working age population dynamics. "If you're worried that secular stagnation might be depressing the natural real rate of interest (the rate consistent with full employment)", he told blog readers[221] "and you think that demography is a big factor, Europe looks really terrible, indeed full-on Japanese."

The basic idea is that working age population dynamics play a big part in determining movements in aggregate demand and hence inflation. This idea received support from a research paper[222] published at the start of August by a group of IMF economists - "Is Japan's Population Aging Deflationary?" The first part of the paper abstract runs as follows:

"Japan has the most rapidly aging population in the world. This affects growth and fiscal sustainability, but the potential impact

[221] ibid
[222] Derek Anderson, Dennis Botman and Ben Hunt, Is Japan's Population Aging Deflationary?, IMF, Washington, 2014
https://www.imf.org/external/pubs/cat/longres.aspx?sk=41812.0

on inflation has been studied less. We use the IMF's Global Integrated Fiscal and Monetary Model (GIMF) and find substantial deflationary pressures from aging, mainly from declining growth and falling land prices. Dissaving by the elderly makes matters worse as it leads to real exchange rate appreciation from the repatriation of foreign assets. The deflationary effects from aging are magnified by the large fiscal consolidation need."

Bottom line, despite all the denials from Mario Draghi that the Eurozone is not another Japan there are plenty of grounds for thinking that it will be.

The Italian Runaway Train

Be that as it may, the principal issue that arises in the Euro Area at the moment is a far more specific one. The ECB is now doing QE, but when will it stop? Or at least when will a debate about the desirability of continuing bond purchases all the way through to 2016 get off the ground? The ECB agreed to the programme more easily than expected, and it is not unlikely it will terminate it sooner. There was a relatively low bar for QE entry, so it would make sense to imagine there might be an equally low one for exit given the lack of consensus over the policy.

But before looking at the question of when it might end, perhaps a case study of the current state of play might be useful. We could, for example, ask ourselves what could happen to Italian debt if the ECB terminates its intervention? Let's take a look at the dynamics.

By now it is pretty common knowledge that Italy's economy continued to contract in 2014, with GDP declining by 0.4% over

2013. Not only did this result mean that Italy had failed to exit recession, it also meant that GDP was back at the same level it had in 2000, when the country entered the Euro currency union. The economy has now contracted in five of the last seven years, as a consequence the trend growth rate is around 0%, and may even be negative.

Worse, nothing which has happened since the financial crisis ended suggests it is going improve radically in the near future, in fact there are good reasons to think that growth could even deteriorate further. In the first place because Italy's working age population is now falling, and secondly because many young educated Italians are leaving to work elsewhere. Both of these are GDP negative, so even if the government implements a number of spectacular reforms it will still be an uphill job offsetting these impacts.

Added to this long term problem a new problem has emerged: low inflation or even deflation. At the time of writing Italy's annual inflation is consistently below zero.

The combination of low inflation and low growth means that it is the evolution of nominal GDP that really matters now. Nominal GDP is non-inflation-corrected GDP (or GDP at current rather than constant prices). If inflation remains low or even becomes negative, then nominal GDP will hardly increase and may even continue to contract (as has happened in Japan). The result is bound to be that the gross government debt to GDP ratio rises above the 130% level registered at the end of 2014.

One of the arguments frequently advanced about how this dynamic could be turned around would be for Italy to run a "large" primary budget surplus. Now the emphasis here is on

large since the country has in fact run a primary surplus (income - expenditure before paying debt interest) since the early 1990s, but that hasn't stopped the weight of the debt climbing and climbing.

The IMF, in their 2013 Fiscal Monitor[223] outlined a scenario in which the obligations of heavily indebted European sovereigns first stabilize, and then fall to the 60% level targeted by the EU's Fiscal Compact by 2030. To achieve this result assumptions are made regarding interest rates, growth rates and other closely related variables, and then the cyclically adjusted primary budget surplus (the surplus exclusive of interest payments) consistent with this scenario is calculated. As the Fund point out, the heavier the debt, the higher the interest rate and the slower the growth rate, the larger the requisite surplus. In fact they found that the average primary surplus required in the decade 2020-2030 was 5.6% for Ireland, 6.6% for Italy, 5.9% for Portugal, 4.0% for Spain, and 7.2% for Greece.

Is it plausible that Italy could run an average primary surplus of 6.6% of GDP over a decade? Hardly - in particular this implies that on average, every year, the government would be draining out 6.6% of GDP in domestic demand via taxation. Yet domestic demand is precisely the weak point in the Italian economy (secular stagnation, ageing population).

As Eichengreen[224] and Panizzi (who studied the plausibility of the IMF projections) conclude:

---

[223] Fiscal Adjustment in an Uncertain World, IMF Fiscal Monitor, 2013, http://www.imf.org/external/pubs/ft/fm/2013/01/pdf/fm1301.pdf
[224] Barry Eichengreen and Ugo Panizza, Can large primary surpluses solve Europe's debt problem?, Vox, 30 July 2014 http://www.voxeu.org/article/can-large-primary-surpluses-solve-europe-s-debt-problem

"These are large primary surpluses. There are both political and economic reasons for questioning whether they are plausible.............History suggests that such behaviour, while not entirely unknown, is exceptional....... On balance, this analysis does not leave us optimistic that Europe's crisis countries will be able to run primary budget surpluses as large and persistent as officially projected."

Italy's situation is to some extent replicated in other countries on the periphery (Ireland sovereign debt to GDP 114.8%, Portugal 131.4%, Spain 96.8% and Greece 176%, all numbers as of September 2014) since almost all official forecasts anticipate an imminent turnaround in the debt dynamic. If secular stagnation and ultra-low inflation really set in this turnaround is going to be impossible to achieve and Europe's leaders will need to decide what to do about it.

Italy's debt now looks certain to climb towards 140% of GDP and beyond (maybe hitting that level as early as in 2016), meaning someone somewhere in the official sector should soon have to recognize that it is not on a sustainable path. The so called AQRs (bank Asset Quality Reviews) didn't generate too many surprises, but what would happen if they did some realistic DSA's (Debt Sustainability Analyses)?

Cases like Greece and Portugal are to some extent containable from an EU perspective since the economies are small enough for EU leaders to engage in some sort of extend-and-pretend via supporting bonds with low coupons and long horizon maturities. But Italy's debt is simply too big to be manageable in this way.

So EU leaders and the ECB now face a dilemma. Trying to make Italy comply with its EU deficit and debt obligations may well mean that the deficit comes down but in all probability the low nominal growth impact of austerity will mean the debt level will go up. Not complying with them opens the possibility to slightly more growth (and possibly mildly stronger inflation) but naturally the debt level will also rise. It's a sort of damned if I do and damned if I don't situation, since either way the debt burden rises.

From the point of view of the country's political leaders though, it is obvious that austerity today has costs (and few visible benefits) while deficit spending may bring some short term benefit at the price of hypothetical longer term debt issues. It shouldn't surprise us then if they go for the latter, especially since Japan's political leaders have been widely applauded for doing something similar.

Naturally, since the difficulties the onset of secular stagnation will produce for heavily indebted countries with ageing and shrinking workforces are not widely understood, hints that deficit objective relaxation calls are growing have not been well received everywhere. During the spring of 2014 the FT published details of a document[225] jointly issued by the German and Finnish finance ministries which strongly rebuked Brussels for easing austerity demands, citing in particular the additional flexibility given to France and Spain for reducing their budgets to within EU deficit limits.

"Since 2012, the commission has substantially changed the way it assesses whether a member state has taken 'effective action' to comply with [EU budget rules]," the memo states. "The recent methodological changes imply the risk of watering down the

---

[225] Berlin attacks EU's easing of austerity demands, Financial Times, 28 February, 2014 http://www.ft.com/intl/cms/s/0/d7b79578-a000-11e3-9c65-00144feab7de.html?siteedition=intl#axzz2v7QHse3y

newly strengthened [rules] at its implementation stage."

As might have been expected, Matteo Renzi was not slow in coming forward to seek similar treatment for his country[226]. According to the Financial Times, the country's finance minister, Pier Carlo Padoan, sent a formal written request to the commission on 16 April 2014 seeking authorization for a change in objectives. Citing the **"severe recession"** that set Italy back in 2012 and 2013, Mr Padoan wrote that Italy wanted to **"deviate temporarily from the budget targets"** and that because of **"exceptional circumstances"** (my emphasis throughout) the government had decided to accelerate the payment of arrears owed by the public to the private sector by €13bn, which would increase the debt to GDP ratio in 2014. The trouble is that these **"temporary factors"** and **"exceptional conditions"** seem to arise with a predictable regularity in Italy's case. The country is currently aiming for a balanced structural budget in 2016 rather than 2015 as agreed with Mario Monti's technocrat government in 2012. A year earlier, the then Prime Minister Silvio Berlusconi had promised a balanced structural budget by 2013. Evidently the likelihood of further postponements is high, and especially with radical political movements on the rise.

Enter Mario Draghi

The relationship between Mario Draghi and Matteo Renzi has long been a source of speculation and gossip in Italy. Shortly after he came to office in February 2014 - following a kind of palace revolution inside his own party whereby the incumbent Prime Minister (Enrico Letta) was unceremoniously defenestrated - the

[226] See: Italy request to push back budget targets dismays Brussels Financial Times 17 April, 2014 http://www.ft.com/intl/cms/s/0/9472a5da-c659-11e3-ba0e-00144feabdc0.html?siteedition=intl#axzz2z7srnzJ8

Financial Times Brussels correspondent published a post on an FT blog[227] with the rather direct title: Does Renzi owe his job to Draghi?

The gist of the article's argument was an attempt to establish some sort of connection between Matteo Renzi's arrival in office and the outcome of the then recent German Constitutional Court ruling which put in question the viability of the central bank's OMT (Outright Monetary Transactions) programme. Spiegel's hypothesis was that the driving force for some kind of "unholy alliance" between the two of them lay in Draghi's interest in getting prime minister Letta out of office before pressure from within Germany about keeping open the offer of a now legally questionable OMT programme to an Italy which was visibly enjoying cheaper bond yields (but was manifestly not advancing with its reform programme) became too strong to withstand.

"Do last week's German constitutional court ruling lambasting – but failing to overturn – the ECB's crisis-fighting bond-buying programme," he asked, *"and Matteo Renzi's ousting of Italy's prime minister Enrico Letta have anything in common?" And he continued, "In the view of many ECB critics, particularly in Berlin, the two are not only related, but one may have caused the other."*

Many German critics, he argued, feel there has been no serious effort by the Italian government – be it in the fading months of Mario Monti's premiership or during Enrico Letta's foreshortened tenure – "to undertake major economic reforms since ECB boss Mario Draghi first announced he would do 'whatever it takes' to save the euro in July 2012."

---

[227] Does Renzi Owe His Job To Draghi, Financial Times, 14 February, 2014 http://blogs.ft.com/the-world/2014/02/does-renzi-owe-his-job-to-draghi/

The key part of the legal and policy background to grasp here is that the German court ruling effectively left OMT - which only ever had a virtual existence and was increasingly seen as an empty bluff since it was clear no one was going to accept the conditionality side - deader than that infamous dead duck. Karlsruhe's objection to the existing bond buying programme was that it went beyond the ECB's mandate since directly financing government debt is prohibited under Maastricht, and the objective of OMT was to help governments finance at an affordable price. Since break-up risk - which could have offered an alternative justification for OMT - is for the moment off the table, OMT lacked definitive legal justification and in practical terms the emperor visibly had no clothes. It was just a question of how long the markets needed to wake up to the fact.

So it was imperative to find some other justification for the initiation of a bond purchases programme should one be needed. Then along came deflation. The important point is that if a programme of bond purchases is implemented as a form of QE it will differ from the earlier OMT programme in terms of the justification offered. Any QE programme introduced to combat deflation can only be implemented as part of an attempt to attain price stability, an objective which does lie within the central bank mandate. Another key difference is that this version of QE involves purchases of bonds from ALL countries in the monetary union (according to their weight in Euro Area GDP), which brings us to the third difference with OMT: there will be no conditionality attached. Given this implementing QE became a "high risk" operation and it was clear that Mario Draghi needed someone else at Italy's helm if he wanted to be able get the Germans on board, someone who could convince them Italy would enact the required reforms. Enter Matteo Renzi.

Now fast forward to August, and we find the former mayor of Florence who had surged to office on the back of promises to enact aggressive labour market reforms, a battery of spending and tax cuts and significant privatizations **had been** strong on talking and very weak on action. Something which is not uncommon in Italy, but people had expected more from him. They thought this time was different.

Mario Draghi's irritation with the situation was visible at the August ECB press conference. When asked by one of the journalists why Italy had fallen back into recession he could hardly contain himself, and was unusually direct in saying a lack of structural reforms was holding the country back and hampering a return to growth. The reference to Renzi was evident.

One week later the two met, in what they had obviously hoped would be a secret meeting but Italy being Italy the press went along for the ride. While no details of what happened at this meeting have transpired it is pretty clear Draghi will have used the opportunity to read his fellow countryman the riot act. Italy has often been full of talk about some kind of Troika intervention, but this is most unlikely, and Renzi made it pretty clear in an interview given to the Financial Times that he personally wouldn't be asking for one.[228]

When asked why Italy's reform pace seemed so slow he rejected Draghi's suggestion that the EU should intervene in countries where reforms were not being implemented fast enough. "I agree with Draghi when he says that Italy needs to make reforms but how we are going to do them I will decide, not the Troika, not the

[228] Matteo Renzi takes a rapier to Italy's bureaucracy", Financial Times, 10 August 2014 http://www.ft.com/intl/cms/s/0/3e790e94-208b-11e4-890a-00144feabdc0.html

ECB, not the European Commission," he said. "I will do the reforms myself because Italy does not need someone else to explain what to do."

The problem is that with the debt dynamics we have seen above the one thing Italy doesn't have at this point is time. It isn't a problem of the impact of a so called "debt snowball" as interest rate payments send debt levels spiraling upwards. If anything it's worse. Mario Draghi can, in theory, contain the debt interest problem, and if needs be with the capital repayments schedule. But the problem Italy has at the moment is one of the credibility of its debt, of the country being able to convincingly argue its trajectory is sustainable, of being able to convince the Germans that if the ECB were to buy bonds these could EVER be redeemed.

While Renzi has waxed eloquently about transforming Italy, buoyed on by the results of the European Parliament elections he seems more concerned with pushing through electoral reform - which is obviously needed but is not perhaps as pressing as the growth and debt problem - leaving the suspicion that he is more interested in getting re-elected than anything else. Indeed the fact that he needs the support of the discredited former Prime Minister Silvio Berlusconi to get reforms through with any kind of urgency[229] has lead critics of the two "institutional parties" to suggest the reform may be more about getting rid of newcomers like Beppe Grillo's Five Star movement than anything else.

To date Renzi's government - which is almost operating outside real historical time in terms of economic issues - has made limited progress on the sort of reforms which might help the country

[229] Italy Slips Back Into Recession, As New PM seeks Berlusconi's Help, Newsweek 8 June 2014 http://www.newsweek.com/italy-slips-back-recession-new-pm-seeks-berlusconis-help-263267

recover some kind of growth, like those to the banking system, the judicial system and the labor market. The only measure that could be considered vaguely "pro-growth" that his government has enacted was the 80 euro bonus delivered to low-wage workers and even this hasn't boosted the economy as its proponents claimed. The measure seems more cosmetic - comparable with José Luis Zapatero's ridiculous "Plan E" - and only reinforces the impression of politicians fiddling while Rome burns. The business lobby Confcommercio, which was highly critical of the measure, calculated that consumption was boosted by just 0.1% in June, the first month in which the tax relief was operative. In their press release they said Italian families were holding back from shopping "because their uncertainty about the future was stronger than the actual increase in funds in their pockets".

Despite this Prime Minister Renzi continues to insist that his government's economic strategy is sound and will lift the country out of crisis. In a lengthy interview broadcast on La7 television following the announcement of the third quarter 2014 GDP results, Renzi said that his government was determined to get the economy back on track, but in due course. "We will work better and harder, but I promised to change direction, not to change the universe in three months time," Renzi said, adding that only a "comic book superhero" could turn around the economy in a matter of months. "Calmly, serenely, we are taking this country by the hand and pulling it out of the crisis," Renzi told listeners.

The problem outside observers are having is not in seeing the complete turnaround - Renzi is right here, this involves a long painful road - but in identifying the first baby steps that are being taken.

And fears about Mr Renzi's grasp on Italy's finances were also fanned last year when spending review commissioner Carlo Cottarelli highlighted the tensions which existed in the government over the prime minister's spending plans. In a post on his blog, Mr Cottarelli - who was appointed by Letta and was previously Director of the Fiscal Affairs Department at the IMF - said that money from earlier savings were already being used by parliament for other expenditure, meaning that in the longer term they could not be used to reduce taxes on employment.

Renzi normally responds to critics that all points of view are valid, but that "11 million Italians think differently" in a clear reference to what he perceives as his strong electoral support. But even this will eventually wane if progress is not seen to be made on the economy. The FT quotes Wolfango Piccoli, analyst at Rome-based think-tank Teneo, to the following effect: "As Prime Minister Matteo Renzi struggles to make progress on political reform, it is becoming increasingly clear that his government lacks an original and coherent plan for the economy,"

So Which Way for the ECB?

Evidently members of the EU Commission, the ECB governing council, and senior political leaders in Berlin, Amsterdam or Paris are neither theoreticians nor intellectuals. The secular stagnation hypothesis is at this point more akin to a theoretical research strategy than a workable template for policy-making, and policymakers are understandably reluctant to take decisions on the basis of what is still largely a hypothesis. As the editors of a recent book on the topic put it in their introduction: "Secular stagnation proved illusory after the Great Depression. It may well prove to be so after the Great Recession – it is still too early to tell. Uncertainty, however, is no excuse for inactivity. Most actions are no-regret policies anyway"[230]. As they suggests the risks here are far from evenly balanced. If countries like Japan, Italy and Portugal are suffering from some local variant of one common pathology, then normal solutions are unlikely to work, and matters can deteriorate fast.

Naturally the ECB can go down the Abenomics path, and power ahead with large scale sovereign bond purchases even while the Commission turns an increasingly blind eye to higher deficit spending at the country level. But it is far from clear that Abenomics works and if it doesn't what happens to all the accumulated debt?

For the time being Europe's leaders seem intent on ploughing a middle course and implementing a version of what could be called Abenomics-light. Mario Draghi's speech at the August 2014 Jackson Hole meeting of central bankers[231] seems to mark some sort of a turning point in this sense. The ECB President accepted for the first time that Euro Area inflation expectations were not as "well anchored" as they might be.

He also stressed that faced with weak GDP growth and inflation, and with interest rates already close to the "zero bound", there was only so much that monetary policy could do to reflate the respective economies. As a consequence, he argued, fiscal policy has an important complementary role to play and he called for

[230] Coen Teulings, Richard Baldwin, Secular stagnation: Facts, causes, and cures, Vox eBook, 15 august 2014 http://www.voxeu.org/article/secular-stagnation-facts-causes-and-cures-new-vox-ebook

[231] Speech by Mario Draghi, President of the ECB, Annual central bank symposium in Jackson Hole, 22 August 2014 http://www.ecb.europa.eu/press/key/date/2014/html/sp140822.en.html

stronger coordination between the different national fiscal stances since that "should in principle allow us to achieve a more growth-friendly overall fiscal stance for the euro area." As he also notes, the Euro Area is "operating within a set of fiscal rules – the Stability and Growth Pact – which acts as an anchor for confidence and that would be self-defeating to break."

What this really means, reformulated in un-coded language, is that Germany could do more to change the overall fiscal stance and make it a more expansionary one. The means Germany should be running a deficit within the 3% rule, while at present Berlin politicians are obsessed with running primary surpluses and paying down the existing debt.

Naturally, the reluctance in Berlin is understandable, since the Abenomics experiment, as we have noted, may well not work. But on the other hand it is obviously most undesirable for countries like Italy and Portugal with government debt levels of over 130% of GDP to be generating more debt. In cases like Spain and France perhaps the best that could be offered within the Stability and Growth Pact would be a slower rate of deficit consolidation. So, at the end of the day it really is down to Germany to do the heavy lifting, if fiscal heavy lifting is to be done while some semblance of policy coherence is maintained.

What is clear from Draghi's speech at Jackson Hole is that the one thing the Euro Area cannot do is stay where it is. Either Germany has to decide to call it a day and leave, which would be a very costly thing to do in the short term - indeed more costly now than it would have been in say 2010 given all the effort which has been put into holding the currency union together. Or fiscal policy needs to be more coordinated, with those who are able to do so adopting a more stimulatory stance. The discourse space which could facilitate this is provided on the one hand by a more difficult than anticipated outlook for German exports in the East (due to the Russia/Ukraine conflict) and the fact that Angela Merkel's coalition partners are now the left of centre SPD and not the economic liberal FDP. With the German economy itself moving between apparent fits of weakness and starts of a strong recovery which never really materializes, a more fiscally simulative stance in Germany could be more palatable than many imagine.

Whatever the end result the transition process is likely to be slow, and accident prone. In this context it is worth bearing in mind that time always has a cost. Letting things drift further means letting debt levels rise, and each additional increment risks testing market patience a factor which is especially important in the cases of Italy and Portugal. The more time passes the more difficult it is going to be for anyone to convince themselves that the debt level of these countries is sustainable.

So there may come a point after which the Germans simply will not allow Mario Draghi to buy more Italian bonds without giving them a prior haircut. OK, they've said they won't do more PSI[232], but they've said a lot of things, and the overall cost of infuriating investors is limited and containable when you have a regional current account surplus and a central bank buying bonds.

Maybe the losses which accrue to Euro "widow maker" trade[233] will be borne by all those eager bond purchasers who thought nothing could possibly go wrong. I am sure German politicians were taking a long hard look at Greece's private sector obligations during the second bailout.

[233] James Mackintosh, The widowmaker doesn't care if this is nuts, FT Alphaville, 17 June 2014 http://ftalphaville.ft.com/2014/06/27/1889702/the-widowmaker-doesnt-care-if-this-is-nuts/

would decide a loss of credibility on PSI would be less costly to them than getting German taxpayers on the hook for current Italian debt levels. Especially in a country where they are now proudly announcing they have reduced government debt for the first time in more than 50 years.

The thing is, despite the meeting between Draghi and Renzi it still appears nothing substantial is going to happen in Italy in the short term. Thanks to bondholders offering supporting ultra-low yields the Italian government is under no pressure to ask for help (and doesn't even feel it needs it).

Naturally in the short term the QE driven "Mario Draghi ultimately has my back" feeling will still prevail, but with markets continuing to finance debt levels that any official study carried out would soon have to recognize any future policy shift from the ECB will only fuel concerns that the size of the pill may become just too big for the ECB to persuade Germany comfortably swallow, leaving the specter of private sector involvement to rear its ugly head. How do you tell people who have just sacrificed hard to get their debt under control that they are now about to help "pardon" 50% of someone else's. It simply doesn't make sense.

In theory it is the intention of the ECB governing council to continue the 60 billion Euros a month bond purchase programme until September 2016, but as became clear in the Q and A session which followed the last Governing Council meeting, this "intention" is in part data, and especially inflation expectations, dependent. This point was forcefully hammered home in an interesting recent article from the FT's ECB correspondent Claire Jones.[234]

[234] Claire Jones, Euro plunge tests ECB inflation forecast, Financial Times, 12 March 2015 http://www.ft.com/intl/cms/s/0/a901fb54-c8ce-11e4-8617-

As Claire points out, "*The [inflation] projections assumed that the exchange rate would stay where it was in the middle of February, about $1.13, until 2017. On Thursday [12 March], the single currency traded at $1.06. According to the ECB's own estimates, a euro that weak would leave policy makers facing a headache about whether to scale down bond buying just months after unleashing their €1.1tn quantitative easing package*".

ECB monetary policy affects the exchange rate, and this affects the inflation outlook. So if, as many analysts are predicting, the Euro were to move towards parity with the USD in the coming months then that fall would give an upside nudge to the bank's inflation expectations, and this would surely provoke a renewed debate on the ECB governing council about the desirability of proceeding as planned with the bond purchases. Remember, Mario Draghi didn't have a majority for proceeding with the programme as recently as December last year. As Claire says: "*The ECB has welcomed the euro's depreciation, which should provide a much-needed boost to the Eurozone's exporters. But a sustained weakening could lead hawks on the governing council to ask some awkward questions about whether policy makers were right to keep on buying €60bn-worth of public and private sector bonds a month*".

According to the forecasts Mario Draghi presented in March inflation is set to reach 1.8% by 2017 and the ECB was heralding QE a success less than a week into its launch. However, as Claire points out, "*under an alternative scenario outlined in the projections, a much weaker exchange rate would probably lead the ECB to miss its target, with inflation likely to rise above 2 per cent by the end of the forecast horizon.*"

00144feab7de.html#axzz3UZhKbXYe

But, as she added, *"the trouble is that the alternative scenario is already in danger of being realised."* This is because it sees the euro dipping to $1.04 by 2017, but if the current rate of decline continues it could reach that level in days rather than weeks.

The next batch of forecasts are not due till June, but already some of those who favour earlier termination are out there testing the water. In fact Governing Council member Bostjan Jazbec, who represents Slovenia, was arguing the purchasing programme could end early one month **before** it started. "I understand it this way ...Once the price mandate is fulfilled, we can end it earlier," he told the Wall Street Journal on 5 February.[235]

Marcel Fratzscher, who is not on the ECB board, but who - as Director of the DIW economic institute - has an influential voice in Germany, agrees. "The idea [in Germany] is that the ECB has been doing too much, and should really try to taper the programme rather sooner and before September 2016", he told Bloomberg TV on 16 March.[236] He went on to say:

"Particularly in Germany the exchange rate is a big issue... the conflict over monetary policy will again intensify over the next couple of months.... The argument of Germany against QE was so far it will not be effective, now the complaint is maybe that it's too effective because it has been driving down 10 year yields in Germany to close to zero it has depreciated the Euro."

[235] ECB's Jazbec says quantitative easing could end before September 2016, Reuters, 5 February 2015 http://www.reuters.com/article/2015/02/05/us-ecb-jazbec-idUSKBN0L91U820150205

[236] German Greek Conflict Becoming Personal, Bloomberg TV, 18 March 2015 http://www.bloomberg.com/news/videos/2015-03-16/german-greek-conflict-becoming-more-personal-fratzscher

even a single government bond had been purchased, but it's worth remembering the programme was approved by the Governing Council against the express wishes of Bundesbank President Jens Weidmann. The fact that Mario Draghi was able to convince his Governing Council to introduce QE on March 5 surprised many observers, who expected Germany to put up more resistance to the idea. In order to get it through the ECB the policy was explicitly tied to the mandate: maintaining price stability. This is the only meaningful objective of QE - not unemployment, not growth - and presented in this way (as Mr Draghi pointed out) not going ahead would have been illegal.

But, in this life, things that come easy are just as easily lost, so the low bar on entry will mean there is also a relatively low one for exit, and as Claire Jones suggests the **tapering debate** could start as early as June, especially with the Euro Area economies looking likely to outperform in the coming months.

The problem - as we are seeing in Japan where it looks like they are about to fall back into deflation again - is getting a short uptick in inflation through currency devaluation is one thing, and solving a problem of deep structural deflation is another. If Europe's brush with deflation is connected with its demography and declining working age population then any tapering that does take place in the purchasing programme won't be the end of the matter, and the bank will probably be forced back into buying again soon enough, driving deeper and deeper into sovereign debt purchases. In addition Europe's present recovery is cyclical, but long term structural impediments to growth remain, so don't expect the wonders to last.

But one thing at a time: you will hear growing talk of ECB tapering as the months pass, and the only real unknown as far as I am concerned is how exactly periphery government bond markets will react to the news.

ABOUT THE AUTHOR

Born in Liverpool Edward Hugh is a macroeconomist of British origin who has lived in Catalonia for over 25 years. For 20 of those years he lived and worked in Barcelona, but since 2010 he has been living in a small village near the town of Figueres.

Hugh, who studied economics at the LSE in the late sixties before going on to do Masters and Doctoral studies in Manchester, is an expert on the impact of demographic change and migratory processes on economic growth. His work came to the attention of a wider audience during the financial crisis when the New York Times described him as the "blog prophet of Euro zone doom". He is an active blogger, and regular contributor to social network platforms like Twitter and Facebook where he is widely followed. He has no political involvement of any kind, and is proud of his reputation as an independent analyst.